edexcel :::

Edexcel International GCSE
English as a Second Language

Student Book

Baljit Nijjar, Janet Searle

D1353367

PEARSON

Published by Pearson Education Limited, a company incorporated in England and Wales, having its registered office at Edinburgh Gate, Harlow, Essex, CM20 2JE. Registered company number: 872828.

www.pearsonglobalschools.com

Edexcel is a registered trademark of Edexcel Limited

Text © Pearson Education Ltd 2011

First published 2011

15 14 13 12 11
IMP 10 9 8 7 6 5 4 3 2

ISBN 978 0 435046 78 1

Original design by Richard Ponsford and Creative Monkey
Typeset by Gantec Publishing Solutions, LLC
Original illustrations © Pearson Education Ltd 2011
Illustrated by Gantec Publishing Solutions, LLC
Cover design by Creative Monkey
Cover photo © Alamy Images: Lisa Moore
Printed in the UK by Scotprint Ltd.

Acknowledgements
The authors and publisher would like to thank the following individuals and organisations for permission to reproduce photographs:

(Key: b-bottom; c-centre; l-left; r-right; t-top)

Fotolia.com: Aleksander 180bl, andrea lehmkuhl 94tr, Andrejs Pidjass 17tr, angela ostafichuk 107bl, Ann Shaw 61tr, Beboy 146, biker3 79t, Carlos Caetano 47tl, claireliz 90, 152br, clearviewstock 8b, Coka 48l, czardases 31tr, Daniel Etzold 1bl, Dariusz Kopestynski 194bl, david melrose 65, drx 1tl, eblue 17br, EcoView 108r, EyeMark 19, FotolEdhar 159l, Fyle 180br, Gabriel Gonzalez G. 194tr, Gilly Smith 152bl, godfer 208bl, goodluz 137r, Hii Boh Teck 120bl, IKO 120tl, James Steidl 78b, 94cr, Jason Stitt 208br, viiibl, Johnny Lye 61bl, kaphotokevm1 78tl, kkaplin 120br, Klaus Eppele 95, Kurhan 51, 159r, Laurence Gough viiibr, Laurentiu Iordache 47bl, lightpoet 184, Lisa Gogolin 108c, lunamarina 57, mangostock 203t, Matthew Collingwood 115, Michael Chamberlin 134bl, micromonkey 8t, 48c, Monkey Business 17tl, 17bl, 47br, 107tl, Nicola Gavin 47tr, Orange Line Media 194tl, Paige Roberts 134tl, Patricia Hofmeester 194br, Pavel Losevsky 195, Petr Mašek 120tr, Phillip Minnis 37, photoclicks 78cl, picsfive 134br, Pontus Edenberg 153, pressmaster 78tr, radarreklama 129, Ruslan Olinchuk 121b, Stephen Coburn 203b, stocker1970 31tl, strider 79c, 79b, Tomasz Trojanowski 61br, Vince Gayman 121t, Violetstar 31br, Warren Price 32r, Yuri Arcurs 152tl, 152tr, yuriyzhuravov 1br, Zoltán Futó 32l; **iStockphoto:** Alina Solovyova-Vincent 208tl, Ana Abejon 1tr, Arthur Carlo Franco 94cl, Barrett Morgan 180tl, Bart Coenders viiit, ene 134tr, kristian sekulic 48r; **NASA:** 94tl; **Pearson Education Ltd:** Creatas 78cr, 167bl, Gareth Boden 137l, Guillaume Dargaud 125, Ian Wedgewood 171, Jules Selmes 94b, 107tr, MindStudio 167tr, Photodisc 180tr, Photodisc. Brofsky Studio Inc. 167br, Ryan McVay. Photodisc 61tl, Studio 8 167tl, 172, 175, 208tr; **Shutterstock.com:** 1000 Words 31bl, erwinova 107br, Geoffrey Lawrence 9, Styve Reineck 108l

All other images © Pearson Education

The authors and publisher would also like to thank the following for permission to reproduce copyright material:

Extracts in Chapter 2 adapted from "My Very Empty Nest", *The Guardian*, 25/09/2010 (McGilvary, M.), copyright © Guardian News & Media Ltd 2010; Extracts in Chapter 3 about Alan Sugar, http://en.wikipedia.org/wiki/Alan_Sugar, granted under the GNU Free Documentation License (GFDL); Extracts in Chapter 5 from *The Kite Runner*, Bloomsbury (Khaled Hosseini, 2003). Copyright © 2003 Khaled Hosseini. Reproduced with permission of Bloomsbury Publishing Group, Doubleday Canada and Riverhead Books, an imprint of Penguin Group (USA) Inc.; Extract in Chapter 6 adapted from "Newly Qualified and Teenage Drivers", http://www.safermotoring.co.uk/NewlyQualifiedTeenageDrivers.html, copyright © SaferMotoring 2000-2011; Extract in Chapter 6 about Tom Daley (Diver), http://en.wikipedia.org/wiki/Tom_Daley_(diver), Granted under the GNU Free Documentation License (GFDL); Extracts in Chapter 8 adapted from "The Carnivore, Nairobi, Kenya", 29 March 2001, http://www.bbc.co.uk/dna/h2g2/A517132, copyright © Ashley Stewart-Noble; Extracts in Chapter 9 adapted from "Can Central Africa's Rain Forests Live With Logging?", *National Geographic News*, 18/11/2004 (Owen, J.), http://news.nationalgeographic.com, copyright © National Geographic, reproduced with permission; Extracts in Chapter 10 adapted from "Twitter, email, texts: we don't talk any more!", the *Guardian*, 14/08/2010 (Hather, M.), copyright © Guardian News & Media Ltd 2010; Extracts in Chapter 11 adapted from Freecycle®, www.uk.freecycle.org. Reproduced with permission from The Freecycle Network; Extract in Chapter 12 adapted from "Demand for gap year schemes soars", *The Guardian*, 01/09/2009 (Tobin, L.), copyright © Guardian News & Media Ltd 2009; Extracts in Chapter 13 about Suduko, http://en.wikipedia.org/wiki/Sudoko, granted under the GNU Free Documentation License (GFDL); Extract in Chapter 14 adapted from "What type of work would suit you?", http://www.direct.gov.uk/en/YoungPeople/Workandcareers/index.htm, © Crown copyright; and Extracts in Chapter 15 adapted from "Be happy", *BBC Focus*, December 2005 (Susan Aldridge), copyright © Susan Aldridge.

Every effort has been made to contact copyright holders of material reproduced in this book. Any omissions will be rectified in subsequent printings if notice is given to the publishers.

Websites
The websites used in this book were correct and up to date at the time of publication. It is essential for tutors to preview each website before using it in class so as to ensure that the URL is still accurate, relevant and appropriate. We suggest that tutors bookmark useful websites and consider enabling students to access them through the school/college intranet.

Disclaimer
This material has been published on behalf of Edexcel and offers high-quality support for the delivery of Edexcel qualifications.

This does not mean that the material is essential to achieve any Edexcel qualification, nor does it mean that it is the only suitable material available to support any Edexcel qualification. Edexcel material will not be used verbatim in setting any Edexcel examination or assessment. Any resource lists produced by Edexcel shall include this and other appropriate resources.

Copies of official specifications for all Edexcel qualifications may be found on the Edexcel website: www.edexcel.com.

Contents

Contents

Listening	Speaking	Writing	Summarising	Exam tips
Changes in popular music	leisure time	formal letter; music review	Outdoors Adventure – Is it for you?	Paper 1: Reading and Writing Part 1: Reading
Friends – related extracts	family; friends; relationships	informal e-mail	My very empty nest	Paper 1: Reading and Writing Part 4: Writing
Living on the road	your home; your town/city; lifestyles	article	The life of Alan Sugar	Paper 2: Listening Part 1: Listening
Long way round	transport; holidays; travelling	formal letter	Golden Sands Holiday Park	Paper 3: Speaking Part 1: Introductory interview
It's not the winning, it's the taking part	sport; exercise	report	The Kite Runner	Paper 1: Reading and Writing Part 2: Reading
Japanese coming-of-age	age; stages in life	formal e-mail	Newly qualified teenage drivers	Paper 1: Reading and Writing Part 5: Writing
Visions of the future	technology	article	Kinect gaming technology	Paper 2: Listening Part 2: Listening
Chewing gum – related extracts	food; cooking; healthy eating	informal letter	Special restaurants	Paper 3: Speaking Part 2: Student talk
March of the Penguins; animal issues	pets; holidays; the natural world	formal letter	Logging	Paper 3: Speaking Creating a mind map
Blogging	texting, social networking sites; communication	report	Twitter, e-mail, texts	Paper 1: Reading and Writing Part 3: Reading
Parents and money	shopping; money; money matters	formal e-mail	Freecycle	Paper 1: Reading and Writing Part 6: Writing
Formal interviews	school; exams; teachers; studying	informal e-mail	Taking a gap year	Paper 1: Reading and Writing Writing a summary
Strange and puzzling – related extracts	books; films	article	The history of sudoku	Paper 2: Listening Part 3: Listening
The human cannonball	jobs; work	letter of application	What type of work would suit you?	Paper 3: Speaking Part 3: Extended discussion
	moods; memory; feelings; memories	article	How to be happy	General exam tips

About this book

This book has several features to help you with International GCSE English as a Second Language.

Getting started

Each chapter has a short Getting started section to help you start thinking about the topic and let you know what is in the chapter.

Language recap

At the end of every chapter is a Language recap section which helps you to review the vocabulary and grammar from the chapter.

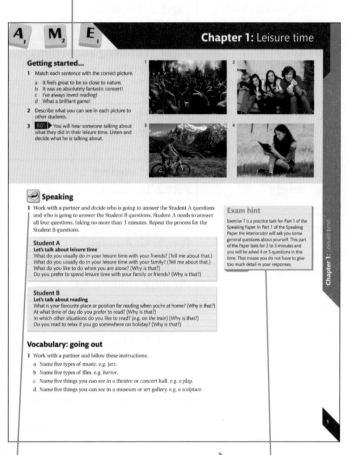

Exercises

There are exercises throughout each chapter, which help you to practise the tasks you will have to do in the exam. In each chapter, there are also topic-related vocabulary exercises and grammar exercises.

Margin boxes

The boxes in the margin give you extra help or information. They might explain something in a little more detail or guide you to linked topics in other parts of the Student Book. The margin boxes include: Exam hint, Language hint, Vocabulary hint and Grammar hint boxes.

Exam tips

At the end of each chapter there is an Exam tips section which focuses on one Part of the Papers. In this section, you are given an example task and shown how to approach the task.

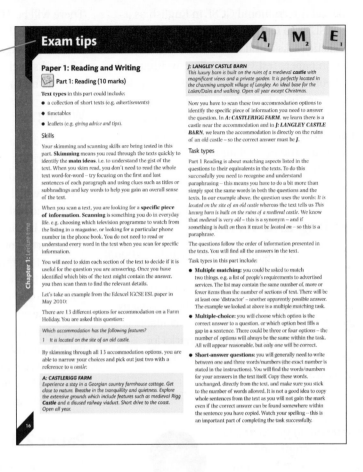

ActiveBook CD

The ActiveBook CD contains:

- a digital version of the book
- all the audio used in the book
- all the audioscripts used in the book
- exam practice questions
- an exam reviser.

Exam practice questions

In this section you will find examples from past papers covering all four skills: Reading, Writing, Listening and Speaking. Do make use of these example questions to make sure you cover as many different examples of tasks as possible.

Exam reviser

This section reviews vocabulary from the Student Book chapter by chapter. In addition, there is a review of functional language (e.g. expressing opinions), phrasal verbs (e.g. to print (something) out) and useful language chunks (e.g. it takes ages). The exam reviser can be used to help you review vocabulary and grammar which will be useful for your exams.

It is very important that you print out a copy of the exam reviser and take it to all of your lessons. You will then be able to add new words/phrases as you learn them in class.

Exam overview

The aim of the Edexcel International GCSE in English as a Second Language (ESL) is to test your English language ability through realistic tasks based on authentic texts. Two separate examination papers test your reading, writing and listening skills and you will be awarded a grade from A* to G for your performance in these two papers. Each of these three skills contributes $33\frac{1}{3}$% to your total score. In addition, you have the option of taking a speaking test for which you will receive a separate grade. You are not allowed to use a dictionary for any of the papers so you will need to make sure you have learnt lots of vocabulary throughout your course!

Paper 1: Reading and Writing

This paper is worth $66\frac{2}{3}$% of the total marks for International GCSE ESL and assesses your reading and writing skills in separate exercises. You will take a 2-hour examination paper which has been set by Edexcel and which will be marked by Edexcel examiners. The total number of marks available is 100: there are 40 marks for reading and 60 marks for writing but these marks are then adjusted to make both reading and writing worth the same.

Reading

In this section, you will find three reading passages of increasing length and difficulty. The passages are taken from a range of sources, including newspapers, websites and fiction, and may include factual information, explanations, opinions and biographical writing. A variety of tasks will be used to check your understanding of these reading texts. These tasks include multiple-choice, note completion and sentence completion. For tasks where you have to write words in English, correct spelling in your answers is very important.

There will be 10 marks available for the first reading passage, and then 15 marks each for the second and third passages.

Writing

There are also three parts to the writing section and you are free to choose the order in which you attempt them. The tasks are different in each of these three parts. For some tasks, a context and target reader are identified in order to give a purpose for your writing and you will need to take these into consideration when you write your answers. It is also important that you make sure you write in a style and register which is suitable for the particular task and lay your answer out correctly – so if you have to write a letter, you should set your answer out as a letter. The word limit for each task is between 100 and 150 words and it is very important that you stick to this limit.

Paper 2: Listening

This skill is assessed through a 45-minute examination paper, set and marked by Edexcel. The total number of marks available is 30 and this represents $33\frac{1}{3}$% of the total International GCSE marks. You will be expected to understand standard spoken English in a range of different situations. The recorded texts may be in the form of monologues, dialogues and occasionally there may be three speakers involved. A variety of tasks will be used to check your understanding of the recorded texts. If you have spelled the word incorrectly, but it is clear which word it is, you will not lose marks.

This paper consists of three parts, each based around a single recorded text. You will be given time to read the questions before each part of the recording begins, and you should answer the questions as you listen. You will hear each recorded text twice.

Paper 3: Speaking

This paper is optional and is separately endorsed. Your achievement in the speaking test will not affect the grade you are awarded on Papers 1 and 2, but you must achieve at least Grade G on Papers 1 and 2 in order to be awarded a grade for the speaking test.

The speaking test assesses your communication skills through a recorded interview between you and an interlocutor, based on task cards supplied by Edexcel. The task cards invite you to express yourself fluently, spontaneously and appropriately in a range of speaking contexts. The interlocutor is selected by your centre and is normally a teacher from the centre.

The total number of marks available is 20. Your recorded interviews will be marked by Edexcel examiners.

The test lasts approximately 12 minutes and is divided into three parts:

● Part 1 is a short introductory interview between you and the interlocutor, lasting 2 to 3 minutes.

● In Part 2, you have 1 minute to prepare a talk in response to a task card plus 1 to 2 minutes to give your talk.

● In Part 3, you are expected to engage in an extended discussion with the interlocutor for a maximum of 5 minutes.

Good luck!

Exam FAQs

You will take the Edexcel International GCSE in ESL in the summer exams session. Find out from your teacher the dates of the papers and when you will be taking the speaking test – this will be a bit earlier than the other papers.

Have you read the Exam overview page at the beginning of the book and the Exam tips at the end of each chapter? If you have, you should have a very clear understanding of what you need to do in the Edexcel International GCSE ESL exam by now. Here is a short quiz to test your knowledge.

General

1　How many papers make up the Edexcel International GCSE in ESL and what are they called?

2　How many marks are available on each paper?

3　How long does each paper last?

4　Are you allowed to use a dictionary in the exam?

Reading

1　How many parts are there in the Reading Paper?

2　How important is it to use correct spelling in your answers?

3　Is the word count important when answering some questions?

Writing

1　How many writing tasks will you have to do?

2　What kind of writing tasks will you have to write?

3　What happens if you write too many words?

4　What might happen if you write too few words?

Listening

1　How many parts are there in the Listening Paper?

2　How many times will you hear each recording?

3　Is the word count important when answering some questions?

Speaking

1　How many parts are there in the Speaking test?

2　Do you have to take the speaking exam?

3　Who will conduct the interview?

4　Are you allowed to ask the interlocutor to repeat the question?

5　Are you allowed to ask the interlocutor to explain a word that you don't understand?

You can check your answers with the answers at the bottom of the page!

Answers

General

1　2 core papers: Paper 1: Reading and Writing; Paper 2: Listening. (Paper 3: Speaking is optional.)

2　Paper 1: Reading and Writing = 100 marks: 40 marks for Reading and 60 marks for Writing, which are then converted to give equal weighting to both Reading and Writing; Paper 2: Listening = 30 marks; Paper 3: Speaking is out of 20 marks

3　Paper 1 lasts 2 hours; Paper 2 lasts 45 minutes; Paper 3 lasts 8–10 minutes

4　No, a dictionary is not allowed to be used for any paper.

Reading

1　3

2　It is very important – you should make sure you spell the words in your answers correctly.

3　Yes – in notes or sentence completion tasks, you will be told the maximum number of words you may use and you must keep to this limit.

Writing

1　3

2　In Part 4 you will have to write a report or an article and in Part 5 either a letter, fax or e-mail. Part 6 will always be a summary task.

Listening

1　Twice

2　3 parts

3　Yes – as in the notes or sentence completion tasks in the reading section of Paper 1, you will be told the maximum number of words you may use and you must keep to this limit.

Speaking

1　No, the speaking paper is optional. You will receive an International GCSE grade based on your performance in Papers 1 and 2.

2　There will be an interlocutor who is most likely to be a teacher at your school.

3　3 parts

4　Yes, you may.

5　Yes, you may – but this should be limited to isolated words rather than big chunks of text.

3　Whatever you have written over the 150 word limit will not be assessed.

4　If you write too few words, you might not cover all the bullet points and your range of language could be limited. If this is the case, it will have a negative impact on your mark.

Getting started...

1 Match each sentence with the correct picture.

a It feels great to be so close to nature.
b It was an absolutely fantastic concert!
c I've always loved reading!
d What a brilliant game!

2 Describe what you can see in each picture to other students.

3 R.01 ▶ You will hear someone talking about what they did in their leisure time. Listen and decide what he is talking about.

 Speaking

1 Work with a partner and decide who is going to answer the Student A questions and who is going to answer the Student B questions. Student A needs to answer all four questions, taking no more than 3 minutes. Repeat the process for the Student B questions.

Student A
Let's talk about leisure time
What do you usually do in your leisure time with your friends? (Tell me about that.)
What do you usually do in your leisure time with your family? (Tell me about that.)
What do you like to do when you are alone? (Why is that?)
Do you prefer to spend leisure time with your family or friends? (Why is that?)

Student B
Let's talk about reading
What is your favourite place or position for reading when you're at home? (Why is that?)
At what time of day do you prefer to read? (Why is that?)
In which other situations do you like to read? (e.g. *on the train*) (Why is that?)
Do you read to relax if you go somewhere on holiday? (Why is that?)

Exam hint

Exercise 1 is a practice task for Part 1 of the Speaking Paper. In Part 1 of the Speaking Paper the interlocutor will ask you some general questions about yourself. This part of the Paper lasts for 2 to 3 minutes and you will be asked 4 or 5 questions in this time. That means you do not have to give too much detail in your responses.

Vocabulary: going out

1 Work with a partner and follow these instructions.

a Name five types of music, e.g. *jazz*.
b Name five types of film, e.g. *horror*.
c Name five things you can see in a theatre or concert hall, e.g. *a play*.
d Name five things you can see in a museum or art gallery, e.g. *a sculpture*.

2 Which of the things in your lists do you like? Why?

I really like dance music. I listen to it all the time. It makes me feel great!

3 Work with a partner and complete the table with the words/phrases in the box. Use a dictionary if necessary.

| a blockbuster   a dance floor   the dress circle   architecture |
| watercolours   a gig   house music   ceramics   a DJ |

film/theatre	art	music
a blockbuster		

4 R.02 ▶ Listen to the words and phrases in Exercise 3. Where is the main stress in each one?

5 Complete the sentences with the correct form of a word/phrase from Exercise 3.

a My family took me to an open air concert at the weekend and we saw a fantastic _____ performed by a local band.

b My sister went to a huge club in Ibiza where there are three separate _____ with different types of music.

c I like most types of dance music. The only one I'm not keen on is _____.

d I went to the school disco yesterday where, surprisingly, the _____ played all my favourite music.

e My dad's got some great tickets for the musical. They're in the _____, so we'll have a very good view.

f I generally enjoy low budget films more than the huge Hollywood _____.

g My favourite kinds of paintings are _____, especially for delicate things like flowers.

h I've decided to do a course in _____ and make a bowl to give to my mum as a birthday present.

i Whenever I visit a foreign city, I like looking at the _____ of the buildings, especially the old ones.

🔊 Listening

1 Work with a partner and discuss these questions:

● When and how do you listen to music?

● Do you buy much music?

● Where do you get it from?

● What music do you enjoy listening to at the moment?

● Are there any particular singers or groups you have always liked? Who are they?

2 R.03 ▶ You will hear part of a radio interview with a music historian. He talks about some of the changes in popular music in the last fifty years. Listen to the interview and answer these questions.

Exam hint

Exercise 2 is a practice task for Part 2 of the Listening Paper. In Part 2 of the Listening Paper you may be asked to listen to a dialogue in the form of an interview and complete the tasks as you listen.

Questions

1–5

Complete these sentences using no more than **three words** and/or **a number**.

1 When Daniel was _____ he used to buy lots of records.

2 Daniel first enjoyed the music of Abba in _____.

3 Madonna asked Abba if she could _____ in one of her songs.

4 Daniel thinks that _____ in Abba has been influenced by the musical *Mamma Mia*.

5 Daniel decided to _____ about Abba after going to a concert given by an Abba 'tribute band'.

6–10

Answer these questions using no more than **three words** or **a number**.

6 During which years was there a significant move towards downloading music?
....

7 How long was *Crazy* by Gnarls Barkley in number one position for?
....

8 How long did it take for *Crazy* by Gnarls Barkley to go to number one?
....

9 How did Sandi Thom use the Internet to promote her music?
....

10 What was Sandi Thom offered in April 2006?
....

3 R.03 ▶ In the Listening Paper, you will hear each recording twice. Listen again and check your answers.

Writing

1 Look up the lyrics to the song *I wish I was a punk rocker (with flowers in my hair)* by Sandi Thom on the Internet. Which of these statements do you think best expresses what the song is saying? Compare your ideas with a partner.

● Music should be more easily available on the Internet.

● Music was a more important way of expressing opinions forty years ago.

● The music business is more interesting now because of new technology.

2 Read this review. Do you agree with the writer's opinion of this song?

MUSIC REVIEW OF THE WEEK

Sandi Thom recorded her first album ***Smile … it confuses people*** in 2006, and it quickly went to number one in the album charts. The hit single ***I wish I was a punk rocker*** from the album also got to number one.

I think this is a really fun album with some catchy pop tunes. Sandi is a good singer and her voice is different from most other singers at the moment. My favourite track is ***I wish I was a punk rocker***, which is lively and has very interesting lyrics. The only negative thing I would say about the album is that the backing band is a bit weak.

This album gets better the more you listen to it. I would definitely recommend downloading it and watching out for any further albums from this talented artist.

3 Read the review again and number three of these paragraph descriptions in the order you read them. (One of them should not be used.)

a Gives a recommendation about whether to download the album or not.

b Gives some information about the album and singer.

c Gives some information about where and when the writer got the album.

d Gives the writer's opinion about the album (both positive and negative).

4 Read the advert and complete the writing task.

Writing reference: see page 260

Reviews Needed!

Have you downloaded any new music recently? If so, could you write us a review of an album? Include information on the singer (or band) and what the music on the album is like, and say whether you would recommend the album to other people.

The best reviews will be published next month.

Writing task

You recently saw this advert in an English-speaking magazine called *Music Monthly*.

Choose an album that you enjoy listening to and use the paragraph descriptions from Exercise 3 to write your review.

In your review you should:

• give some information about the singer/band

• give your opinion of the album

• say whether you would recommend the album.

Write your review using between 100 and 150 words.

5 In groups of four, read out the review of your album and discuss the following:

- Has anybody else in the group listened to the album you described?

- If yes, do they agree with your review?

- If no, is it an album they would like to listen to?

Grammar: question forms

1 Work with a partner and look at the question pairs i–ii, then answer the questions about them.

Grammar reference: see page 229

a How is the word order of these two questions different? Why do we use indirect questions?

   i Direct question: ***How did you first get interested in popular music?***

   ii Indirect question: ***Could you tell us how you first got interested in popular music?***

b How do you typically form these questions?

   i *Yes/No* question: ***Does anybody buy singles these days?***

   ii *Wh-* question: ***What was the first single you bought?***

c What is different about these questions?

   i Subject question: ***Who are the original members of Abba?***

   ii Object question: ***Which song do you prefer?***

d Which question is not natural everyday English? Where in a question do we often put a preposition (if there is one)?

   i ***Where did you get that CD from?***

   ii ***From where did you get that CD?***

2 There is a mistake in each of these questions. Find the mistakes and correct them. Use the information in Exercise 1 to help you.

a Does she be going to the theatre with us on Friday?

b You can play the guitar well?

c What you have been doing all day?

d What you think of that skateboarding display yesterday?

e What did happen at the end of the film?

f About what are you talking?

g Could you tell me how much is the entrance fee?

h Would you mind telling me whether is there a performance this evening?

3 Rewrite these direct questions as indirect questions starting with the words given.

Grammar reference: see page 230

a What is your favourite type of music?

   I'd like to know _____ .

b Do you like dancing?

   Could you tell me _____ ?

c What are you going to do this weekend?

   Would you mind telling me _____ ?

d Have you been cycling recently?

Could you tell me _____?

e Did you enjoy the last film you saw?

I'd like to know _____? ✳

f What did you do for your last birthday?

Would you mind telling me _____?

4 Look at the answers which the pop star Shakira gave in an interview. Write the questions you think the interviewer asked. Write at least six indirect questions. Compare your questions with a partner.

a It's Shakira Isabel Mebarak Ripoll.

What's your full name?

b Yes, I have. My friends call me Shaki.

I'd like to know if you've got a nickname.

c My father is from Lebanon and my mother is from Colombia.

d I was born in Barranquilla in Colombia in South America and I still live there.

e I've got four brothers and four sisters.

f I would say I'm a perfectionist and maybe a bit bossy. ✳

g No, I don't smoke, or drink alcohol or coffee. ✳

h I'm five foot two inches.

i I was thirteen.

j I suppose you would call it Latin/pop-rock.

k I write all my songs myself.

l One great moment was when I was given the award for Latin Female Artist of the Year at the World Music Awards in 1998.

🗣 Speaking

1 Work with a partner and each choose one of the topics below. Prepare to time your partner – give them 1 minute to prepare and then ask them to start speaking. Tell them to stop speaking after 2 minutes. Did your partner answer the question on the card?

Student A

You are going to talk about **leisure time**. You can use some or all of the ideas listed below in your talk but <u>you must answer this question</u>:

Which outdoor leisure activity do you most enjoy and why?

You must talk for 1 to 2 minutes. You have 1 minute to think and make notes before your talk begins.

Here are some ideas to help you:

• Exercise
• Excitement
• Relaxation
• Social aspect

Exam hint

Exercise 1 is a practice task for Part 2 of the Speaking Paper. In Part 2 of the Speaking Paper, you will be asked to speak about a topic for 1 to 2 minutes and you will be given **a question that you have to answer** on the topic. You will be given some ideas to help you talk about the topic, but you don't have to use them if you don't want to. You will have 1 minute to think about what you want to say before you start speaking.

Exam hint

In your 1-minute preparation time remember to make some notes of what you want to say. One way of doing this is to make a mind map. (See page 133 for how to make a mind map.)

Student B

You are going to talk about **leisure time**. You can use some or all of the ideas listed below in your talk but <u>you must answer this question</u>:

Which outdoor leisure activity would you most like to try and why?

You must talk for 1 to 2 minutes. You have 1 minute to think and make notes before your talk begins.

Here are some ideas to help you:

- Excitement
- Exercise
- Relaxation
- Social aspect

2 Work with a partner and take it in turns to ask and answer the following questions. Remember to give as much information as possible and try to keep talking for at least 5 minutes.

Part 3

We have been talking about **leisure time** and I would like to ask you some more questions on this topic.

- Do you think that it is important for young people to spend time outdoors? (Why is that?)
- Do you think that young people are spending less time outdoors? (Why is that?)
- How could young people be encouraged to spend more time outdoors?

- How has technology influenced what people do in their leisure time?
- Do you think these changes have been positive or negative? (Why is that?)
- Do you think that young people spend more time alone? (Why is that?)

- What changes have there been in the way that people communicate? (Tell me about that.)
- What are the positive aspects of these changes? (Tell me about that.)
- What are the negative aspects of these changes? (Tell me about that.)

Reading

1 Work with a partner and look at the descriptions of different reading skills in the box, then discuss the questions.

Reading Skills

Skimming: reading quickly to get the general idea of a text

Scanning: picking out specific pieces of information (e.g. *numbers*)

Detailed reading: reading closely for details contained in a text

- Which one or two of the skills would usually be appropriate for reading the following types of texts in everyday life?

  a a newspaper

  b an e-mail from a friend you haven't seen for a long time

  c a train timetable

  d a novel

  e a note or message

  f instructions (e.g. *for a DVD player*)

Exam hint

Exercise 2 is an example task for Part 3 of the Speaking Paper. In Part 3 of the Speaking Paper, you will be asked to discuss more questions on the same topic that you spoke about in Part 2. It is important that you give as much information as possible in your answers. This discussion lasts for approximately 5 minutes.

Language hint

Expressing opinions
I think that …
I don't think that …
I've always thought that …
In my opinion, …
From my point of view, …
As far as I'm concerned, …
I strongly believe that …
I have my doubts about …

- What do you usually do when you find a word or phrase in a text that you don't understand? Why?

- How do you think you could get better at reading in English? Compare your ideas with other students.

2 Work with a partner and discuss these questions:
- Do you enjoy outdoor leisure activities?

- Have you ever been on an outdoor course? (e.g. *rock climbing or canoeing*)

- If yes, tell your partner about it.

- If no, do you think you would enjoy it?

3 Read the leaflet about *The Outdoors Centre* and complete the tasks that follow.

Exam hint

Exercise 3 is a practice task for Part 2 of the Reading and Writing Paper. In Part 2 of the Reading and Writing Paper, you will be asked to read a passage (e.g. *a leaflet, advert or article*) and then complete the tasks that follow.

Outdoors Adventure – Is it for you?

The Outdoors Centre runs a range of outdoor courses aimed at both groups of young people from schools and colleges and individuals of the same age who want to join a group once they arrive here. All courses are led by an instructor and focus on promoting problem solving, leadership and communication skills. The courses run for 3–7 days and we can tailor make a course for you if you have a group of 12 participants. All our courses are residential and we have separate six-bed dormitories for male and female participants.

Why 'Adventure all the way'?

This is a 7 day course and is our most popular course. It provides a combination of outdoor activities, the chance to meet new people and the opportunity to have some fun. We guarantee that you will be proud of what you have achieved by the end of the week.

Arrival is in time for the evening meal, followed by a welcome to the centre and introductions to other group members and your instructors. You will be issued with the necessary kit and then shown to your allocated bed and locker so that you can acquaint yourself with the dormitory arrangements. Once you have unpacked, your instructor will set up some 'get-to-know-you' activities in the centre grounds. These will be short and fun so you can start getting to know each other quickly and the adventure begins.

After a filling breakfast on the second day you will be ready to try more of the centre's exciting outdoor activities. You will start with some simple problem-solving activities in the grounds and build up to higher challenges as the day progresses. Later in the day, depending on the time of year, you may prepare a shelter in the woods or near the beach which you will sleep out in.

Days three and four may either be spent rock climbing or enjoying water activities. If climbing, there will be a range of climbs to challenge everyone and you will get the chance to abseil down the rock you have just climbed up. Water activities will initially focus on safety in the water and learning how to paddle a kayak, before moving on to take part in fun-filled team tasks on the water, including scrambling up a waterfall to end the fourth day.

On days five and six there is a chance to gain firsthand experience of navigation, teamwork and leadership. The group, divided into two teams, will set out on an overnight expedition. Each person will carry a rucksack with their personal kit including sleeping bag as they head off into remote mountain areas. The teams will jointly navigate their way to a log cabin where they will spend the night. The following morning each team will be given their own finish point, which they will have to reach by a given time to have successfully completed the task.

The last day will require all of the skills gained during the week with a three team challenge involving climbing, kayaking and a map-reading treasure hunt around the centre grounds and immediate local area. In the afternoon, all participants help in a big clean up both indoors and out before having some free time. After an evening meal, the course will officially finish with the presentation of certificates and a group photograph.

Is this course for you?

To gain the full rewards of this course no previous experience is required. The days are quite long and are full of activity so they can be physically challenging. However, they are not beyond the reach of average fitness. You need to be open-minded to new experiences and prepared to get on with people from a wide range of backgrounds.

There is little time to shop whilst on the course, mainly due to our busy schedule and our locations. Therefore only a small amount of spending money is required. Each centre has a shop selling confectionery, toiletries, etc.

We actively discourage smoking; those under 16 are not allowed to smoke. There is no smoking allowed during activities or on expeditions. In addition, the drinking of alcohol while on any of our courses is prohibited at our centre.

Questions

1–3

Choose **three** correct answers.

According to the passage, *The Outdoors Centre*

a   runs one type of course over the year.

b   has separate courses for colleges.

c   hosts courses for individuals and groups.

d   works only with schools and colleges.

e   can design specific courses if needed.

f   takes participants from all age groups.

g   provides accommodation for guests.

4–6

Choose **three** correct answers.

On day one of the *Adventure all the way* course, participants

a   decide which dormitory bed they want.

b   get the chance to meet others on their course.

c   are expected to arrive mid afternoon.

d   have a meal with the Centre instructors.

e   are given the equipment they will need.

f   take part in some introductory sessions.

g   are shown around the surrounding area.

7   Choose **one** correct answer.

On day two, group members

a   spend the day indoors learning new team skills.

b   take part in progressively more difficult tasks.

c   spend the night in a shelter in the centre grounds.

8   Choose **one** correct answer.

On days three and four, there is

a   a single climb and abseil session for the group.

b   a choice between two different outdoor activities.

c   time spent learning a new skill with a partner.

9   Choose **one** correct answer.

While on the expedition, the teams

a   work together on day five.

b   walk mainly on flat ground.

c   have the same final destination.

10–12

Choose **three** correct answers.

On the last day of the course, group members

a   have nothing to do in the afternoon.

b   use all their newly acquired skills.

c   are divided into teams of three.

d   finish the course in the evening.

e   are tested on the week's events.

f   receive a memento of their visit.

g   remain on the centre grounds.

13–15

Answer these questions using no more than **three words** or **a number**.

13 In what way should you approach unfamiliar situations?

....

14 Give two reasons why you do not have much time for shopping.

....

15 While a course is running, what are all participants not allowed to do?

....

Vocabulary: staying in

1 Work with a partner and check the meaning and pronunciation of the words and phrases in the table. Use a dictionary to help you if necessary. Add two more words/phrases for each of the headings.

reading	a novel an autobiography non-fiction
computers	to download music to shop online to send e-mails
TV	a soap (opera) a documentary a chat show
friends	to have friends round (for a meal) to go round to a friend's (for a meal) to have a barbeque

2 Complete the sentences with the correct form of the words/phrases in Exercise 1.

a Have you read *My Side*, David Beckham's book about his life?

b No, I don't read many _____. I prefer _____, especially books about historical events.

c We've done a class survey about what people use their computers for.

d What's the most popular thing?

e Receiving and _____ is number one, and second is _____ onto their iPods.

f What's on TV tonight?

g Well, there's a ____documentary____ about some kind of medical research, and then at ten there's a ____chat show____ with Shakira as the guest.

h That should be good!

i Did you have a good weekend?

j It was great, thanks. We _____ a friend's for lunch. She lives in Cambridge, so we didn't have far to go. The weather was good so we _____ in the garden.

3 R.04 ▶ Listen to four conversations. What answer does each person give to these questions?

Conversation 1: What kind of programmes do you like watching on TV?

Conversation 2: Do you prefer reading fiction or non-fiction?

Conversation 3: What do you use computers for mostly?

Conversation 4: Do you often socialise with friends at home?

4 Ask and answer the questions in Exercise 3 with a partner. Encourage your partner to give more details by asking more questions.

Grammar: prepositional phrases

1 Look at the highlighted prepositional phrases in these sentences. Which one is about time, which about place and which about movement?

a I like reading with my feet up *on the sofa*.

b Sometimes I get *into bed* to watch a film.

c *In the old days*, there wasn't such a range of leisure activities.

2 Complete each phrase with the appropriate preposition of time: *at, in* or *on*.

a _____ 7.15 a.m.

b _____ Tuesday

c _____ 2001

d _____ the winter

e _____ New Year

f _____ March 17th

3 Complete each phrase with the appropriate preposition of place: *at, in* or *on*.

a _____ the bus stop

b _____ page 56

c _____ the middle

d _____ the radio

e _____ home

f _____ Germany

4 Complete each sentence with the appropriate preposition of movement: *at, to, into* or *towards*.

a We arrived _____ the theatre very late.

b She got _____ bed and fell asleep.

c Welcome _____ Australia!

d A huge dog ran _____ me and I screamed.

e Throw the ball _____ me and I'll catch it.

f We're working _____ reaching an agreement.

Grammar hint

at the end/in the end

Complete each sentence with *at the end* or *in the end*.

1 _____, I found my wallet under the sofa.

2 _____ of the book, they went to live in Canada.

3 There will be time for questions _____.

Grammar reference: see page 229

5 Read Julia's e-mail to Giovanna quickly and answer these questions.

a What film is she describing?

b What is her general opinion of it?

c What did she like most about the film?

Dear Giovanna,

I wanted to tell you about an amazing film I saw *on/at*[1] Friday. It's the second *Pirates of the Caribbean* film, *Dead Man's Chest* – have you seen it? It came out *in/at*[2] 2006, but I missed it then.

Maria and I went to see it *in/on*[3] Friday evening. We nearly missed the beginning because Maria arrived *to/at*[4] the cinema *on/at*[5] 8.00 p.m. – just before it started. When we went *to/into*[6] the cinema, it was all dark and we couldn't see where we were going! But *at/in*[7] the end, we sat right *on/at*[8] the front so we could get the full effect of the big screen.

Anyway, let me tell you about the film itself. It's set *at/on*[9] the same time and *at/in*[10] the same place as the first film and *in/at*[11] the beginning, it continues from where the first film finished. Do you remember Will and Elizabeth were going to get married? Well, something happens *in/at*[12] the middle of the wedding and everything changes! Well, I won't tell you what happens *on/at*[13] the end, because that would spoil it.

At/In[14] one point, I felt that the film was too long and I must say that the plot is a bit weak. But the action is fantastic, especially as you get *at/towards*[15] the end. There are some really good fight scenes and other stunts.

I hope everything is OK with you. I'll write again *at/in*[16] a couple of weeks.

Best wishes,
Julia

6 Complete the e-mail with the correct prepositions.

 Writing

1 The Principal of your school wants suggestions for films to show in a new 'Film Club' that the school is starting next term. Write a *letter* to your principal with a film suggestion.

In your letter you should:

● give some general background about the film

● give your opinion about the film

● say why you think other students will like it.

Write your letter using between 100 and 150 words.

Exam hint

Exercise 1 is an example task for Part 5 of the Reading and Writing Paper. In Part 5 of the Reading and Writing Paper you will be asked to do a short piece of writing in response to a given situation. The writing can take the form of a *letter, fax* or *e-mail* and you may have to provide information and/or ask for required information.

Writing reference: see page 256

Summarising

1 Read the article about *The Outdoors Centre* and then write a summary for the student magazine.

In your summary you should:

- say who *The Outdoors Centre* runs courses for
- tell students two things that happen when they first arrive
- tell students about two activities to expect.

Write your summary using between 100 and 150 words.

Outdoors Adventure – Is it for you?

The Outdoors Centre runs a range of outdoor courses aimed at both groups of young people from schools and colleges and individuals of the same age who want to join a group once they arrive here. All courses are led by an instructor and focus on promoting problem solving, leadership and communication skills. The courses run for 3–7 days and we can tailor make a course for you if you have a group of 12 participants. All our courses are residential and we have separate six-bed dormitories for male and female participants.

Why 'Adventure all the way'?

This is a 7 day course. It provides a combination of outdoor activities, the chance to meet new people and the opportunity to have some fun. We guarantee that you will be proud of what you have achieved by the end of the week.

Arrival is in time for the evening meal, followed by a welcome to the centre, other group members and your instructors. You will be issued with the necessary kit and then shown to your allocated bed and locker. Once you have unpacked, your instructor will set up some 'get-to-know-you' activities in the centre grounds. These will be short and fun so you can start getting to know each other quickly.

After breakfast on the second day, you start with some simple problem-solving activities in the grounds and build up to higher challenges as the day progresses. Later in the day, depending on the time of year, you may prepare a shelter in the woods or near the beach which you will sleep out in.

Days three and four may either be spent rock climbing or enjoying water activities. If climbing, there will be a range of climbs to challenge everyone and you will get the chance to abseil down the rock you have just climbed up. Water activities will initially focus on safety in the water and learning how to paddle a kayak, before moving on to take part in fun-filled team tasks on the water, including scrambling up a waterfall to end the fourth day.

On days five and six, the group, divided into two teams, will set out on an overnight expedition. Each person will carry a rucksack with their personal kit including sleeping bag as they head off into remote mountain areas. The teams will jointly navigate their way to a log cabin where they will spend the night. The following morning each team will be given their own finish point, which they will have to reach by a given time to have successfully completed the task.

The last day includes a three team challenge involving climbing, kayaking and a map-reading treasure hunt around the centre grounds and immediate local area. In the afternoon, all participants help in a big clean up before having some free time. After an evening meal, the course will officially finish with the presentation of certificates and a group photograph.

Language recap

Grammar

1 Complete the questions with the correct alternative. Ø means no word should be added.

a Where _____ Linda gone? *have/has/Ø*
b Is he _____ to come to the party? *going/go/went*
c Could you tell us _____ what time the swimming pool opens? *does/if/Ø*
d _____ she play the guitar? *Can/Do/Ø*
e What _____ happened to him yesterday? *has/did/Ø*
f Do you know where _____ the butter is? *does/is/Ø*
g Can you tell me _____ you've finished with that book? *if/what/Ø*
h When does the film _____? *start/starts/started*
i I'd like to know whether _____ you're going to the party? *if/are/Ø*
j Would you mind telling me who _____ gave you this money? *did/have/Ø*

2 There are mistakes in eight of the prepositions in the phrases in *italics*. Find the mistakes and correct them.

a We went out for a lovely meal *at Valentine's Day.*
b I spent the whole day lying *at the beach* and reading my book.
c He stood up and left *in the middle* of the film.
d I've been *at Rome* twice.
e We're *working to an agreement* about pay at work at the moment.
f I'm really looking forward to seeing you all *on New Year.*
g She arrived *to the party* really late because her train was delayed.
h Everyone went quiet the minute she *walked to the room.*
i He's lived *in South Africa* for ten years.
j It was difficult to get tickets but *at the end*, we got some on the Internet.

Vocabulary

3 Complete this e-mail with the correct form of a word/phrase from the box. Three items cannot be used.

> blockbuster   dress circle   gig   ceramics   architecture   watercolours   dance floor   DJ   house music

Dear Kate,

Sorry I haven't written for so long – I've been so busy!

Last weekend, it was my friend Charlie's birthday and his parents invited the whole class to a party at his house on Friday night. It was in a big marquee in his garden. The _____ (1) was really good and played all my favourites – I couldn't stop dancing! You would have loved it; he played _____ (2) all night. In fact the whole class was up on the _____ (3) for the whole evening. I can't wait for his birthday next year.

What else? Oh yes, a couple of weeks ago, I went to see a friend of mine who's in a band. They've just started doing _____ (4) at local venues and they were performing in the village hall. It was really fun and quite a lot of people turned up.

How's your art course going? I must say I really loved the _____ (5) you showed me last time – especially that set of plates you'd made. They were lovely. I think you said you were working on different styles of painting like _____ (6) and things now. Is that right?

OK, I'd better go. I'll ring you soon and we'll fix up a weekend for you to come down.

Alex

4 Complete the crossword using the clues.

ACROSS

2 Receive information or programme on a computer from the Internet (8)
7 An occasion when you cook and eat food outside (8)
8 Books about real facts or events (3, 7)
9 A TV drama that is on regularly about the same group of people (4, 5)
10 A book that someone writes about their own life (13)

DOWN

1 I'm going to have the neighbours _____ for coffee. (5)
3 A long story written about characters and events that are not real (5)
4 A TV programme that gives information about a subject (11)
5 A TV show in which people are asked questions about themselves (4, 4)
6 I'll _____ you an e-mail tomorrow. (4)

Paper 1: Reading and Writing

 Part 1: Reading (10 marks)

Text types in this part could include:

- a collection of short texts (e.g. *advertisements*)
- timetables
- leaflets (e.g. *giving advice and tips*).

Skills

Your skimming and scanning skills are being tested in this part. **Skimming** means you read through the texts quickly to identify the **main ideas**, i.e. to understand the gist of the text. When you skim read, you don't need to read the whole text word-for-word – try focusing on the first and last sentences of each paragraph and using clues such as titles or subheadings and key words to help you gain an overall sense of the text.

When you scan a text, you are looking for a **specific piece of information**. **Scanning** is something you do in everyday life, e.g. choosing which television programme to watch from the listing in a magazine, or looking for a particular phone number in the phone book. You do not need to read or understand every word in the text when you scan for specific information.

You will need to skim each section of the text to decide if it is useful for the question you are answering. Once you have identified which bits of the text might contain the answer, you then scan them to find the relevant details.

Let's take an example from the Edexcel International GCSE ESL paper in May 2010:

There are 13 different options for accommodation on a Farm Holiday. You are asked this question:

Which accommodation has the following features?

1 It is located on the site of an old castle.

By skimming through all 13 accommodation options, you are able to narrow your choices and pick out just two with a reference to a *castle*:

A: CASTLERIGG FARM

*Experience a stay in a Georgian country farmhouse cottage. Get close to nature. Breathe in the tranquillity and quietness. Explore the extensive grounds which include features such as medieval Rigg **Castle** and a disused railway viaduct. Short drive to the coast. Open all year.*

J: LANGLEY CASTLE BARN

*This luxury barn is built on the ruins of a medieval **castle** with magnificent views and a private garden. It is perfectly located in the charming unspoilt village of Langley. An ideal base for the Lakes/Dales and walking. Open all year except Christmas.*

Now you have to scan these two accommodation options to identify the specific piece of information you need to answer the question. In **A: CASTLERIGG FARM**, we learn there is a castle near the accommodation and in **J: LANGLEY CASTLE BARN**, we learn the accommodation is directly on the ruins of an old castle – so the correct answer must be **J**.

Task types

Part 1 Reading is about matching aspects listed in the questions to their equivalents in the texts. To do this successfully you need to recognise and understand paraphrasing – this means you have to do a bit more than simply spot the same words in both the questions and the texts. In our example above, the question uses the words: *It is located on the site of an old castle* whereas the text tells us *This luxury barn is built on the ruins of a medieval castle*. We know that *medieval* is very *old* – this is a synonym – and if something is *built on* then it must be *located on* – so this is a paraphrase.

The questions follow the order of information presented in the texts. You will find all the answers in the text.

Task types in this part include:

- **Multiple matching:** you could be asked to match two things, e.g. a list of people's requirements to advertised services. The list may contain the same number of, more or fewer items than the number of sections of text. There will be at least one 'distractor' – another apparently possible answer. The example we looked at above is a multiple matching task.

- **Multiple-choice:** you will choose which option is the correct answer to a question, or which option best fills a gap in a sentence. There could be three or four options – the number of options will always be the same within the task. All will appear reasonable, but only one will be correct.

- **Short-answer questions:** you will generally need to write between one and three words/numbers (the exact number is stated in the instructions). You will find the words/numbers for your answers in the text itself. Copy these words, unchanged, directly from the text, and make sure you stick to the number of words allowed. It is not a good idea to copy whole sentences from the text as you will not gain the mark even if the correct answer can be found somewhere within the sentence you have copied. Watch your spelling – this is an important part of completing the task successfully.

Getting started...

1 Look at the pictures. What does each one make you think about?

2 Complete each sentence with a word from the box. Work with a partner and explain the meaning of each highlighted phrase.

| fallen close get start distant touch |

a My sister is hoping to _____ a family after she gets married next year.

b We're a very _____ family. We tell each other everything.

c She's a _____ cousin, but I'm not exactly sure how we're related.

d Jo is the only one my brother has stayed in _____ with since leaving university.

e Dan and Cara have _____ out. Apparently, it was to do with money.

f I don't really _____ on with Anna's boyfriend, so I see her on her own.

Speaking

1 Work with a partner and decide who is going to answer the Student A questions and who is going to answer the Student B questions. Student A needs to answer all four questions, taking no more than 3 minutes. Repeat the process for the Student B questions.

Exam hint

Exercise 1 is a practice task for Part 1 of the Speaking Paper.

Student A
Let's talk about your family
How many are there in your immediate family?
Would you describe your family as close? (Why is that?)
Who do you get on with best in your family? (Why is that?)
When do you see other members of your family, such as your cousins/aunts/uncles? (Tell me about that.)

Student B
Let's talk about your friends
How many close friends do you have?
Why are they your close friends? (Tell me about that.)
Which friend do you get on best with? (Why is that?)
Do you prefer spending time with one close friend or a group of friends? (Why is that?)

 **Listening**

1 R.05 ▶ Listen to part of a discussion. Which of these statements do the speakers discuss?

  a I think I will stay friends with my best friends forever.

  b I tell my best friend everything.

  c I prefer going out with a group of friends rather than just one friend.

  d My oldest friends are my best friends.

  e I talk to different friends about different things which are important to me.

  f I don't like spending a lot of time on my own.

2 R.05 ▶ Now listen again. Which expressions from the box do the speakers use?

> **Responding to opinions**
>
> That's more or less what I think.
>
> I'm not quite sure what I think about that.
>
> ✓It depends really.
>
> That's sometimes true for me but not often.
>
> Absolutely not.
>
> ✓That used to be true for me but it isn't any more.
>
> ✓That's never been the case for me.
>
> Definitely.

3 Match the expressions in Exercise 2 with the statements in Exercise 1, according to what is closest to your opinion. (If none of them fits, write sentences of your own.)

4 Work in groups of four. Discuss and explain the reasons for your responses to the statements in Exercise 1. Find the person who has the most similar attitudes to you.

Grammar: present tenses

1 Look at these examples of present tenses. Match them with the uses i–vi.

  a Melanie works two nights a week as a midwife.

  b They live together with their children.

  c If I want my kids to do something, they just do it.

  d I believe that it is very important to try new experiences.

  e We do enjoy doing things as a family.

  f I'm changing the way I deal with their untidy rooms.

  i The present continuous is used to describe actions or events going on now or around now.

  ii The present simple is used to describe permanent (not temporary) situations.

  iii The simple form is used with verbs that do not have continuous forms.

  iv The present simple is often used in subordinate clauses which refer to the future.

  v Do can be used to add emphasis.

  vi The present simple is used to talk about things that happen regularly or all the time.

2 Choose the correct alternative in these sentences.

  a I usually *go/am going* and visit family in Cyprus, but this summer I *work/am working* as a tour guide to try to make some money.

  b *Do you know/Are you knowing* what 'affection' means?

  c Do *get/getting* in touch with Justin before he *moves/is moving* to Ireland.

  d This cake *tastes/is tasting* delicious. *Does/Is* your brother often *make/making* cakes?

  e I *don't think/'m not thinking* Tina understands exactly what you *want/are wanting* her to do.

  f I hope it *doesn't/isn't* still *rain/raining./*I *'m not wanting/don't want* to get wet on the way to my sister's wedding.

3 There are mistakes in each of these sentences. Find the mistakes and correct them.

  a I'm seeing my grandmother at least once a month.

  b We'll phone home when we'll get to the hotel.

  c I hate the way his girlfriend often replys for him.

  d Grandparents aren't usually living with their families in this country.

  e Your brother dosen't need to wait for us.

  f I'm really liking Mike's cousin.

  g The average number of children per family falls.

  h He do like you but he's just very shy.

  i I'm promising that I'll try to get on with your parents, but it's not easy.

  j At last my sister is begining to enjoy her new job.

 Reading

1 Work with a partner and look at the pictures and the title of the text. Tell your partner what you think the text will be about.

2 Now read the article and answer the questions that follow.

Grammar hint

'State' verbs

Which of the following sentences are possible and which are not (or very unlikely)? Why?

1 A What do you think about?
   B What are you thinking about?
2 A Do you feel OK?
   B Are you feeling OK?
3 A I see what you mean.
   B I'm seeing what you mean.

Grammar reference: see page 231

Exam hint

Before reading a text, it can often help to look at the title and sub-titles and any illustrations to get an idea of what the text will be about. When reading, look for words or phrases in the text which express the same ideas as the key words in the questions.

Exam hint

Exercise 2 is a practice task for Part 3 of the Reading and Writing Paper. In Part 3 of the Reading and Writing Paper you will be asked to read a passage (e.g. *a report or article*) and then complete the tasks that follow.

My very empty nest

My name is Sonia and I am now 52. I went from my parents' house to my sister's house, to a succession of shared flats and houses with friends and then to a home with my husband and children.

After nearly three decades in which I have hardly had a second's privacy, the youngest of my four children is now leaving for university. I should be cheering and, inside, in a very small place, I am jubilant, patting myself on the back on a job well done, raising four kids alone and seeing them all off safely to university and successfully into the world.

I think of what life will be like now my daughter has gone. The laundry will be only mine, folded and put away the minute it's dry. There will be no dirty dishes in the sink. There will be one single cup drying on the draining board instead of a dozen growing penicillin under the bed. The bedroom will prove to have a carpet instead of messy mountain ranges of 'nothing to wear'. There will be no

half-full glasses; no stalagmites of loose change; and the sheets will always match the pillowcases. When I put down a lipstick it will still be there the next day, and when I reach for the conditioner I will find it at the side of the bath instead of upside down in the shower, dripping into the mouth of the open drain.

So why do I feel this crushing sense of grief? The reality is that my children hated my cooking, were fussy eaters and those five o'clock meals were a torture of pushed-around food for all of us. The park was cold and boring. I never had enough money or time or patience, and mornings were a noisy nightmare of me urging them to hurry up, get ready, finish faster. And now they have.

I keep the children's bedroom doors firmly closed so I don't see the walls dotted with a constellation of tiny Blu-Tack stars that once held 100 snapshots of teenagers or the remnants of childhood. The wardrobes reveal a line of empty hangers and boxes that didn't make the final ascent to the attic.

When someone walks across the floor upstairs it will be a ghost, and, instead of music and hoots of laughter from telephone calls in which I occasionally overhear myself referred to in less than glowing terms, it will just be the creaks and groans of the central heating pipes. When I leave the sitting room at night, in perfect order with the cushions plumped up on sofas only I sit on, instead of a Las Vegas skyline of left-on light bulbs, it will be dark in the hall and dark on the stairs and dark in the bedroom where I still sleep on the right side of the bed, though it's been years since I lost my husband.

Nobody will eat all the raspberries or finish the yoghurt. I need never hide the cooking chocolate again. I need never buy milk. The bread will go mouldy, and I'll come home in the evening and instead of making a meal for someone who doesn't want it and prefers instant noodles, I can have crackers and cheese, and eat apples. I can finally write the book I've always dreamed of writing, and decorate the spare room, of which I now have four. And once it's all done, I can look back on 26 years full of

kids and a husband and wonder what to do with the next 26 without either of them.

I realise that I've gone from having a home to living in a warehouse. I've moved into the next stage of life in which I'm not a mother or a wife but a caretaker. When you get made redundant from other jobs you get a golden handshake and a carriage clock, but when your time is up as a live-in parent, all you get is an attic full of rubbish. You lose a child and gain a storage facility.

What am I moaning about? I've always had a very full life of my own. I love my job, have great friends and do more activities than there are days in the week. But still I can't suppress a pang that the children are all grown up and it's over. However, it could be worse. So, though the shelves may be lined with leftovers, I also have privacy, and this big empty house seems suddenly full of wonderful, delicious possibilities. It's just going to take me some time to appreciate them. That and a lot of tissues.

Questions

1–5

Choose **true**, **false** or **not given** for each statement.

	True	False	Not given
1 Sonia has experienced living alone in the past.	☐	☐	☐
2 Sonia raised her children with her husband.	☐	☐	☐
3 Sonia's children have all gone to university.	☐	☐	☐
4 Sonia's daughter left used plates under the bed.	☐	☐	☐
5 Sonia's daughter often borrowed her clothes.	☐	☐	☐

6–10

Answer these questions using no more than **three words** or **a number**.

6   How does Sonia describe her children's relationship with food?

....

7   Which two items remain in the children's wardrobes?

....

8   What is the source of the only noise in the house now?

....

9   Which words tell you that Sonia's children were not energy conscious?

....

10   What will Sonia not have to think about doing when she gets in at night?

....

11–15

Complete these sentences using no more than **three words** or **a number**.

11   Sonia now plans to _____ which will fulfil her long term ambition.

12   Sonia hopes to _____ some of the rooms in her house.

13   In her new role as _____ Sonia is still looking after her children's belongings.

14   Sonia still leads a _____; she is busy with work, friends and activities.

15   It is going to _____ for Sonia to get used to living alone.

◁))) Listening

1   Work with a partner and discuss these questions:

● Do all your friends live near to you?

● Do you often fall out with your friends?

● Have you ever been on holiday with your friends?

2   R.06 ▶ Listen to five different people talking about friends as part of a radio programme and complete the notes that follow using no more than **three words** or **a number** for each answer.

Exam hint

Exercise 2 is a practice task for Part 1 of the Listening Paper.

Speaker 1
● friends for nearly 15 years and like sisters
● not always _____ (1) with one another
● would help each other if _____ (2)

Speaker 2
● used to have a close, best friend but fell out
● didn't talk _____ (3) and then went to live overseas
● friend got in touch as she wanted _____ (4)

Speaker 3
● group of friends went on a summer holiday to _____ (5)
● thought they would all have a good time
● couldn't agree on what to do and had _____ (6)

Speaker 4
● has lots of friends instead of one close friend
● doesn't like it when people stop seeing _____ (7) to spend time with only one person
● favourite thing is to go out _____ (8) with his friends

Speaker 5
● best friend is her mum
● call each other _____ (9) for a long time
● _____ (10) not happy with her relationship with her mum

3   R.06 ▶ Listen again and check your answers.

Vocabulary: suffixes

1 Match the words with the suffixes in the box to make nouns. Which combinations need a spelling change?

| -ness -ment -ion -ship -hood -ity |

friend*ship*   sad_____
child_____   member_____
happy_____   enjoy_____
affect_____   reliable_____
stupid_____   kind_____
excite_____   forgetful_____
father_____   relation_____

2 Complete these sentences with one of the answers from Exercise 1.

a I had a wonderful _____. We were very close as a family and all got on incredibly well.

b My grandma's memory is not as good as it used to be; her _____ is becoming a real problem.

c I think the _____ of the party was all too much for your little cousin. She fell asleep as soon as her head touched the pillow.

d David's _____ is one of the things I value most about him. If he says he will do something, he does it.

e I'm afraid the _____ of the local tennis club has fallen to 250 this year.

f As children we were shown a lot of _____; we are a very open and loving family.

g It was with great _____ that they waved their daughter off to university; she would be missed.

h I'll never forget the _____ shown to me by two complete strangers when I fell off my bike.

👄 Speaking

1 Work with a partner and each choose one of the topics below. Prepare to time your partner – give them 1 minute to prepare and then ask them to start speaking. Tell them to stop speaking after 2 minutes. Did your partner answer the question on the card?

Student A

You are going to talk about **relationships**. You can use some or all of the ideas listed below in your talk but you must answer this question:

Who is your oldest friend and why are you still friends?
You must talk for 1 to 2 minutes. You have 1 minute to think and make notes before your talk begins.

Here are some ideas to help you:
· When you met
· How you met
· How often you see each other
· What you have in common

Student B

You are going to talk about **relationships**. You can use some or all of the ideas listed below in your talk but <u>you must answer this question:</u>

Which special occasion did you last enjoy with your family?
You must talk for 1 to 2 minutes. You have 1 minute to think and make notes before your talk begins.

Here are some ideas to help you:
- Reason for occasion
- Who was there
- What happened
- How you felt

2 Work with a partner and take it in turns to ask and answer the following questions. Remember to give as much information as possible and try to keep talking for at least 5 minutes.

Exam hint

Exercise 2 is a practice task for Part 3 of the Speaking Paper.

Part 3

We have been talking about **relationships** and I would like to ask you some more questions on this topic.

- Do you think it is important to spend time together as a family? (Why is that?)
- How important do you think it is to eat meals together? (Why is that?)
- What is the main reason why families do not spend enough time together? (Tell me about that.)

- Do you think it is better to have a few close friends or a group of not so close friends? (Why is that?)
- Do you think you have to know somebody for a long time for them to be a close friend? (Why is that?)
- Do you think that the use of technology (e.g. *chat rooms*) encourages or discourages real friendships? (Why is that?)

- What technological changes have there been in the last 20 years which have affected family relationships? (Tell me about that.)
- Do you think families are as close now as they were 20 years ago? (Tell me about that.)
- What changes in family relationships do you think will have occurred in another 20 years? (Why is that?)

Grammar: modifiers

1 Look at the highlighted words in these sentences. Which three of the words in the box are similar in meaning to *incredibly*? Which two are similar to *quite*? Which one is similar to *bit*?

Grammar hint

A modifier is an adjective, adverb or phrase that gives additional information about another word.

> pretty   terribly   little   extremely   fairly   really

a I'm incredibly close to my best friend.

b My brother and I are quite similar.

c My sister is a bit taller than me.

Grammar hint

quite

Quite often means *fairly*, but it can also mean *completely*. In which of the following sentences does it mean *fairly* and in which does it mean *completely*?

1 You are quite right. We should visit your uncle.
2 Is Paul quite certain that he wants to leave school?
3 Julie is quite amazing the way she runs her own business as well as bringing up three small children.
4 I see my sister a lot as we live quite close.

Grammar reference: see page 231

2 There are mistakes in seven of these sentences. Find the mistakes and correct them.

a She is quite likes Steve but she doesn't know him well.

b It was terribly freezing in Jill and Dave's new house. They don't have central heating yet.

c I'm bit thirsty. I think I'll have an orange juice.

d He was fairly surprised to hear that I had passed my driving test.

e Sam's cousin is quite a nice. I hope he can come to the party tonight.

f My new car is a little smaller my old one but it's fine.

g The food's pretty good in that new Thai restaurant. We went there with friends last night.

h I enjoyed the film but it was a fairly long and a bit sentimental.

i Tim is extremely clever, but he still needs to study more.

j I met fairly an interesting distant cousin for the first time yesterday.

3 Read this extract from an e-mail message. Which option, a, b or c, best fits each gap?

> I went on holiday this summer with my family and it was _____ (1) fantastic! We were staying in this little hotel on the south coast of Turkey. It was_____ (2) close to the sea, ten minutes' walk at the most. It was _____ (3) comfortable and had a great pool. They also did _____ (4) delicious food in the evenings.
>
> A lot of the time we stayed around the hotel and the pool and sunbathed, but I did go paragliding once – off the side of a cliff. It was _____ (5) scary I can tell you! We also spent a couple of days learning to scuba dive, which was good fun and _____ (6) relaxing in comparison.

1	a very	b a bit	c really
2	a fairly	b little	c absolutely
3	a completely	b incredibly	c horribly
4	a fairly	b a bit	c really
5	a pretty	b bit	c totally
6	a absolutely	b terribly	c quite

4 Tell another student about the last time you found something:

- really interesting
- pretty expensive
- a bit annoying
- fairly dull
- incredibly exciting

Vocabulary: describing people

1 Work with a partner and look at the words for describing physical appearance. What other words/phrases can you add to the table?

hair	build	general appearance
shoulder-length	slim	well-dressed
clean-shaven	well-built	smart
a beard	stocky	in her mid-30s

2 Work with a partner and look at the words/phrases in the box.

> good-looking bright sensible laid-back stylish stingy
> full-of-him/herself reliable shy odd stubborn open-minded sensitive

For the words/phrases you don't know, check the meaning and pronunciation in a dictionary.

3 Match six words/phrases from the box in Exercise 2 with these sentences.
  a He always tries to get out of paying for drinks when we go out even though I know he's got plenty of money at the moment.
  b Nothing seems to bother him. He's always very relaxed about everything.
  c Once she's made up her mind, it's terribly difficult to get her to change it!
  d Basically, you know that if she says she'll do something, she will definitely do it.
  e Ever since she won a prize for her first novel she's become quite annoyingly arrogant.
  f He doesn't really like social situations where he doesn't know other people. He finds it quite difficult to make polite conversation.

4 Write example sentences for three of the other words/phrases in Exercise 2. Ask your partner to match your sentence with a word/phrase from the box.

5 R.07 ▶ You will hear two people (one male/one female) describing someone they have met at a party. Write down the words/phrases they use to describe him. Do the speakers both feel the same way about him? Compare your answers with a partner.

6 Work with a partner and think of a teacher you both know. Don't tell other students who you have chosen. Write down six words/phrases that you would use to describe his/her physical appearance.

7 Take it in turns to read out your words to the rest of the class. Other pairs of students should quietly write down who they think it is. Which pair got the most correct answers?

 Writing

1 Informal e-mails and letters can be very similar in style. Which of these statements are true of them both?
  a The writer usually knows the person they are writing to.
  b Contractions (e.g. *isn't*, *there's*, etc.) are used.
  c Exclamation marks are sometimes used.

d The style is sometimes like spoken language.

e Informal language is used, e.g. *Can you meet me at 6.00 p.m.?* rather than more formal language, e.g. *Would it be possible for you to meet me at 6.00 p.m.?*

f They usually end either *Yours faithfully* or *Yours sincerely*.

2 Look at the letter in the Writing reference on page 254. What is the main subject of each paragraph?

3 Work with a partner and read the following e-mail. How many paragraphs do you think it should be divided into? Where would you begin and end each paragraph? (Don't worry about punctuation at this stage.)

○○○

Hi there!

Thanks for your last e-mail and all your news. You sound like youve been really busy with college work. I hope you get all your assignments finished before I arrive. Its not long now until the 25th – I cant wait! It seems like ages since I last saw you – and since I had a proper holiday. I know you wont be able to meet me at the airport; its really kind of your brother to say he doesnt mind coming instead. Just so I have some idea of who to look out for, could you give me a rough idea of what he looks like? I dont want to go home with the wrong person! The other thing I wanted to ask you about was your family. Id like to bring them one or two small presents from England, but Im not sure exactly what yet. If you could give me some suggestions for what your parents and brother might like, that would be really helpful. I do hope everythings going OK with you. Ill tell you the latest about whats happening with me when I see you (and theres lots to tell!).

Jo

---

4 Work with a partner and look at these sentences. Discuss when we use the apostrophe (') in English.

a The dog looks happy. It's just found its bone.

b I haven't been on my brother's new boat yet. He's very proud of it!

c My parents' house is very old. Apparently it was built in 1785.

5 Look at the e-mail in Exercise 3. There are thirteen apostrophes missing. Where should each one go?

6 You are going to write a reply to the e-mail in Exercise 3. In your *e-mail* to Jo you should:

● describe your brother's general appearance

● state what gift your parents would like and why

● state what gift your brother would like and why.

Write your e-mail using between 100 and 150 words.

Exam hint

Exercise 6 is a practice task for Part 5 of the Reading and Writing Paper.

Exam hint

Decide how you are going to organise your reply. How many paragraphs are you going to have? What is going to be the subject of each one? Does it have a friendly opening and closing paragraph? Is it written in an informal style? Does it address the bullet points?

Summarising

1 Your English teacher has asked you to write a summary of the article 'My very empty nest' below.

In your summary you should:

● say what Sonia's life was like before her children left home

● give **two** good points for Sonia living alone

● give **two** bad points for Sonia living alone.

Write your summary using between 100 and 150 words.

Exam hint

Exercise 1 is a practice task for Part 6 of the Reading and Writing Paper.

My very empty nest

My name is Sonia and I am now 52. I went from my parents' house to my sister's house, to a succession of shared flats and houses with friends and then to a home with my husband and children.

After nearly three decades in which I have hardly had a second's privacy, the youngest of my four children is now leaving for university. I should be cheering and, inside, in a very small place, I am jubilant, patting myself on the back on a job well done, raising four kids alone and seeing them all off safely to university and successfully into the world.

I think of what life will be like now my daughter has gone. The laundry will be only mine, folded and put away the minute it's dry. There will be no dirty dishes in the sink. There will be one single cup drying on the draining board instead of a dozen growing penicillin under the bed. The bedroom will prove to have a carpet instead of messy mountain ranges of 'nothing to wear'. When I reach for the conditioner I will find it at the side of the bath instead of upside down in the shower, dripping into the mouth of the open drain.

So why do I feel this crushing sense of grief? When someone walks across the floor upstairs it will be a ghost, and, instead of music and hoots of laughter from telephone calls in which I occasionally overhear myself referred to in less than glowing terms, it will just be the creaks and groans of the central heating pipes. When I leave the sitting room at night, in perfect order with the cushions plumped up on sofas only I sit on, instead of a Las Vegas skyline of left-on light bulbs, it will be dark in the hall and dark on the stairs and dark in the bedroom where I still sleep on the right side of the bed, though it's been years since I lost my husband.

I'll come home in the evening and instead of making a meal for someone who doesn't want it, I can have crackers and cheese, and eat apples. I can finally write the book I've always dreamed of writing, and decorate the spare room, of which I now have four. And once it's all done, I can look back on 26 years full of kids and a husband and wonder what to do with the next 26 without either of them.

What am I moaning about? I've always had a very full life of my own. I love my job, have great friends and do more activities than there are days in the week. But still I can't suppress a pang that the children are all grown up and it's over. However, it could be worse. So, though the shelves may be lined with leftovers, I also have privacy, and this big empty house seems suddenly full of wonderful, delicious possibilities. It's just going to take me some time to appreciate them.

Language recap

Grammar

1 Read this e-mail. Put the verbs in brackets into either the present simple or present continuous.

Dear Jo,

Great to hear from you. I'm very pleased to hear that all the surprise birthday party preparations for your dad _____ [1] (go) well. I _____ [2] (know) he will get quite a shock on the night but he will definitely enjoy having all his family and friends around him. I must say I _____ [3] (look) forward to it so much – I can't wait!

Did I tell you that we _____ [4] (move) out of our flat? Mum and Dad have decided to sell it and we are buying a house not far from here. I get my own room too and it's big enough for friends to be able to comfortably stay over. It _____ [5] (have) a lovely big garden which my mum is really excited about. She really _____ [6] (like) gardening and I've promised her that I will help her to get the garden looking nice once we move in.

How's school? _____ [7] (you still have) problems with your project? I hope not! My studies _____ [8] (go) really well and I _____ [9] (look) forward to our school trip to France next month. We are going camping for a week and doing lots of outdoor activities.

Do say 'Hi!' to Dave when you _____ [10] (see) him. I look forward to catching up with him at the party.

Love,
Paula xx

---

2 Put the word *quite* in the best place in these sentences.

a It was a surprise to discover a tiny kitten in my bedroom.
b I couldn't believe how many people were at the concert. It was incredible.
c He's good at tennis. He plays at least twice a week.
d I agree with you. We should have a big party for Dad's fortieth birthday.
e Why did the referee allow that goal? It was clearly offside. It's ridiculous!
f We enjoyed last night's film, but it should have been half an hour shorter.

Vocabulary

3 Match the words in the box with the dictionary definitions a–h.

| sensible   stingy   odd   bright   laid-back   sensitive   stylish   stubborn |

a thinks about how other people will feel about something; easily offended or upset
b intelligent, clever
c strange or different from what you expect
d attractive and fashionable
e not generous, especially with money
f refusing to change your mind even when other people criticise you or try to persuade you
g relaxed and not seeming to worry about anything
h able to make good and practical decisions

4 Put the word in brackets at the end of each sentence into the correct form.

  a Would you say you had a happy _____? (child)
  b Barry felt great _____ for his grandmother. (affect)
  c I can't believe my _____ last night. I should never have shouted at Fiona. (stupid)
  d How much does annual _____ of the club cost? (member)
  e I'm getting very _____ . Now I can't find my glasses! (forget)
  f I wish Tony was a bit more _____ . This is the third time he's not turned up for a game of tennis. (reliability)
  g In his _____ he had forgotten to switch the camcorder on. (excite)
  h Do you have a good _____ with your sister? (relation)

5 Mark the stress on the correct syllables in these words.

  a _sen_sitive
  b stubborn
  c stylish
  d extremely
  e definitely
  f reliability
  g excitement

Paper 1: Reading and Writing

 Part 4: Writing (20 marks)

This section requires you to produce a semi-formal, factual piece of writing based on your own knowledge and interests – but you are quite free to invent relevant material. This piece of writing will take the form of a **report** or an **article**.

You are given a short description of a situation which:

1 sets out the context and purpose – i.e. where your piece of writing will appear or what it is for

2 sets out the target reader – i.e. who will read it

3 outlines what you should include in your response.

You must respond to all these instructions when producing your piece of writing as these will dictate the tone and register as well as the format and style of the response required. It is essential to keep to the number of words: if you write too few words, it is unlikely that you will have covered all the points in sufficient detail and you will not be able to access the full range of marks available for this section. Similarly, there are penalties for exceeding the word limit.

All these aspects form part of the writing assessment, so you must bear them all in mind.

Your report or article will be marked according to four criteria. These are:

● **Communicative quality:** this looks at how successfully you have fulfilled the requirements of the task. It is very important then to make sure you have addressed all the bullet points within the word count.

● **Lexical accuracy and range:** this assesses the range of vocabulary you have used and how accurately you have used it.

● **Grammatical accuracy and range:** this looks at the range of grammatical structures you use and how accurately you have used them.

● **Effective organisation:** this looks at the way you have organised your response in terms of paragraphing, cohesion and coherence.

Let's look at this question in the Edexcel IGCSE ESL paper in November 2009:

Your school has decided to support a charity* this year. Write an article for the school newspaper.

- *Give details of your chosen type of charity.*

- *Say why your school should support it.*

- *Suggest two ways that the school could raise money for that charity.*

*Charity – An organisation that gives money, goods or help to people who are poor, sick or in need of support.

*You should write between **100 and 150 words**.*

You learn that the context is a school magazine and the purpose is to persuade others at school which charity the school should support. From this, you know that fellow school students and teachers at the school are the target audience. You will need to bear this in mind when you are thinking about the tone, style and language you will use – it should not be too formal as your fellow students will be reading it. On the other hand, it cannot be too chatty as teachers will also read it.

You will note that there are essentially four things you must mention in your report since the third bullet point asks you to suggest two ways of raising money. The best way to produce a clear and well-structured text is to work your way through the bullet points one by one, ticking each one off when you are happy you have addressed it fully. Since you have a maximum of 150 words for your report and four pieces of information to give, you might want to consider writing approximately 35 words for each piece of information. Clearly, you have to be a bit flexible on this as one bullet point might require a bit more detail than the others, but as a guideline, this should work.

Getting started...

1 Work with a partner. Name as many different places that people live in (e.g. *cottage*) as you can in 1 minute.

2 Match each of the following words/phrases with the correct definition.

a   houseboat
b   caravan
c   studio flat
d   cottage
e   bungalow
f   detached house
g   semi-detached
h   terraced house house
i   flat
j   motorhome

i   a house that is joined to another by one shared wall
ii   a house that is built on one level
iii   a house that is not attached to another house
iv   a vehicle that you live in while on holiday that you can drive around in
v   a house that is one of a row of houses joined together
vi   a vehicle that a car pulls behind it and in which you can live while on holiday
vii   a set of rooms for someone to live in that is part of a larger building
viii a special boat that you can live in
ix   a large single room that contains the kitchen, living room and bedroom. The bathroom is separate.
x   a small house especially in the country

3 R.08 ▶ Listen to three people describing their lifestyles. Which two words in the box could you use to describe each one?

| sociable   hard   busy   leisurely   high-pressure   lonely |

Vocabulary hint

lifestyle – the way that someone lives, including their work and home life, and the things they own

---

 ## Speaking

1 Work with a partner and decide who is going to answer the Student A questions and who is going to answer the Student B questions. Student A needs to answer all four questions, taking no more than 3 minutes. Repeat the process for the Student B questions.

Exam hint

Exercise 1 is a practice task for Part 1 of the Speaking Paper.

Student A
Let's talk about your home
Who do you live with?
How would you describe the house/flat you live in?
Which is your favourite room? (Why is that?)
What changes would you like to make to your bedroom? (Why is that?)

Student B
Let's talk about your town/city
How would you describe the town/city you live in?
What is the best thing about your town/city? (Why is that?)
What is the worst thing about your town/city? (Why is that?)
Which one thing would you change about your town/city? (Why is that?)

🔊 Listening

1 Look at the photos and read the text. Write two questions which you would expect to be discussed in the radio interview.

IT'S YOUR LIFE MONDAY

LIFE RADIO, 10.15 A.M. Today's programme is about 'living on the road'. We have an interview with Greg and Marcia Dowling, a couple who have been living, and working, on the road for over ten years. After nearly two years of living a 'normal' life, they swapped their comfortable house for a motorhome and took to the highways of the United States. Find out about how they feel about the ups and downs of life on the road.

Exam hint

Exercise 2 is a practice task for Part 2 of the Listening Paper.

2 **R.09** ▶ Listen to the radio interview and answer the following questions.

Questions

1–5

For each question, choose the best answer, **a, b** or **c.**

1 What do Greg and Marcia do for a living?

  a They are travel writers.

  b They are photographers.

  c Greg is an explorer and Marcia is a photographer.

2 They enjoy living in the motorhome because they

  a go back to the same location every day.

  b can take photos of new people they meet.

  c enjoy the fact that the surroundings change.

3 What does Marcia say about going to bed at night?

  a She finds it exciting to sleep in different places all the time.

  b She doesn't usually sleep very well in new places.

  c She likes sleeping in the same bed each night.

4 What is Marcia's main point about communicating with family and friends?

  a She communicates by phone and e-mail but she misses face-to-face contact.

  b It isn't a problem because it's easy to contact people using the Internet and mobile phones.

  c It's too difficult to stay in touch with people so they don't usually try.

5 Greg says living on the road is hard because

  a the van often needs repairing.

  b you have to get to know each new place.

  c it's stressful not knowing where you're going next.

6–10

Complete the notes using no more than **three words** or **a number**.

Compromises they have to make:
● they enjoy a challenge and wanted to live _____ (6) so don't miss many home comforts
● Marcia misses those features of a house that people normally _____ (7)
● Marcia really misses a real bathroom and hot running water
● Marcia finds it _____ (8) and hard to do hand washing
● both of them have to be _____ (9) due to the size of the van
● both of them need their own _____ (10) as they are together all the time.

3 R.09 ▶ Listen again and check your answers.

4 Work with a partner and discuss these questions:

  ● Did the interviewer ask the questions you expected?

  ● Can you imagine ever deciding to live 'on the road'? Why/Why not?

  ● What do you think you would miss most if you lived on the road?

Grammar: making comparisons

1 There is a mistake in each of the comparative and superlative forms in these sentences. Find the mistakes and correct them.

  a This lifestyle is more harder work than you might think.

  b We can live a much more flexibler life than before.

  c I certainly have to be tidyer than I was before.

  d Living on the road was most sensible thing to do.

  e Speaking on the phone is not good as having a friend pop round.

  f Is living in a van as exciting than he says?

Grammar reference: see page 232

2 Read the e-mail quickly and decide how the writer feels about getting a bicycle: completely positive, completely negative or both positive and negative?

● ● ●   📧

Dear Mike,

Just writing to say you must buy that bike you were thinking about! I'm using mine _more often than_[1] (often) I thought. I just intended to use it for having fun, but in fact, now I cycle to college every day – and I'm enjoying every minute!

I get to college _____[2] (quickly) and it's definitely _____[3] (cheap) mum having to give me a lift. It's obviously _____[4] (healthy), too and I'm already feeling _____[5] (fit) before – especially because I've got two long hills to cycle up! On Fridays, I study in a different location which is _____[6] (far) away, but it still only takes me half an hour by bike. It's probably _____[7] (quick) going by car because in a car you often get stuck in traffic all the way.

I was worried about safety at first, but _____[8] (scary) moment so far was when I rode over a hole in the road. I wobbled a lot and nearly fell off, but managed to keep going! I was a bit concerned, too, that I might get too hot and sweaty but it's _____[9] (bad) I imagined. I just take some spare clothes and, if necessary, I have a quick shower at college!

I really think getting a bike is _____[10] (good) decision I've made in a long time. You won't regret it I'm sure. Let me know what you decide – I look forward to hearing all about it.

All the best,
Sam

---

3 Complete the e-mail with the correct form of the word in brackets, using comparatives, superlatives or (*not*) *as ... as*.

4 Look at the information in the box and match these headings with the correct parts A, B or C. Then complete the example sentences 1–7.

  a Describing things which are the same

  b Describing a small difference

  c Describing a big difference

Modifying comparatives and superlatives
A _____
1 *far, much, a lot* + comparative adjective/adverb
He's far _____ interested in making money than anything else.
2 *by far, easily* + superlative adjective/adverb
This is easily _____ most friendly town I've ever lived in.
3 *not nearly as ... as*
I'm not nearly as addicted to watching TV _____ you are.
B _____
4 *a bit, a little, slightly* + comparative adjective/adverb
You get there slightly _____ quickly by car.
5 *not quite as ... as*
This neighbourhood isn't quite _____ affordable as it used to be.
6 *nearly as ... as*
My new flat is _____ as big as my old one.
C _____
7 *(just) as ... as*
His new house is just as expensive _____ the previous one.

5 Rewrite these sentences using the prompts in brackets to make comparative/superlative forms.

a I'd be _____ (a bit / interested) in trying to live without technology if I could just keep my phone.

b I think it would be _____ (much / interesting) to live on a houseboat than in a motorhome.

c I think _____ (easily / good) thing about living on the road would be meeting different people.

d I don't think I'd be _____ (quite / willing) to give up my television as other people I know.

e I'd find it _____ (far / easy) to give up my mobile phone than my computer.

f I think that in the end living on the road would be _____ (just / boring) living in a house.

6 Work in small groups. Look at your completed sentences in Exercise 5. Do you all agree with the sentences? Find our what other students think. Do you have the same opinions?

Vocabulary: at home

1 Add six words or phrases to each of the columns.

rooms and places at home	machines and objects at home
living room	*washing machine*

2 You are now going to test your partner. First, write definitions for four words/phrases from your table in Exercise 1. Then take turns to test each other on your words.

Example:

A: A machine that washes cups and plates, etc.
B: A dishwasher.

3 Work with a partner and explain the difference in meaning between the verb phrases in *italics* in each pair of sentences. Use a dictionary if necessary.

a i My brother's just back from Australia so we're having a party to *welcome him home*.

   ii Sit down and *make yourself at home* while I make us some dinner.

b i The living room *overlooks* a lovely square.

   ii The kitchen *opens out onto* the garden at the back of the house.

c i When we *have a loft conversion*, we'll have a spare bedroom for visitors.

   ii We're *having an extension built* this year, so the kitchen will be much bigger.

d i When I moved in, I *did up* the whole house, including putting in a new kitchen.

   ii I've decided to *redecorate* all the bedrooms this year.

4 Two different people have written about houses or rooms. Complete each paragraph with the correct form of the words/phrases in Exercise 3.

Janet 120 | Posted: 4th August 2007 3.47 p.m.

When I was a child, I loved going to my grandmother's house. Nothing had changed for years and I used to hope that she'd never <u>do it up</u> (1). All the paintwork was old and faded – I don't think she ever _____ (2) at all. I slept in a tiny bedroom which _____ (3) the sea and I loved listening to the waves during the night.

Peter B. | Posted: 17th September 2007 1.12 p.m.

Did I tell you that James and Susi have just had a lot of work done on their house? They've had a _____ (4) and made a new spare bedroom under the roof. It's great! They've also _____ (5) at the back of their house. So now they've got a lovely sunny room to sit in which _____ (6) the garden. When I came back from studying abroad last month, they had a party for me to _____ (7). It was lovely weather so we were half-in and half-out. It was very relaxed and everyone just _____ (8)!

🗣 Speaking

1 Work with a partner and each choose one of the topics below. Prepare to time your partner – give them 1 minute to prepare and then ask them to start speaking. Tell them to stop speaking after 2 minutes. Did your partner answer the question on the card?

Exam hint

Exercise 1 is a practice task for Part 2 of the Speaking Paper.

Student A
You are going to talk about **lifestyles**. You can use some or all of the ideas listed below in your talk but <u>you must answer this question</u>:

What type of place would you like to live in and why?
You must talk for 1 to 2 minutes. You have 1 minute to think and make notes before your talk begins.

Here are some ideas to help you:
- Property type
- Features
- Location
- Outside space

Vocabulary hint

lifestyle – the way that someone lives, including their work and home life, and the things they own

Student B
You are going to talk about **lifestyles**. You can use some or all of the ideas listed below in your talk but <u>you must answer this question</u>:

What type of lifestyle would you most like and why?
You must talk for 1 to 2 minutes. You have 1 minute to think and make notes before your talk begins.

Here are some ideas to help you:
- Money
- Family life
- Career
- Social life

2 Work with a partner and take it in turns to ask and answer the following questions. Remember to give as much information as possible and try to keep talking for at least 5 minutes.

Exam hint

Exercise 2 is a practice task for Part 3 of the Speaking Paper.

Part 3

We have been talking about **lifestyles** and I would like to ask you some more questions on this topic.

- Do you think it is important for children to move out of their parents' home and become independent? (Why is that?)
- What is a good age for children to move out of their parents' home? (Why is that?)
- Do you think parents should give their children money once they have left home? (Why is that?)

- How important is it to have lots of money in life? (Tell me about that.)
- Do you think that people attach too much importance to money? (Tell me about that.)
- Do you think having a lot of money can cause problems? (Why is that?)

- Do you follow famous people and their lifestyles in the media? (Why/Why not?)
- Do you think that showing famous people and their lifestyles in the media has a positive effect on young people? (Why is that?)
- Do you think that people are becoming too materialistic? (Why is that?)

 # Reading

1 Work with a partner and discuss these questions:

- Do you know of any successful business people?

- What line of business do they work in?

- What has made them so successful?

2 Now read the text on the life of Alan Sugar and answer the questions that follow.

The life of Alan Sugar

Alan Sugar was born on the 24ᵗʰ March 1947 to Fay and Nathan Sugar. He is the youngest of four children. As a child, Alan and his family lived in a *council flat* and his father was a tailor in a garment industry. Alan left school at 16 and worked briefly as a statistician at the *Ministry of Education*. He then started selling car aerials and electrical goods out of a van he had bought with his savings of £100.

Alan Sugar met his wife Ann when he was 17 and she was 16. They married on the 29ᵗʰ April 1968, when Alan was only 21. During the same year Alan founded the electronics company Amstrad, the name being an acronym of his initials (**A**lan **M**ichael **S**ugar **Tr**ading). By 1970, the first manufacturing venture was underway. This venture focused on the production of audio equipment. He managed to achieve lower production prices for hi-fi turntable covers, severely undercutting competitors who used a different production process. Manufacturing capacity was soon expanded to include the production of audio amplifiers and tuners.

In 1980, Amstrad was listed on the London Stock Exchange and during the 1980s, Amstrad doubled its profit and market value every year. By 1984, recognising the opportunity of the era of home computers, Amstrad launched its first personal computer, competing against strong rivals such as the Commodore 64, the Sinclair ZX Spectrum and the BBC Micro. Despite this, three million units were sold worldwide with a long production life of eight years. In 1985, Alan had another major breakthrough with the launch of an Amstrad word processor which, although made of very cheap components, retailed at over £300. In 1986, Amstrad bought the rights to the Sinclair computer product line and produced two more ZX Spectrum models in a similar style to their own machines.

At its peak, Amstrad achieved a stock market value of £1.2 billion, but the 1990s proved a difficult time for the company. The launch of a range of business personal computers was marred by unreliable hard disks, which gave rise to a high level of customer dissatisfaction and great damage to Amstrad's reputation in the personal computer market, from which it never recovered.

In the early 1990s, Amstrad began to focus on portable computers rather than desktop computers. Also, in 1990, Amstrad entered the gaming market with the Amstrad GX4000, but it was a commercial failure, largely because there was only a very poor selection of games available on it. Additionally, it was immediately superseded by the Mega Drive and Super Nintendo, which both had a much more comprehensive selection of games. In 1993, so as to place the focus on telecommunications rather than computers, Amstrad released the PenPad, a Personal Digital Assistant and then released the first of two combined telephone and e-mail devices.

On the 31ˢᵗ July 2007, it was announced that broadcaster BSkyB had agreed to buy Amstrad for about £125 million. On the 2nd July 2008, it was announced that Alan was standing down from Amstrad as chairman, to focus solely on his other business interests.

As well as having Amstrad as a business interest, Alan Sugar has a number of other business interests. The first of these called Amsair Executive Aviation was founded in 1993 and is run by one of Alan's sons. This company offers business and executive jet charters. A second business interest owned by Alan Sugar, but controlled by the same son, is Amsprop. This is an investment firm. In September 2006, it bought the IBM South Bank building from private investors for £115 million. The IBM Centre occupies a prime site in London. IBM's lease runs for another eight years. The trade press speculates that the site is likely to present a major redevelopment opportunity.

Lord Sugar is also the owner (and Chairman of the board) of Viglen Ltd, an IT services provider catering primarily to the education and public sector. Following the sale of Amstrad PLC to BSkyB, Viglen is now Alan Sugar's sole IT establishment. He is also Chairman of Amscreen, a company run by a second son, specialising in selling advertising space based around screens that they provide to schools and bars.

As well as being aware of his business history, many people are familiar with Alan Sugar through his TV career. Alan Sugar became the star of the reality show *The Apprentice* which has had six series broadcast, one in each year between 2005 and 2010. Sugar fires a candidate each week until one candidate is left, who is then employed in one of his existing business interests. In May 2010, a successful *Junior Apprentice* was introduced, in which a group of ten young people, between the ages of 16 and 17, compete to win £25,000 from Alan Sugar. Both shows have been extremely popular.

Questions

1–5

Complete these sentences using no more than **three words** or **a number**.

1 Nathan Sugar earned money as _____.

2 After finishing school, Alan was soon working for himself, using _____ to get him started.

3 When Alan was 21, he started _____.

4 By employing a _____, Amstrad was able to price its products more competitively than its rivals.

5 By the mid 1980s _____ were becoming more desirable and Amstrad moved into this market.

6–10

Complete these notes using no more than **three words** or **a number**.

1980s
● Amstrad peaked in value

1990s
● Launched business PCs
● Problem with their _____ (6)
● Customers not happy and _____ (7) affected
● Emphasis shifted from _____ to _____ (8) computers
● The move into _____ (9) was unsuccessful due to an inferior product and the emergence of alternatives
● Telecommunications products released to reduce _____ (10) on computers.

11–15

Answer these questions using no more than **three words** and/or **numbers**.

11 Which of Alan's business interests was started in 1993?

....

12 Why did Amsprop buy the IBM Centre?

....

13 What role does Viglen Ltd play in the education and public sector?

....

14 How many of Alan's companies are run by his sons?

....

15 When was *Junior Apprentice* launched?

....

Grammar: reflexives

1 Look at these sentences. In which two is the highlighted word necessary for the meaning, and in which one is it just added for emphasis?

Grammar reference: see page 233

a The company itself was extremely successful.

b He made himself a multi-millionaire by working hard.

c It's sometimes hard to make things happen by ourselves.

2 Choose the correct alternatives in these sentences.

a If you use the automatic timer, the oven turns *it/itself* off.

b I don't think anybody else is going to help *us/ourselves*.

c Try to *concentrate/concentrate* yourself on what you really want to do.

d The idea *itself/oneself* is a good one, but it will be difficult to get enough people interested.

e　We'll see *us/each other* at the library later today.

f　John and I e-mail *ourselves/each other* every week.

g　I really don't want to go to the meeting *by/on* myself.

h　I organised the party *by/on* my own, which was tiring.

Grammar hint

on your own/alone/lonely

Look at the phrases in *italics*. Which two mean 'without any other people' and which means 'unhappy because you are without any other people'?

1　I've never lived *on my own* before.

2　I like spending at least one day a week *alone*.

3　I think I would feel *lonely* if I didn't live with people.

3　Complete the text using the words in the box.

| each　own　on　by　her　herself　itself　them　themselves　their |

Communal living

Louise Hackey lives in a community where everyone takes turns to do tasks like cooking and washing up. They grow fruit and vegetables _____ (1) and even have _____ (2) own cows and sheep. She loves the communal aspect of life there, but she _____ (3) admits that it's sometimes hard work.

The group consists of forty-five adults and thirteen children. A large old building in the countryside provides _____ (4) with the chance to live a cooperative, self-sufficient lifestyle. Their intention is not to be isolated from the wider community, however, or to live _____ (5) themselves. Far from it – the group sees _____ (6) as part of the wider community, not separate from it, with the children attending local schools and many people having jobs locally.

Many of the main living areas are communal, although Louise appreciates her _____ (7) private living area, too. 'Sometimes I need to get away and be _____ (8) my own for a while,' she says. Members work for a minimum of 12–15 hours a week. Although they help _____ (9) other with some of the bigger tasks (e.g. the potato harvest), people mostly do individual tasks. You need plenty of commitment for happy co-existence. Louise thinks the hard work is worth it, however, because it gives _____ (10) the kind of lifestyle she believes in.

4　Read the text again and answer these questions.

a　What is unusual about where Louise lives?

b　How are the tasks divided up?

c　How does Louise feel about living there?

5　Work with a partner. Ask and answer these questions.

a　What would be your ideal amount of time (e.g. *in a day or in a week*) to spend on your own and with friends/family?

b　Which of these things do you prefer to do by yourself? Explain why?

- shopping
- studying
- travelling
- cooking
- going to the cinema

Vocabulary: town and country

1　Complete the sentences with the words in the box.

| overcrowded　remote　historic　upmarket　rural
inner-city　tranquil　suburb　quaint　community |

a　This street is famous for its modern, _____ shops which are used by the rich and famous.

b　We visited a wonderfully _____ city with a cathedral. The whole city is surrounded by walls originally dating back to Roman times.

c My grandmother lives in a _____ stone cottage with a beautiful garden; she has lived there all her life.

d A lot of money is now being spent on regenerating _____ areas that are run-down, making them more attractive places to live.

e There are many _____ islands in the world which are uninhabited and difficult to get to.

f The underground in rush hour is so _____ that I usually walk home to avoid the chaos.

g We moved from an apartment in the city centre to a house in a leafy _____ so that we could have a garden.

h We left city life and our jobs to move to a small village in a _____ area surrounded by fields.

i The holiday cottage overlooked the sea; it was so _____ the only sounds we could hear were those of the sea and the birds overhead.

j There is a greater sense of _____ living in a village as everybody knows each other.

2 How do you pronounce the words in Exercise 1? Say them to a partner and decide in which column in the table each word would go. Then mark the main stress.

1 syllable	2 syllables	3 syllables	4 syllables

 Writing

1 Read this task and answer the questions.

> **Writing task**
>
> You have had a class discussion about the following statement:
>
> *Life is better without technology.*
>
> Your teacher has now asked you to write an article for the school magazine, discussing points for and against the statement.

a Who will be reading your article? What style do you need to use?

b Which of these two paragraph plans do you think is best? Why?

Paragraph plan 1

● Introduction (try to involve the reader, possibly by using a question)

● Positive points about the statement

● Negative points about the statement

● Conclusion (your opinion based on your arguments)

Paragraph plan 2

● Introduction (your opinion about the statement)

● Positive points about the statement

● Negative points about the statement

● Conclusion (what most people think about the statement)

2 Read the article. Does it follow the best paragraph plan?

Life is better without technology

I'm sure you'll all agree that technology is now an integral part of our lives. However, have you ever thought about how different your life would be without technology?

There are many advantages to lessening our reliance on technology. Many people think they need their televisions and computers to have fun in their leisure time. In spite of people believing this, they almost always enjoy themselves more by being more physically active and sociable.

On the other hand, there are some drawbacks to not using technology. Although we might not like it, a lot of communication in the modern world revolves around technology. E-mailing and phoning are efficient means of communicating, whereas writing letters is less so. Other household equipment, such as washing machines and cars, also contribute to a comfortable lifestyle.

I believe that there are dangers in over-using technology. Nevertheless, if we are sensible we can enjoy its benefits.

3 Make a note of the six linkers of contrast used in the article in Exercise 2.

4 Combine the ideas in these two sentences using each of the linkers of contrast. Refer to the article in Exercise 2 to help you. Be careful about punctuation.

a The countryside is more peaceful than the city.

b You can have more fun in the city.

1 however

The countryside is more peaceful than the city. **However**, *you can have more fun in the city.*

2 nevertheless   5 whereas

3 although   6 on the other hand

4 in spite of

5 You are going to write an article about living in the countryside. First write some notes as in the table.

Advantages of living in the countryside	Disadvantages of living in the countryside
It's peaceful. You're more likely to get to know your neighbours.	There's not much to do.

6 Work with a partner. Discuss whether you would prefer to live in the countryside or the city? Do you agree with each other?

7 Your teacher has asked you write an *article* for the school magazine. The title of the article is 'Life in the countryside is boring'.

In your article you should:

- give **two** advantages of living in the countryside
- give **two** disadvantages of living in the countryside
- give your opinion about life in the countryside.

Write your article using between 100 and 150 words.

Exam hint

Exercise 7 is a practice task for Part 4 of the Reading and Writing Paper.

Writing reference: see page 252

Summarising

1 Read the article about the well known business man Alan Sugar and then write a summary for your teacher.

In your summary you should:

- talk about how Amstrad performed in the 1990s
- give two details about Alan's other business interests
- give two details about Alan's TV career.

Write your summary using between 100 and 150 words.

Exam hint

Exercise 1 is a practice task for Part 6 of the Reading and Writing Paper.

The life of Alan Sugar

Alan Sugar founded Amstrad in 1968. He was only 21 and this was his first serious business venture. At its peak, Amstrad achieved a stock market value of £1.2 billion, but the 1990s proved a difficult time for the company. The launch of a range of business personal computers was marred by unreliable hard disks, which gave rise to a high level of customer dissatisfaction and great damage to Amstrad's reputation in the personal computer market, from which it never recovered.

In the early 1990s, Amstrad began to focus on portable computers rather than desktop computers. Also, in 1990, Amstrad entered the gaming market with the Amstrad GX4000, but it was a commercial failure, largely because there was only a very poor selection of games available on it. Additionally, it was immediately superseded by the Mega Drive and Super Nintendo, which both had a much more comprehensive selection of games. In 1993, so as to place the focus on telecommunications rather than computers, Amstrad released the PenPad, a Personal Digital Assistant and then released the first of two combined telephone and e-mail devices.

On the 31st July 2007, it was announced that broadcaster BSkyB had agreed to buy Amstrad for about £125 million. On the 2nd July 2008, it was announced that Alan was standing down from Amstrad as chairman, to focus solely on his other business interests.

As well as having Amstrad as a business interest, Alan Sugar has a number of other business interests. The first of these called Amsair Executive Aviation was founded in 1993 and is run by one of Alan's sons. This company offers business and executive jet charters. A second business interest owned by Alan Sugar, but controlled by the same son, is Amsprop. This is an investment firm. In September 2006, it bought the IBM South Bank building from private investors for £115 million. The IBM Centre occupies a prime site in London. IBM's lease runs for another eight years. The trade press speculates that the site is likely to present a major redevelopment opportunity.

Lord Sugar is also the owner (and Chairman of the board) of Viglen Ltd, an IT services provider catering primarily to the education and public sector. Following the sale of Amstrad PLC to BSkyB, Viglen is now Alan Sugar's sole IT establishment. He is also Chairman of Amscreen, a company run by a second son, specialising in selling advertising space based around screens that they provide to schools and bars.

As well as being aware of his business history, many people are familiar with Alan Sugar through his TV career. Alan Sugar became the star of the reality show *The Apprentice* which has had six series broadcast, one in each year between 2005 and 2010. Sugar fires a candidate each week until one candidate is left, who is then employed in one of his existing business interests. In May 2010, a successful *Junior Apprentice* was introduced, in which a group of ten young people, between the ages of 16 and 17, compete to win £25,000 from Alan Sugar. Both shows have been extremely popular.

Language recap

Grammar

1 For questions 1–9, read the text and decide which answer, a, b or c, best fits each gap.

A company in Cornwall is now offering an exciting alternative to the traditional hotel. *The Mighty Oak Tree Climbing Company* now offers 'tree camping' – you don't camp under the trees, but right up in the trees _____ (1). Special hammocks or 'tree-boats' are suspended in the branches of oak trees.

Alan and Bethany Stock decided to start their _____ (2) tree camping company in Britain after coming across the idea in the USA. There is no need to feel nervous up in the trees, as everyone attaches _____ (3) to the hammock with ropes and harnesses. 'I tried _____ (4),' says Mike from London, 'and I enjoyed _____ (5) enormously. It's like being right inside nature. I went with two friends – I don't think I'd like to be there _____ (6) myself all night. At first, we scared _____ (7) other a bit by rocking the tree-boats, but you get used to it!

The instructor _____ (8) stays with you anyway, so you definitely feel safe. In the morning, they bring you breakfast in the trees. It's not cheap – £200 a night if you're on your _____ (9), or £140 per person for a group of up to five – but it's worth the money for such a once-in-a-lifetime experience.'

1	a itself	b himself	c themselves
2	a a	b own	c one
3	a themselves	b them	c it
4	a it	b itself	c them
5	a me	b my	c myself
6	a on	b by	c with
7	a each	b one	c own
8	a itself	b himself	c themselves
9	a own	b himself	c self

2 Complete the second sentence so that it has a similar meaning to the first sentence, using the word given. Do not change the word given. You must use between two and five words, including the word given.

a Mexico City is more polluted than Tokyo.
as
Tokyo _____ Mexico City.

b This neighbourhood isn't as friendly as it used to be.
less
This neighbourhood is _____ it used to be.

c I've never lived in a flat as big as my new flat before.
easily
My new flat is _____ place I've ever lived in.

d I live a lot nearer work than she does.
lot
She lives _____ away from work than I do.

e James doesn't play football quite as well as Marco.
footballer
Marco is _____ than James.

f I've never been to such a bad restaurant as this one.
far
This is _____ restaurant I've ever been to.

g My sister is slightly taller than me.
tall
I'm _____ my sister.

h He didn't drive nearly as quickly as he did last time.
than
He drove _____ he did last time.

Vocabulary

3 Complete these sentences with the correct word in the box.

> leafy   community   upmarket   run-down   remote   overcrowded   quaint   historic

a   I live in a very _____ area; the nearest town is miles away.

b   There are lots of trees around where I live; it's a very _____ suburb.

c   The city centre was _____ last night as a World Cup football match was being shown on a large screen.

d   The problem with fast city life is the lack of _____ as people are too busy to get to know the others in their neighbourhood.

e   I like visiting _____ buildings and finding out about what happened in the past.

f   The local government has put a lot of money into redeveloping the _____ areas of the city.

g   We stayed in a _____ little cottage on holiday – it looked like something from a postcard.

h   I love looking in all the _____ shops in Paris, even if I can't afford to buy anything!

Paper 2: Listening

The listening paper gives you the opportunity to demonstrate your understanding of standard spoken English, which could be live or broadcast, on both unfamiliar and familiar topics in personal, social, academic or vocational contexts. You will hear the recording of each section twice.

 ## Part 1: Listening (10 marks)

Text type

In this part you will listen to a **short monologue** giving information, for example:

- public announcements
- radio reports
- telephone messages
- pre-recorded information.

Skills

You will be expected to listen for relevant detailed information. On the recording, the speaker will talk – at normal speed – on a range of topics which you can expect to meet in social, school or work situations. You should be able to recognise the context of the listening extract so that you can concentrate on understanding the content.

Task types

There are 10 marks available in Part 1 and there will be 10 questions, each worth one mark.

Task types in this section include:

- **Notes or sentence completion:** you will need to write your answers out in words for this task type. The prompts show clearly what parts of speech you should use in your answer. The answers are all words heard in the recording, and you should not change the form of the words you hear. The answer required will be either a number or one, two or three words (check the instruction for the exact number).

- **Table or form completion:** this task type is very similar to notes or sentence completion and you must write your answers out in words here as well. Each question is presented differently, according to the context and to allow for real-life type tasks. The answers are all words which you will hear in the recording, and, again, you should not change the form of the words you hear. The answer required will be either a number or one, two or three words – again, check the instruction.

- **Multiple-choice questions:** you have to decide which option is the correct answer to the question, or which option best fills a gap in a sentence. There are generally three options for each question.

Let's look at this extract from a notes completion task from the Edexcel IGCSE ESL Listening Paper in November 2008:

In this section, you will hear an education officer talking to a group of students who have just arrived at a study centre in the countryside where they will stay for three nights.

*Listen and complete the notes. Write no more than **THREE** words for each answer.*

BIOLOGY AND GEOGRAPHY FIELD TRIP
Programme for today:

Activities for Geography students
a.m.
Counting visitor numbers to
[3.] .... *businesses in Brodick.*
p.m.
Interviewing visitors at the farm's
[4.] .... *centre.*

This is the extract which contains the answers to Questions 3 and 4 from what you will hear on the recording:

*So, let's move on to the **programme** now. You are here for the short programme so let me warn you – you are in for a rather packed schedule. I understand that you are a mixed group of geography and biology students. Well, today, you will spend part of the day working on a joint project and, tomorrow, you will be focusing on your own subject more.*

***Today**, you will all be examining the impact of tourism on the area. **Geography students**, you will be walking over to Brodick **village** to conduct counts on visitor numbers to certain places in the village. You will be concentrating on **food** businesses. This will include the cafes, snack bars, restaurants and all take-aways. In the afternoon, you are conducting another study at the deer farm. You will be going to the **information** centre at the farm to ask visitors about their shopping habits.*

First, the speaker makes it very clear that she is going to talk about the **programme** – so you know to turn your focus to that section of the questions. A bit further on, she announces that she will be outlining details for **today** – and then she mentions the **Geography students** specifically. So now, you should be listening out for the answers to Questions 3 and 4. Although the question is not worded in exactly the same way as the information is given in the recording, you should be able to pick out that Question 3 is **food** and Question 4 is **information**.

Getting started...

1 Work with a partner and look at the pictures. Tell your partner which situation you like the most and why.

2 Work with a partner and answer the questions. Check any words you are not sure about in a dictionary.

  a What different things are usually included in a *package* holiday?
  b What is the difference between *half-board* and *full-board* accommodation?
  c When do you need to *check in*?
  d What kind of transport can *take off* and *land*?
  e What do you think *ecotourism* is?

1
2
3
4

 ## Speaking

1 Work with a partner and decide who is going to answer the Student A questions and who is going to answer the Student B questions. Student A needs to answer all four questions, taking no more than 3 minutes. Repeat the process for the Student B questions.

Exam hint

Exercise 1 is a practice task for Part 1 of the Speaking Paper.

Student A
Let's talk about transport
Which form of transport do you use the most? (Why is that?)
Is there anything you dislike about this form of transport? (Why is that?)
Which form of transport do you prefer for long journeys? (Why is that?)
What do you do to pass the time on long journeys? (Tell me about that.)

Student B
Let's talk about going on holiday
Who do you usually go on holiday with? (Tell me about that.)
When did you last go on holiday and who did you go with? (Tell me about that.)
What did you do on your last holiday? (Tell me about that.)
Do you have a favourite kind of holiday? (Why is that?)

Reading

1 Work with a partner and discuss these questions:

- Do you prefer active or relaxing holidays?

- Do you prefer to stay in a busy or quiet place?

- What would be your ideal holiday?

2 Read the list of holiday places and match each of the statements that follow to one of the places. You must choose answers based on the information given. You should only use each holiday place once.

Exam hint

Exercise 2 is a practice task for Part 1 of the Reading and Writing Paper. In Part 1 of the Reading and Writing Paper you will be asked to read a collection of short texts (e.g. *advertisements*), a timetable or a leaflet and then answer the questions that follow.

Holiday places

A   Club Palmeras

Very spacious tropical grounds dotted with palm trees. Two pools. Activities, shows and a full entertainment programme. A kids' club and mini-disco. Brand new gym with sauna.

Accommodation available: one bedroom apartments, studio apartments and rooms with a sea view

B   Playa Del Sol

Modern apartment complex. Big pool surrounded by terraces and palm trees. Children's soft play room and playground. Satellite TV room and games room offering table tennis, snooker and darts. Tennis and squash courts also available.

Accommodation available: one bedroom apartments and junior suites

C   Ferrera Menorca

Stylish accommodation made up of blocks connected by pathways, with flower filled grounds. Three main pools and two kids' pools. Sports and organised entertainment are available. Bundles of bars, restaurants and shops just one kilometre away.

Accommodation available: standard rooms and suites

D   **Viva Blanca**

Modern design and friendly atmosphere. A fantastic choice for families. Lagoon-like pool, PADI diving school and loads of activities for kids. Buffet restaurant, handful of bars and restaurants and massage and beauty treatments available.

Accommodation available: one bedroom apartments

E   **Almirante Nuramar**

On a cliff edge overlooking a bay and a short walk away from a nature reserve. Neat green lawns, large outdoor pool and sunbed-covered terrace. Stacks of sports and evening entertainment programme.

Accommodation available: standard rooms, family rooms, superior rooms

F   **Farragut**

Brightly coloured décor. Close to local amenities and the marina. Free day passes to the nearby family water park. Swimming pool, snack bar, activities and entertainment. New health suite including sauna, steam room and jacuzzi. It's a great family escape.

Accommodation available: standard and family apartments

G   **Royal Blanca**

Set in attractive gardens, in a peaceful setting. This hotel is a real find for families. A free daily bus service to the beach a short distance away. Kids' club, climbing area and playground. Tennis and volleyball available.

Accommodation available: one and two bedroom bungalows

H   **Miami Son Bou**

Family friendly and in a wonderful setting. It's a short walk to the nearby beach. There is a supermarket, souvenir shop and restaurant right next door to the quiet complex.

Accommodation available: standard rooms, sea-view rooms, single rooms and interconnecting rooms

I   **Barcelo Village**

Good value and family friendly. Great location – just a stroll from the man-made beach and even closer to shops, bars and restaurants. The pools are surrounded by attractive gardens.

Accommodation available: standard and one bedroom apartments and studio apartments

J   **Royal Galea**

Completely refurbished and renovated. Spacious modern complex offers good quality, comfortable accommodation. Warm and friendly atmosphere. Excellent location overlooking the beach. Peaceful setting with easy access to nearby amenities. Close to two large shopping centres with cinema complex.

Accommodation available: standard rooms

K   **Playa Joel**

Large family holiday park with lively atmosphere. Well kept grounds with lots of open space for kids to play. Kids' clubs offer organised activities and teenagers will love the cellar disco. Numerous sporting facilities from horse-riding to mini golf.

Accommodation available: 1050 tent pitches, static caravans

	Statements	Holiday places										
		A	B	C	D	E	F	G	H	I	J	K
1	This location is a camp site.											
2	This site offers children their own rooms.											
3	There are swimming pools just for children here.											
4	You can learn how to scuba dive here.											
5	It would be easy to go and see a film from here.											
6	This place has rooms with adjoining doors.											
7	This place offers a transport service to the beach.											
8	If you are interested in wildlife, this is the place for you.											
9	You do not pay to use a nearby attraction if you stay here.											
10	This site is near an artificial beach.											

Grammar: tenses

1 Read the blog about Tom's camping weekend. Work with a partner. Look back at Tom's blog and find one example of:

- the past simple
- the past continuous
- the past perfect simple
- the past perfect continuous.

Tom S.

Posted 7th March 2011 11.35 a.m.

Hi everybody,

I've just got back from camping for the weekend. It was fantastic. We travelled to the campsite on Friday after Mum and Dad had finished work and we were there within two hours. We stayed in a static caravan and it was just like being at home but right next to the sea. While Mum and Dad were unpacking the car, Emily and I went exploring.

There was a campsite club where all the adults go in the evening and they do lots of activities for our age group at the same time. It meant we could all be in the same place in the evening and still do our own thing. During the day we tried surfing and body boarding and in the evenings we went to the club. On the Saturday night there was a dance competition that Emily was going to enter but because she had hurt her leg during the day, she couldn't. I had been surfing all day and hadn't even thought about entering the competition. Everybody knows I can't dance, but somehow Emily convinced me to enter. I didn't win but I really enjoyed taking part. It really was a great weekend.

It would be good to hear from you all.

Tom

2 Which tense is used to refer to each of these?

Grammar reference: see page 233

a something which happened before another past action

b a finished action or situation

c an action in progress at a definite time in the past

d something in progress up to the time in the past we are talking about

3 Read this text. Put the verbs in brackets into the correct tense.

Holiday for Gambian toad

The sight of an open suitcase and the opportunity to find somewhere to escape the heat _____ ¹ (be) too much for an adventurous toad from Gambia. Without a second thought, it _____ ² (jump) into the suitcase, which a British tourist _____ ³ (pack) at the end of his holiday. Without realising it, the toad got a free ride all the way back to the UK.

When Mike and his girlfriend _____ ⁴ (get) home, they were not expecting the appearance of their new have guest. 'It looked like he _____ ⁵ (sleep) inside one of my trainers. I _____ ⁶ (just take) some souvenirs out of the suitcase and _____ ⁷ (chat) with my girlfriend about how good the holiday _____ ⁸ (be) when we heard a noise and _____ ⁹ (see) this little toad jump out.

'We couldn't believe it! It was the same toad we _____ ¹⁰ (see) on the hotel balcony the night before while we _____ ¹¹ (play) cards. At the time we thought that was his home – we didn't think we'd be bringing him back to ours.'

As the toad _____ ¹² (hop) around the bedroom to explore its new surroundings it was quickly trapped in a container. 'It was 40°C when we left Gambia, so the priority now is to keep him warm. We _____ ¹³ (get) some advice about

his diet and we're feeding him worms from the garden, which he seems to like!'

Vocabulary: travel and transport

1 Work in groups of four. Each choose one of the groups of words a–d. Explain the meaning and pronunciation of your words to the other members of your group.

a yacht / canoe / ferry / surfboard

b jumbo jet / parachute / helicopter / hot-air balloon

c minibus / scooter / mountain bike / coach

d wind-surfing / paragliding / water-skiing / white-water rafting

2 Add the words in the box to the correct columns.

> chauffeur cabin crew aisle compartment boot runway
> guard cockpit cruise anchor mast bonnet lay-by deck

Car	Train	Plane	Ship

3 Match each of these words with the correct definition a–f.

> travel trip journey voyage flight tour

    a the time spent travelling from one place to another

    b a long journey by sea or in space

    c a journey by air

    d a journey for pleasure in which you visit several different towns, areas, etc.

    e a (short) journey to visit a place or for a specific purpose

    f general activity of moving from one place to another

4 Complete the sentences with the words in Exercise 3.

    a Sarah's got an important business _____ to Brussels at the weekend.

    b My _____ to work is quite long and tiring.

    c We went on a fourteen day _____ of all the most famous Egyptian sites.

    d Our _____ to Barcelona was delayed by technical problems with the plane.

    e I think it's very true that '_____ broadens the mind'.

    f She made her transatlantic _____ in a specially designed boat.

5 Read the text about Jack's travels after leaving school. Complete each gap with one of the words and phrases from Exercises 1–3.

> _Travel_____ (1) has always been a passion of mine. My first big adventure was to South Africa in the late 1970s. I went out as a young volunteer and got a place as a member of the _____ (2) on a large ship carrying electrical equipment. During the _____ (3) I spent most of the time on _____ (4), getting a suntan!
>
> While I was in South Africa, I did a lot of hitch-hiking. I remember getting a lift with one elderly man in his 1950s car. We'd gone about one kilometre when smoke and flames started coming out from under the _____ (5). He was very relaxed about it and just stopped and got a fire extinguisher out from the _____ (6). Another time, a beautiful Rolls-Royce picked me up. I couldn't believe my luck. It belonged to the Bishop of Swaziland and was being driven by his personal _____ (7).
>
> At the end of my time, I flew back home. The _____ (8) only took about sixteen hours and was quite full. I was sitting next to a woman called Liz, who told me she didn't like flying. After a few minutes, she got out of her seat and started walking up and down the _____ (9). I think the cabin _____ (10) were a little concerned, but after a while Liz sat down and seemed OK. Later on, as we approached our destination, she asked me if she could hold my hand. During the landing, the plane bumped along the _____ (11) as normal, but I could feel Liz squeezing my hand so tightly I thought my fingers were going to break!

◁))) Listening

1 Work with a partner and answer these questions:

- Do you enjoy travelling? Why/Why not?

- If you were going travelling for six months, who would you choose to go with?

- What form(s) of transport would you choose for your trip?

2 R.10 ▶ Listen to a radio interview and answer the following questions.

Exam hint

Exercise 2 is a practice task for Part 2 of the Listening Paper.

Questions

1–5

Answer these questions using no more than **three words** and/or **numbers**.

1 What jobs do the guests on the radio show have?

....

2 How long was their journey?

....

3 Where did they go on their journey?

....

4 Why did they choose to make the journey on motorbikes?

....

5 How old was Charley when he was first introduced to motorbikes?

....

6–10

Complete these sentences using no more than **three words** or **a number**.

6 The two guests first got to know each other while making _____.

7 The guests were _____ for nearly four months.

8 Their partners were _____ on their own at home.

9 The guests decided that _____ they would not have made the journey.

10 Both guests appreciated having a break from _____.

3 R.10 ▶ Listen again and check your answers.

4 Work with a partner and discuss these questions:

● What were the main reasons they wanted to go on this journey?

● Do you think it would be an exciting thing to do? Why/Why not?

 Speaking

1 Work with a partner and each choose one of the topics below. Prepare to time your partner – give them 1 minute to prepare and then ask them to start speaking. Tell them to stop speaking after 2 minutes. Did your partner answer the question on the card?

> **Student A**
>
> You are going to talk about **travelling**. You can use some or all of the ideas listed below in your talk but <u>you must answer this question</u>:
>
> **Talk about a journey you enjoyed. Why did you enjoy it so much?**
> You must talk for 1 to 2 minutes. You have 1 minute to think and make notes before your talk begins.
>
> Here are some ideas to help you:
> · Where you were going
> · Who with
> · Reason for journey
> · What happened

> **Exam hint**
>
> Exercise 1 is a practice task for Part 2 of the Speaking Paper.

Student B

You are going to talk about **going on holiday**. You can use some or all of the ideas listed below in your talk but <u>you must answer this question:</u>

Talk about a holiday you enjoyed. Why did you enjoy it so much?
You must talk for 1 to 2 minutes. You have 1 minute to think and make notes before your talk begins.

Here are some ideas to help you:
- Where you went
- Who with
- How long for
- What happened

Exam hint

Exercise 2 is a practice task for Part 3 of the Speaking Paper.

2 Work with a partner and take it in turns to ask and answer the following questions. Remember to give as much information as possible and try to keep talking for at least 5 minutes.

Part 3

We have been talking about **travelling and holidays** and I would like to ask you some more questions on this topic.

- From what age do you think young people benefit from visiting other countries? (Why is that?)
- Do you think that it is important for young people to travel without their parents? (Why is that?)
- At what age should young people be able to travel with their friends? (Why is that?)

- Do you think you should follow the customs of the country you are visiting? (Why is that?)
- How important is it to learn about other cultures? (Why is that?)
- With television and the Internet, do you think you have to travel to a country to learn about the culture? (Why is that?)

- What are the positive effects of tourism on a holiday destination? (Tell me about that.)
- Do you think there are any negative effects? (Tell me about that.)
- What are the advantages/disadvantages of taking holidays in your own country? (Tell me about that.)

Grammar: time linkers

1 Match the sentence halves a–i with i–ix to make one complete holiday story. Notice how the time linkers in *italics* are used to link the text together.

a *When* Miranda and her brother got to the airport,

b *Finally*, their plane took off

c *After* looking for somewhere to stay for several hours,

d *To begin with* they were quite happy with their hotel,

e That afternoon they went out to get something to eat,

f The next morning, *by the time* they had had a shower and some breakfast,

g They decided to go to the beach, but *as soon as* they got there,

h They left the beach and went into town, but *while* they were looking around a local museum,

i *After that*, Miranda and her brother

i   but everywhere was closed as it was a public holiday.

ii   decided it was time to finish their holiday and go home.

iii Miranda's bag was stolen.

iv   they realised it was nearly midday.

v   it started to pour with rain.

vi   but later they realised that there were lots of things wrong with it.

vii they *eventually* found a room in a small but cheap hotel.

viii and a few hours later they arrived at their holiday destination.

ix   they were told their plane would be delayed for at least three hours.

2 Which two time linkers are possible in each of these sentences?

a   One day, _____ I was walking to work, I noticed a large group of people coming towards me.

   i after   ii when   iii as   iv by the time

b   I waited in line for nearly an hour and _____ it was my turn.

   i eventually   ii finally   iii as soon as   iv while

c   _____ I got to the party, all the food had been eaten.

   i While   ii Afterwards   iii By the time   iv When

d   I heard a strange noise. _____ I thought it was my cat.

   i Then   ii At first   iii Suddenly   iv To begin with

e   _____ I saw him, I realised I had made a terrible mistake.

   i As soon as   ii While   iii When   iv Finally

Vocabulary: synonyms

1 Put three words from the box into each of the columns in the table.

stunned	spellbound	expedition	shocked	fed up
fascinated	quarrel	excursion	amazed	depressed
intrigued	row	dispute	trip	upset

a journey	an argument	interested	unhappy	surprised

Grammar hint

after, afterwards, after that

Which one of the following sentences is not possible?

1 After we arrived at the hotel, we decided to go for a swim.
2 After arriving at the hotel, we decided to go for a swim.
3 Afterwards arriving at the hotel, we decided to go for a swim.
4 We arrived at the hotel and unpacked our bags. Afterwards, we decided to go for a swim.
5 We arrived at the hotel and unpacked our bags. After that, we decided to go for a swim.

Grammar reference: see page 234

2 Choose the best alternative in each sentence.

a The hotel has arranged an *excursion/expedition* for us to go and see the volcano on the next island.

b I was a little *surprised/stunned* when Paul said he was interested in coming on holiday with us.

c Paula and Ian had a bad *row/dispute* on Friday and they haven't spoken to each other since.

d When the hotel said we couldn't have a room with a seaview, Mike got quite *upset/depressed*.

e She was *spellbound/intrigued* to know whether he would take the job.

f Flights have been cancelled due to a pay *quarrel/row/dispute* between the pilots' union and the airline.

3 Write three true sentences which each include one of the words from Exercise 1. Share your sentences with a partner.

I have always been fascinated by volcanoes.

I'd love to go on some kind of scientific expedition to the Amazon rainforest.

 Writing

1 You are going to write a letter of complaint to the travel agency about a holiday you have been on with your family.

Work with a partner and answer these questions:

● Do you need to use formal or informal language?

● How should you start and finish the letter?

In your letter you should:

● give **two** details about the holiday you went on

● state **two** problems you had with the holiday

● say what you want the company to do.

Writing reference: see page 254

2 Work with a partner and decide which of these paragraph plans you should follow when writing your letter.

Paragraph plan 1

● What you want the company to do.

● Give the reason why you are writing.

● Details of the holiday you went on.

● Problems you had with the holiday.

Paragraph plan 2

● Give the reason why you are writing.

● Details of the holiday you went on.

● Problems you had with the holiday.

● What you want the company to do.

3 Write your letter using between 100 and 150 words.

Exam hint

Exercise 3 is a practice task for Part 5 of the Reading and Writing Paper.

Summarising

1 You are doing a project on holiday destinations. Read the following information about Golden Sands Holiday Park and write a summary for your teacher.

In your summary you should:

- give details about the area around Golden Sands Holiday Park
- say what facilities there are for children at the Holiday Park
- say what facilities there are for adults at the Holiday Park.

Write your summary using between 100 and 150 words.

Exam hint

Exercise 1 is a practice task for Part 6 of the Reading and Writing Paper.

Golden Sands Holiday Park is situated on a picturesque headland with parts of the park overlooking the sea. From the park you can walk to the nearest bay which is sheltered and at one end there is a pub which serves food and a popular surf shop. From this bay you can access the adjacent bay which is smaller and more suitable for young children. If you walk out of the holiday park and head up the road, it is a ten-minute stroll to another two bays which are connected at low tide. All the bays are safe and exceptionally clean. There is something for everybody: swimming, surfing, body boarding or just lazing about on the beach, reading your favourite book. The larger bays are life guarded by the Royal National Lifeguard Institution (RNLI) from May to September. Dogs are welcome on all beaches in the area. The headland itself offers fantastic coastline walks not only for walking enthusiasts but also for those who just want a stroll with their dog.

Golden Sands Holiday Park is a family-owned park, catering specifically for families. In the centre of the park is a children's play area with swings, slides and climbing frames, and also an area for bike riding. The entire park is child-friendly with speed limits of 5 mph and well placed speed bumps so that children are not restricted to the play area alone. In the mornings and afternoons there is a kids' club where children can get to know one another through doing fun activities. The park also has two indoor swimming pools, one of which is a baby pool. Even if the weather is not too good, you can always have fun in the pool. There is also a large barn with two badminton courts and table tennis area.

After enjoying the beach, or going on a day trip to a nearby fishing village or shopping in a more modern town centre, there is plenty to do in the evening at the park. If the weather is fine you can always have a barbeque. The on-site shop has a good range of food and drink and a DVD rental section is open to all park guests. As an alternative we have an on-site restaurant to give Mum and Dad a break from cooking where they can sit back and relax. The clubhouse provides children's entertainment for the first part of the evening so that parents can socialise while also being able to keep an eye on what the children are doing. Later in the evening, there is entertainment for adults – either a live band, a quiz session, a comedian, or music and dancing. There is also an adults only games room with snooker tables and dart boards.

We can guarantee you a real family holiday at **Golden Sands Holiday Park**. We only allow families to stay on the park and there are limits placed on the number of teenagers per booking. There is also a strict curfew policy for teenagers to make sure that everybody enjoys their holiday.

Language recap

Vocabulary

1 Use the clues to complete the crossword.

ACROSS

1 I like catching the _____ across to France. You can get out of your car, have a walk around and then get something to eat and drink. (5)

4 _____ we'd been in the coach all morning, we were very glad to get out and stretch our legs. (5)

6 Let's have a walk on _____ and watch the sun set before we go down below for a drink. (4)

10 We need to go down the river by _____. There is no path from this point. (5)

11 If you _____ through that window you can just see the trees at the end of the garden. (4)

12 Did the boys enjoy their _____ to Florida? (4)

DOWN

2 He loves sailing and last year he bought his own _____ . He plans to sail around the Greek islands this summer. (5)

3 This afternoon we're going on a short _____ of the old part of town. Apparently, we'll visit the houses of some famous local artists. (4)

5 James is quite _____ up about breaking his leg on the first day of his skiing holiday. (3)

7 The main problem with the cruise was our _____ , which was very small and very hot. (5)

8 Sarah was very _____ when she found out that Simon had lied to her. (5)

9 Did you know that the train _____ is almost double if you leave before 9.30 a.m.? (4)

10 Even today the _____ and the officers don't mix much on board ship. (4)

13 Tim and I had a _____ this morning and now he's not speaking to me. (3)

Grammar

2 There are mistakes in these sentences. Find the mistakes and correct them.

    a After he'd checked in his luggage, he was deciding to go and get a coffee.

    b Holly and Mary were out jogging when they had noticed the man on the motorbike.

    c They taken around all the local tourist sites and had a wonderful time.

    d After they found their seats, they had started arguing about who should have the MP3 player.

    e We were just driving into Rome when we were hearing the announcement on the radio.

    f The two brothers had been sat in silence for several minutes before one of them spoke.

    g By the time Derek arrived home, he was being tired, wet and exhausted.

    h James had thought nothing else could go wrong with their holiday, but he had been forgotten one very important thing.

3 Complete the story with these time linkers. There is an extra one that you do not need.

as soon as	while	to begin with	by the time	eventually	afterwards

It's great to be home, but the journey back was terrible! _____ (1), just as we were leaving, Flo said she couldn't find her passport. So then we had to turn the flat upside down to find it. _____ (2) we discovered it down the back of the sofa. _____ (3) we had found it, it was too late to get to the airport by bus. So I tried to call a taxi, but the earliest a taxi could come was in an hour, which would mean missing our flight. _____ (4) I kept ringing taxi firms, Carol went next door to see if our neighbours could give us a lift. Amazingly, they could and we raced off to the airport. _____ (5) we got to the main airport building, we jumped out of the car and ran for the check-in desk. We needn't have rushed though as the plane was delayed by three hours!

Paper 3: Speaking

The speaking examination is in three parts and lasts about 12 minutes in total. You will be interviewed individually by an interlocutor – in most cases the interlocutor will be a teacher within your centre. Your speaking exam will be recorded on a cassette or CD and sent to an Edexcel examiner to be assessed.

Part 1: Speaking: Introductory interview (2 to 3 minutes)

In Part 1, the interlocutor will introduce him/herself first and then ask you a set of straightforward introductory questions on a familiar topic such as television, the weekend, sports and games, and music. This is really a warm-up activity to get you used to speaking in English and to allow you to become familiar with the voice of the interlocutor in case it is not your usual teacher. The interlocutor works from a set of prompt questions which have been provided by Edexcel to guide the conversation. The answers you give to these questions should be more than just *yes* or *no* (and in fact the questions are devised in such a way as to make it very difficult to answer them properly with just a single word), but in this part you do not have to give extended replies – that comes later on in the test.

You may ask for an explanation of an occasional word if you really can't work out what it means, but the interlocutor is not allowed to give you a long and detailed explanation, nor to paraphrase the question you have been asked. You may ask for the question to be repeated but don't worry if you still can't understand it – the interlocutor will simply move on to a different question.

Your oral is assessed as a whole – taking into account all three parts. This means that the three different parts are not assessed individually. Your overall performance will be marked on each of four criteria:

- **Communicative ability and content:** your ability to express opinions and information, to initiate and to respond to questions appropriately.

- **Pronunciation and fluency:** your ability to produce clear and understandable language.

- **Lexical accuracy and range:** how accurately and appropriately you use vocabulary to communicate, and how well you cope with any vocabulary problems, e.g. if you forget a word during the test.

- **Grammatical accuracy and range:** range and accuracy of the grammatical structures you use.

In Part 1, you need to respond to the questions appropriately by giving both information and opinions. You also need to communicate clearly – so think about your pronunciation and intonation. You should also try to use a range of vocabulary – try not to use the same words over and over again. We all have favourite words, but, in the speaking exam, you should try to use a variety. You should also bear in mind the kind of grammatical structures you use – again the examiners will be listening out for a variety of structures.

This part of the exam should last about 2 to 3 minutes.

Have a look at this Part 1 Interlocutor's card from the Edexcel International GCSE ESL Speaking Paper in November 2009:

PART ONE

In this first part, I'd like to ask you some questions about yourself.

Let's talk about school holidays.

- *What do you like most about school holidays?*
- *What did you do during your last school holiday?*
- *What was the most interesting thing you did during the last school holiday?*
- *What would be your idea of a perfect school holiday?*

Thank you. That is the end of Part One.

The topic of holidays is a familiar, everyday one; the questions asked are straightforward in terms of both language used and responses required. They all invite an answer from you which will be more expansive than just a simple *yes*. The questions give you the opportunity to offer both information and opinion and allow you to use a range of structures, e.g. present tense, past tense, conditional tense, superlative – as well as a range of vocabulary as you mention the different activities.

Getting started...

1 Which of these activities would you *not* call a sport? Why? Add the words to the table.

> hang-gliding   ten-pin bowling   snooker
> ice-hockey   skiing   golf   motor-racing
> tennis   archery   baseball   squash   chess
> snorkelling   bird-watching   boxing
> badminton   rock-climbing   jogging   yoga

Do	Play	Go

1

2

3

4

2 Choose the correct alternatives in these sentences.

a   We've got some very good players in our football *band/team* this year.
b   What was the final *score/mark* at the end of the match?
c   Did you *beat/win* your chess match?
d   Tim is an excellent tennis *coach/tutor*.
e   Sandrine is very *competition/competitive*, isn't she?
f   I've just bought some new golf *clubs/rackets*.

Speaking

1 Work with a partner and decide who is going to answer the Student A questions and who is going to answer the Student B questions. Student A needs to answer all four questions, taking no more than 3 minutes. Repeat the process for the Student B questions.

Exam hint

Exercise 1 is a practice task for Part 1 of the Speaking Paper.

Student A
Let's talk about sport
Which sports do you play regularly? (Tell me about that.)
Which sport do you enjoy the most? (Tell me about that.)
Where do you play _____ (Tell me about that.)
Who do you play with? (Why is that?)

Student B
Let's talk about sport
Which team sports do you play? (Tell me about that.)
Which single player sports do you play? (Tell me about that.)
Do you prefer team sports or single player sports? (Why is that?)
Do you and your family play any sports together? (Tell me about that.)

◁))) Listening

1 Work with a partner and look at this saying, then discuss the questions with your partner.

'It's not the winning, it's the taking part that counts.'

● What do you think the saying means?

● Do you agree with it? Why/Why not?

2 R.11 ▶ Listen to an extract from a radio programme and answer the questions.

Exam hint

Exercise 2 is a practice task for Part 2 of the Listening Paper.

Questions

1–2

Choose **one** correct answer.

1 The commentators on the radio programme
   a take part in the programme once a month.
   b change with every edition of 'Newsround'.
   c are the same people for each programme.

2 The Scottish Football Association's proposals
   a are fully supported by those aware of it.
   b target children at primary school.
   c reinforce the importance of winning.

3–5

Choose **three** correct answers.

The Association's proposals could involve
   a changing the score at half time.
   b not rewarding the winning team.
   c not running school tournaments.
   d increasing the number of players.
   e not counting the number of goals.
   f decreasing the number of players.
   g awarding trophies to all players.

6–15

Complete these notes using no more than **three words** or **a number**.

Terry Porter
● used to be _____ (6) for a football squad
● did not take the proposals _____ (7) at first
● feels that the proposals do not reflect _____ (8)
● thinks we live in a _____ (9) and this means learning about competition
● thinks this involves both _____ (10)
Sarah Goodwood
● agrees with Terry's comments
● thinks that _____ (11) has many competitive levels
● thinks children need to learn from the _____ (12) of losing
● feels those _____ (13) could be put off playing their sport
Arnold Cartwright
● thinks that the proposals could make games _____ (14)
● agrees that children should not receive _____ (15) in competitions

3 `R.11` ▶ Listen again and check your answers.

4 Work with a partner and answer these questions:

- What is the Scottish Football Association proposing?
- Is each of the three members of the panel for or against the proposals?

Grammar: obligation and permission

1 Read the description of a sport. What two names is the sport known by?

Grammar reference: see page 234

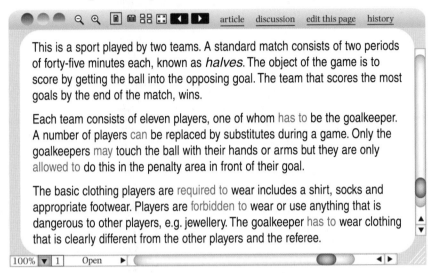

This is a sport played by two teams. A standard match consists of two periods of forty-five minutes each, known as *halves*. The object of the game is to score by getting the ball into the opposing goal. The team that scores the most goals by the end of the match, wins.

Each team consists of eleven players, one of whom has to be the goalkeeper. A number of players can be replaced by substitutes during a game. Only the goalkeepers may touch the ball with their hands or arms but they are only allowed to do this in the penalty area in front of their goal.

The basic clothing players are required to wear includes a shirt, socks and appropriate footwear. Players are forbidden to wear or use anything that is dangerous to other players, e.g. jewellery. The goalkeeper has to wear clothing that is clearly different from the other players and the referee.

2 Read the text again. Which of the highlighted words and phrases express obligation? Which express prohibition? Which express permission? Put the words/phrases in the correct column in the table.

Obligation	Prohibition	Permission

3 Work with a partner and discuss these questions.

a Which sentence is the odd-one-out in these two groups? Why?

Group 1

i You can't have any brakes on your bike.

ii You mustn't have any brakes on your bike.

iii You don't have to have any brakes on your bike.

Group 2

iv You're required to wear special glasses to protect your eyes.

v You're supposed to wear special glasses to protect your eyes.

vi You ought to wear special glasses to protect your eyes.

b Which three of these sentences are correct?

i I have to start doing more sport.

ii I've got to start doing more sport.

iii I often have to train on Saturday evenings.

iv I often have got to train on Saturday evenings.

c Put these sentences into the past.

    i I *have* to collect my tennis racket on Thursday.

    ii I *must* play Tony at golf again because we had such a good time.

    iii *I've got* to buy a new cycle helmet.

d Which sentence is incorrect in each of these groups? Find it and correct it.

Group 1

    i You don't need to be a member to use the courts.

    ii You needn't to be a member to use the courts.

    iii It isn't necessary to be a member to use the courts.

Group 2

    iv You can wear protective clothing.

    v You're allowed to wear protective clothing.

    vi You're permission to wear protective clothing.

e In which case, i or ii, was a tennis court definitely booked?

    i We didn't need to book a tennis court as lots of courts were free.

    ii We needn't have booked a tennis court as lots of courts were free.

4 Complete the second sentence so that it has a similar meaning to the first sentence, using the word given. Do not change the word given. You must use between two and five words, including the word given.

a It's necessary for you to be at the stadium by 11.00 a.m.

    got

    You _____ to be at the stadium by 11.00 a.m.

b It's fine to get advice in between games.

    allowed

    You _____ to get advice in between games.

c You cannot stop another player from getting to the ball.

    permitted

    It _____ you to stop another player from getting to the ball.

d It is not necessary for you to wear any special kind of clothing.

    have

    You _____ to wear any special kind of clothing.

e We would advise you to stretch well before and after a game.

    should

    You _____ well before and after a game.

f It's very important to avoid eating a lot before you play.

    must

    You _____ a lot before you play.

g You're supposed to wear a crash helmet.

    ought

    You _____ wear a crash helmet.

h It wasn't necessary for me to bring a spare racket.

    have

    I _____ brought a spare racket.

Vocabulary: success

1 Complete the report from a high school headteacher with the words in the box.

> pass   prize   achievement   won   record   successful
> achieved   result   did   success

We are proud to report another _____ (1) year in all areas at Headland High. Starting with sports, our football first team, under the expert guidance of Joss Partley, _____ (2) the Sussex Schools Trophy for the second year running. And in athletics, Sarah Mayhew broke the junior national 800 metre _____ (3).

The end-of-year school concert was also a great _____ (4) with over 150 children taking part in various ways and £375 being raised for charity. In addition, our sixth form students _____ (5) extraordinarily well this year. For the first time, 100% managed to _____ (6) their A-level exams and nearly 75% _____ (7) the necessary grades for them to go to the university of their choice. 35% were awarded 'A' grades, which is a remarkable _____ (8).

The Brodie _____ (9) for all-round _____ (10) goes to Francis Brown. Francis has worked consistently hard at all his academic subjects and has also been active both musically and on the sports field. He is an example to all of us of the fruits of hard work.

2 There is a mistake in each of these sentences. Find the mistakes and correct them.

  a The performance was a great successful and everyone was very pleased.

  b To our surprise, we won the other team 3–0.

  c Winning the trophy was one of the school's greatest achieves.

  d He is the most succeeding football player I have ever known.

  e I won first record in a competition – it's a new mountain bike!

  f Do you know the achievement of the England versus Italy game?

  g Everyone in our class took the maths exam with an 'A'.

  h Ian beat the 1,500 metres although he isn't really fit.

Vocabulary hint

win, gain, earn

Complete the sentences with the correct form of *win*, *gain* or *earn*.

1 I _____ nearly twice as much in my new job.
2 You can _____ €25m in this week's lottery.
3 She _____ a lot of useful experience by working in her father's firm.

📖 Reading

1 Work with a partner and discuss these questions.

  a Have you ever flown a kite? When/Where? Did you enjoy it?

  b Have you ever heard of/been to a kite-flying tournament?

  c How do you think someone could 'win' a kite-flying tournament?

Exam hint

Exercise 2 is a practice task for Part 2 of the Reading and Writing Paper.

2 Read the extract from the novel *The Kite Runner* and answer the questions that follow.

The Kite Runner

Every winter, districts in Kabul held a kite-flying tournament. And if you were a boy living in Kabul, the day of the tournament was the highlight of the cold season. I never slept the night before the tournament. I'd roll from side to side, make shadow animals on the wall, even sit on the balcony in the dark, a blanket wrapped around me. I felt like a soldier trying to sleep in the trenches the night before a major battle. And that wasn't so far off. In Kabul, fighting kites was a little like going to war.

As with any war, you had to ready yourself for battle. For a while, Hassan and I used to build our own kites. We saved our weekly allowances in the fall and dropped the money in a little porcelain horse Baba had given me. When the winds of winter began to blow and snow fell in chunks, we went to the bazaar and bought bamboo, glue, string and paper. We spent hours every day shaving bamboo for the center and cross pieces, cutting the thin tissue paper which made for easy dipping and recovery. And then, of course, we had to make our own string, or *tar*. If the kite was the gun, then *tar*, the glass-coated cutting line, was the bullet in the chamber. We'd go out in the yard and feed up to five hundred feet of string through a mixture of ground glass and glue. We'd then hang the line between the trees, leave it to dry. The next day, we'd wind the line around a wooden spool. By the time the snow melted and the rains of spring swept in, every boy in Kabul had numerous cuts on his fingers from a whole winter of fighting kites. I remember how my classmates and I used to huddle, compare our battle scars on the first day of school.

The kite-fighting tournament was an old winter tradition in Afghanistan. It started early in the morning on the day of the contest and didn't end until only the winning kite flew in the sky – I remember one year the tournament outlasted daylight. People gathered on sidewalks and roofs to cheer for their kids. The streets filled with kite fighters, jerking and tugging on their lines, squinting up to the sky, trying to gain position to cut the opponent's line. Every kite fighter had an assistant – in my case, Hassan – who held the spool and fed the line. The rules were simple: No rules. Fly your kite. Cut the opponents. Good luck.

Except that wasn't all. The real fun began when a kite was cut. That was where the kite runners came in, those kids who chased the windblown kite drifting through the neighborhoods until it came spiraling down in a field, dropping in someone's yard, on a tree, or a rooftop. The chase got pretty fierce; hordes of kite runners swarmed the streets, shoved past each other like those people from Spain I'd read about once, the ones who ran from the bulls. And when a kite runner had his hands on a kite, no one could take it from him. That wasn't a rule. That was custom.

For kite runners, the most coveted prize was the last fallen kite of a winter tournament. It was a trophy of honor, something to be displayed on a mantle for guests to admire. When the sky cleared of kites and only the final two remained, every kite runner readied himself for the chance to land this prize. He positioned himself at a spot that he thought would give him a head start. Tense muscles readied themselves to uncoil. Necks craned. Eyes crinkled. Fights broke out. And when the last kite was cut, all hell broke loose.

Vocabulary hint

Kabul – the capital city of Afghanistan
Baba – grandfather
bazaar – a market or a group of shops especially in the Middle East

Questions

1–5

Choose **one** correct answer.

1   The kite-flying tournament takes place
   a   all around Afghanistan.
   b   on one day every year.
   c   during the autumn season.

2   How did the narrator feel the night before the kite-flying tournament?
   a   relaxed
   b   excited
   c   uncomfortable

3   How did they get the materials to make their kites?
   a   They bought them using their savings.
   b   Baba gave them the money to buy them.
   c   The boys collected what they needed.

4   To make the kites
   a   bamboo had to be thinned.
   b   tissue paper had to be dipped.
   c   string had to be glued together.

5   The cuts on their hands were caused by
   a   stripping bamboo.
   b   winter weather.
   c   handling lines.

6–10

Complete these sentences using no more than **four words** or **a number**.

6   The kite-fighting tournament finished when there was _____ remaining.

7   Observers occupied _____ to watch the tournament.

8   The kite fighters have to _____ to bring down their kites.

9   In the tournament, each kite fighter works alongside _____.

10   The tournament does not have any _____.

11–15

Answer these questions using no more than **three words** or **a number**.

11   What did the kite runners do once a kite had been cut?

....

12   Which two words in the text tell you that there are lots of kite runners?

....

13   Which two words in the text tell you that the kite runners were not gentle with each other?

....

14   What are the kite runners not allowed to do when one of them wins a kite?

....

15   Which is the most important kite to a kite runner?

....

3   Work with a partner and discuss these questions:
   ● Would you be interested in watching or taking part in a kite-fighting tournament? Why/Why not?

   ● Do you know of any customs or sports that are special to your country? Describe them.

   ● Did you like the way the extract above was written? Would you be interested in reading more from this book? Why/Why not?

4   American spelling is sometimes a little different from British spelling. Find the American spelling for these words in the last two paragraphs of the story.

> neighbourhoods   spiralling   honour

5 Work with a partner. Look at these pairs of words. In each pair, which word is American and which is British? (Use a dictionary if necessary.)

  a   center – centre
  b   theatre – theater
  c   color – colour
  d   favour – favor
  e   catalog – catalogue
  f   dialogue – dialog
  g   skillful – skilful
  h   enrol – enroll
  i   travelled – traveled
  j   defence – defense
  k   paralyze – paralyse

6 Can you see any patterns in the way American spelling is often different from British spelling? Do you know any other examples of American spelling? Discuss your ideas with your partner.

Grammar: *would* and *used to*

1 R.12 ▶ Listen to five people talking about their attitude to sports/games as children. Match sentences a–f with the speakers 1–5. Use the letters only once. There is one extra letter which you do not need to use.

  a   He/she describes a game he/she played.
  b   He/she is surprised by how things have changed.
  c   The rules of his/her sport have changed recently.
  d   He/she misses a past activity.
  e   Things changed a lot for him/her after leaving school.
  f   He/she can feel frustrated when playing his/her sport.

2 R.13 ▶ Complete these sentences from Exercise 1. Put one word in each gap. Then listen and check your answers.

  a   I never _____ to do much sport.
  b   I used _____ love finding a good book.
  c   We _____ all get to school really early.
  d   I didn't have time for any sport. It took ages to _____ used to that.
  e   I _____ to be pretty good in my teens.
  f   I'm not as fit as I was . . . I can't really get _____ to that.
  g   When I was younger we _____ always be outside.
  h   I _____ used to getting up an hour or so before I go to work.

3 Match the structures a-d with their uses i-iv.

  a   *would* + infinitive (without *to*)
  b   *used to* + infinitive (without *to*)
  c   *be used to* + noun/gerund
  d   *get used to* + noun/gerund

Grammar hint

used to

Which of these sentences is not correct? Why?
1 Did you used to play much sport?
2 I'm not used to getting up before 7.00 a.m.
3 He used to be the fastest boy in my school.

i   to say you are accustomed to something because you have been doing
it for some time

ii to say you are becoming accustomed to a new situation

iii to talk about past habits and repeated actions but not about past states

iv to talk about past habits and states that do not occur now or no longer exist

4 Work with a partner. Decide on a particular age (e.g. *ten years old*). Take turns to
ask and answer these questions in relation to that age:

● What sports did you use to play?

● What other things did you use to do in your free time?

● How would you typically spend your weekends?

5 Write a summary of what your partner told you. Read out your summaries
in small groups.

*When José was ten, he used to play lots of sports including football and tennis. He also
used to enjoy going bird-watching with his father in the mountains . . .*

Speaking

1 Work with a partner and each choose one of the topics below. Prepare to time
your partner – give them 1 minute to prepare and then ask them to start
speaking. Tell them to stop speaking after 2 minutes. Did your partner answer
the question on the card?

Exam hint

Exercise 1 is a practice task for Part 2 of the
Speaking Paper.

Student A
You are going to talk about **sport and exercise**. You can use some or all of the ideas
listed below in your talk but <u>you must answer this question</u>:

How important is physical exercise in your life and why?
You must talk for 1 to 2 minutes. You have 1 minute to think and make notes before
your talk begins.

Here are some ideas to help you:
· Type of exercise
· Social aspect
· Health/fitness
· Enjoyment

Student B
You are going to talk about **sport and exercise**. You can use some or all of the ideas
listed below in your talk but <u>you must answer this question</u>:

Which type of physical exercise do you enjoy most and why?
You must talk for 1 to 2 minutes. You have 1 minute to think and make notes before
your talk begins.

Here are some ideas to help you:
· How often
· Social aspect
· Health/fitness
· Relaxation

Exam hint

Exercise 2 is a practice task for Part 3 of the Speaking Paper.

2 Work with a partner and take it in turns to ask and answer the following questions. Remember to give as much information as possible and try to keep talking for at least 5 minutes.

Part 3
We have been talking about **sport and exercise** and I would like to ask you some more questions on this topic.

- Do you think it's important to play sport regularly? (Why is that?)
- What do you think you learn from playing team sports? (Tell me about that.)
- Do you think you have to be good at sport to enjoy it? (Why is that?)

- Do you think you play enough sport at school? (Why is that?)
- How could schools encourage students to be more active? (Tell me about that.)
- Are there any types of exercise that you would like to see introduced in school? (e.g. *yoga*). (Tell me about that.)

- Do you think that exercising using games consoles (e.g. *Nintendo Wii Fit*) is as effective as traditional forms of exercise? (Why is that?)
- What are the advantages of exercising using games consoles? (Tell me about that.)
- What are the disadvantages of exercising using games consoles? (Tell me about that.)

 # Writing

1 Read the task and look at the information about writing reports in the Writing reference on page 250.

Writing task

A recent survey has shown that the fitness and health of young people where you live is suffering because they are not as active as they use to be. You have been asked to write a report for teachers at local schools which a) gives some reasons why this is happening and b) makes some suggestions as to ways of tackling this problem. Write your report using between 100 and 150 words.

2 Read this advice for writing a good report. Which is not a good piece of advice?

a Highlight key words in the instructions.

b Think about who you are writing the report for.

c Plan how many paragraphs you will have.

d Decide on the purpose of each paragraph.

e Include an introduction to your report.

f Decide if you want to use sub-headings.

g Write in an informal style.

3 Work with a partner. Which of the phrases in *italics* do you think could be useful in a report?

a *A recent survey has revealed* serious problems with the local transport system.

b *The aim of this report is to* look at ways of encouraging more recycling by local people.

c *I would be very grateful if you would consider* my recent application.

d *One possible way of approaching this problem is to* provide more litter bins in public places.

e *Another idea which has been effective elsewhere is to* install CCTV cameras along busy shopping streets.

f *On the other hand,* many young people are heavily involved in voluntary work with local organisations.

g *They had been sitting by the side of the road* for several hours before someone gave them a lift.

h *In conclusion then, I would recommend that* a survey of foreign tourists is carried out to discover exactly which are the most popular local tourist sites.

4 Change the endings of the 'useful' sentences to make them appropriate for *your* report.

5 There is a mistake in each of these sentences. Find the mistakes and correct them.

a *Not only* should parents play different sports with their children, *but* they should *also* to avoid taking them everywhere by car.

b *As well as* include sports activities as part of the normal curriculum, schools should organise sports matches with other local schools.

c *In addition* the effect on the physical health of young people, sport can improve mental alertness.

d Sport helps prevent many kinds of illness. *Furthermore,* can teach young people to work effectively in teams.

6 Now write your report for the teachers of local schools.

In your report you should:

● state the purpose of your report

● give **two** reasons why the health/fitness of young people is suffering

● suggest **two** ways that schools could help with the problem.

Write your report using between 100 and 150 words.

Exam hint

Exercise 6 is a practice task for Part 4 of the Reading and Writing Paper.

Summarising

1 Read the extract from the novel *The Kite Runner* and then write a summary for your English teacher.

In your summary you should:

- say how the boys made their kites

- say how a kite-fighting tournament is won

- explain the role of the kite runners.

Write your summary using between 100 and 150 words.

The Kite Runner

As with any war, you had to ready yourself for battle. For a while, Hassan and I used to build our own kites. We saved our weekly allowances in the fall and dropped the money in a little porcelain horse Baba had given me. When the winds of winter began to blow and snow fell in chunks, we went to the bazaar and bought bamboo, glue, string and paper. We spent hours every day shaving bamboo for the center and cross pieces, cutting the thin tissue paper which made for easy dipping and recovery. And then, of course, we had to make our own string, or *tar*. If the kite was the gun, then *tar*, the glass-coated cutting line, was the bullet in the chamber. We'd go out in the yard and feed up to five hundred feet of string through a mixture of ground glass and glue. We'd then hang the line between the trees, leave it to dry. The next day, we'd wind the line around a wooden spool. By the time the snow melted and the rains of spring swept in, every boy in Kabul had numerous cuts on his fingers from a whole winter of fighting kites. I remember how my classmates and I used to huddle, compare our battle scars on the first day of school.

The kite-fighting tournament was an old winter tradition in Afghanistan. It started early in the morning on the day of the contest and didn't end until only the winning kite flew in the sky – I remember one year the tournament outlasted daylight. People gathered on sidewalks and roofs to cheer for their kids. The streets filled with kite fighters, jerking and tugging on their lines, squinting up to the sky, trying to gain position to cut the opponent's line. Every kite fighter had an assistant – in my case, Hassan – who held the spool and fed the line. The rules were simple: No rules. Fly your kite. Cut the opponents. Good luck.

Except that wasn't all. The real fun began when a kite was cut. That was where the kite runners came in, those kids who chased the windblown kite drifting through the neighborhoods until it came spiraling down in a field, dropping in someone's yard, on a tree, or a rooftop. The chase got pretty fierce; hordes of kite runners swarmed the streets, shoved past each other like those people from Spain I'd read about once, the ones who ran from the bulls. And when a kite runner had his hands on a kite, no one could take it from him. That wasn't a rule. That was custom.

For kite runners, the most coveted prize was the last fallen kite of a winter tournament. It was a trophy of honor, something to be displayed on a mantle for guests to admire. When the sky cleared of kites and only the final two remained, every kite runner readied himself for the chance to land this prize.

Grammar

1 Read the text and complete the gaps. You have been given the first letter of each missing word.

Sport was taken very seriously at our school. Everybody h_____ (1) to wear a navy blue sports kit, which we all hated. We were always told that you didn't n_____ (2) to be good at sport to enjoy it, but I would disagree. We usually had t_____ (3) take our sports lessons outside, unless the weather was bad, and it had to be really bad for us to stay in the gym. We were s_____ (4) to take part in all school sports events and the most dreaded of these was the annual school run. Everyone was r_____ (5) to do the run unless you had special written permission to miss it. There was a set route and we weren't a_____ (6) to deviate from this. This meant that we were not s_____ (7) to take any short cuts, although we always managed to find one. After finishing the run we were p_____ (8) to go straight to the changing rooms and have a hot shower. It was miles long and it always rained.

2 Complete these sentences using the prompts.

a   I / used / do / lots /different sports / I / be / younger.
b   Every Sunday afternoon / my brother and I / would / go / local park / play football.
c   She / gradually get / used / work for / large multi-national corporation.
d   We / still / not used / live / in / country.
e   You / use / enjoy /go /school?
f   My family / would / always spend / summer holidays / south of France.
g   Simon / slowly / get / used / long train journey / his new job.
h   You used / drive / left-hand side / road / yet?

3 Connect the pairs of sentences with the words/phrases in brackets. Change the grammar of the sentences as necessary.

a   She plays a lot of badminton. She is in her school swimming team. (As well as)
b   You must lose some weight. You need to make sure you do regular exercise. (Furthermore)
c   The Olympic Games generates enormous interest in sport. It can have a very important economic effect on the host country. (Not only)
d   He won the European title. He would like to get a medal at the World Championships. (In addition)

Vocabulary

4 Complete these sentences with the words in the box. There are two extra words that you do not need to use.

| beat   succeed   result   competitive   prize   successful   record   score   pass   achievement |

a   I can't believe that Jan managed to _____ all her exams. It's fantastic.
b   Simon has become quite a _____ salesman. He can be quite persuasive.
c   Do you know what the world _____ is for the 100 metres?
d   She won a _____ of £2,000 for her first novel.
e   I get a real sense of _____ when I know I have taught a class well.
f   This election has been a good _____ for the Green Party.
g   We need to _____ the London Lions by fifteen points if we're going to go through to the next round of the tournament.
h   She's given herself two years to _____ in becoming a published writer.

5 Name the sport which is being described.

a   You play on ice and try to hit a hard flat round object into the other team's goal with special sticks.
b   Two people use long sticks to hit coloured balls into holes at the sides and corners of a table.
c   You hold on to a large frame covered with cloth and fly slowly through the air without an engine.
d   Two people use rackets to hit a small rubber ball against the walls of a square court.
e   You shoot arrows from a bow and attempt to hit the centre of a target.
f   You roll a ball along the floor and try and knock down objects at the other end.
g   You hit a small white ball with a special stick across the course and try to get the ball into the hole.
h   Lots of people drive as fast as they can in special cars around a track.
i   You go very fast down a snowy mountain standing on special long pieces of wood or plastic.
j   You go underwater wearing a special mask and plastic tube to help you breathe to look at things living in the sea.

Paper 1: Reading and Writing

 Part 2: Reading (15 marks)

Text types

Text types in this part include **longer** pieces of text (about 700 words) such as:

● articles

● leaflets

● adverts

Skills

Your ability to read for both **gist** and **detail** is being tested here. **Gist** is the general meaning, purpose or intention of a text. Reading for gist is the same as skimming, but with a longer text. We read for gist to gather the central themes and ideas quickly – we skip over the detail. It is not necessary to read and understand every word – we focus on significant words.

Reading for **detail** is like scanning – you are looking for specific information or detail in longer texts. Now it is important that you read and understand each word, number or fact because you are trying to learn something specific from the text. This is careful reading.

So, you skim first to get the gist, then go back to the text to read for detail.

Task types

You have to match information listed in the questions to their equivalents in the texts. It is not a question of spotting the same words in both questions and text – you must recognise and understand paraphrasing. All the answers are in the text and the questions follow the order of information presented in the texts.

Task types include:

● **Multiple-choice:** you choose which option is the correct answer to a question or best fills a gap in a sentence. There could be three or four options which will all appear reasonable, but only one will be correct.

● **Short-answer questions:** generally you will write between one and three words/numbers (the exact number is given in the instruction). The words/numbers for your answers come from the text itself and you should copy these words exactly as they stand in the text, making sure you keep to the number of words allowed. Don't copy whole sentences from the text – you will not gain the mark even if the correct answer is included in the sentence you have copied. Watch your spelling – this is an important part of completing the task successfully.

Let's take an example from the Edexcel International GCSE ESL paper in May 2010:

Having been told **Write no more than THREE words taken from the text**, you read this section of the text:

> *... A Hungarian scientist, Dr. Szent Gyorgyi, won a Nobel Prize in 1937 for his work with paprika pepper pods and Vitamin C research. He found that paprika peppers have seven times as much Vitamin C as oranges.*

You then have to answer this question:

> *What is paprika high in?*

The sentence you have to complete uses a paraphrase – if something is *high in* it means it *contains* or *has a lot of something*. We read in the text that paprika has seven times as much Vitamin C as oranges – this is a lot. Therefore we know paprika must contain a lot of vitamin C or be *high in Vitamin C* – so the answer here is *Vitamin C*.

● **True/False/Not Given:** you have to decide whether information given in each statement is True, False or Not Given according to the text. *Not Given* means there is no information within the text as to whether the statement is true or false.

Let's continue with our example from the Edexcel International GCSE ESL paper in May 2010. You read this section of the text:

> *Christopher Columbus ... found it [the sweet pepper] on the island he called Hispaniola (present-day Haiti) in 1493. He also came across Capsicum frutescens, the fiery shrub known as chilli. One of the aims of Columbus's voyage was to find an alternative trade route for importing black pepper ... Columbus's new-world peppers did not immediately appeal to the taste buds of Europeans, but they continued to be exported to Europe as there was a ready market for them further east in Arabia, Asia and Turkey.*

Then you have to decide if this statement is True, False or Not Given according to the text:

> *Columbus took the peppers back to Europe.*

If we read carefully for detail, we find the specific information we are seeking is not given – we know Columbus discovered paprika (sweet pepper) and chillies and that peppers were exported to Europe although many Europeans did not like them at first – but there is nothing to suggest Columbus himself took the peppers to Europe, so we have to choose *Not Given*.

● **Notes and sentence completion:** you complete the notes or sentences with one or more words (specified in the instruction) – these words are in the text, and, again, you should copy the words exactly. The notes or sentences to be completed will paraphrase information in the text. Again, avoid copying whole sentences from the text.

1 There is a mistake in each of these sentences. Find the mistakes and correct them.

a I put all the bags in the bonnet of the car and drove off.
b She is a very welcoming host and always makes me feel in home.
c He is so big-of-himself and always tells everyone how great he is.
d I went ten-pin boxing with some friends last night.
e Could you pop me off at the train station on your way to work?
f We've got tickets for the ballet on Saturday. The seats are at the front of the dress balcony.
g We don't need any petrol. I made the car up yesterday.
h They live in a self-centred community where they grow all the food they need.
i They are always arguing. This is the third time this week they've fallen off.
j He's a far cousin of mine – the son of someone in my family, but I'm not sure who.
k I'm doing friends round for dinner tonight so I'd better start the cooking.
l His car was a white-off, but luckily he escaped the accident completely unhurt.

2 Choose the correct alternative in these sentences.

a I *listen/'m listening* to music every morning in the car on my way to work.
b When I *get up/'ll get up* in the morning, I always feel tired.
c I *live/'m living* with my parents until my new flat is ready to move into.
d He almost always wins his races because he totally *believes/is believing* in himself.
e I get bored on beach holidays, but my sister really *do loves/does love* them.
f While we were sitting on the bus, we *heard/had heard* a strange noise.
g We had *had/had been* looking forward to this day for a long time.
h I soon realised I*'d left/'d been leaving* my bag at home.
i I *cycled/was cycling* up the hill when I hit a hole in the road and fell off.
j When I saw her, I knew she *had done/had been doing* some painting.
k When I was a child, I *must/had to wear* a green uniform at school.
l You are not allowed *use/to use* dictionaries in the exam.
m You often *don't have to/mustn't pay* for downloading music from the Internet.
n We *didn't need/needn't* have taken any ski equipment because it was possible to hire it in the resort.
o You really *should/ought* to keep in touch with your parents more.

3 There is a mistake in each of these questions. Find the mistakes and correct them.

a What you usually do at weekends?
b Do you know if are the tickets available yet?
c Who did tell you about the party?
d Do you can pick me up at about 8 o'clock?
e To who did you give the letter?
f Would you mind telling me where is the leisure centre?
g Where did you used to live when you were a child?
h You had been worrying about me before I phoned?
i Are you work at that shop again for the summer?
j Did you had to do a lot of homework last term?

4 Read the text and decide which answer, a, b, c or d, best fits each gap.

Cities fascinate me and I have a great interest in the history of urban areas, particularly the transport systems and how they change. It is interesting to see the way small towns of the past have changed into huge, _____ (1) cities. I am especially _____ (2) by the history and background of the London Underground.

On one of my first _____ (3) to London many years ago, I was _____ (4) to discover that some parts of the Underground system are over 140 years old. It is certainly the oldest and also one of the busiest underground railway networks in the world. _____ (5) I have found out more about the 'Tube', as it is known, my _____ (6) for it has grown and grown.

Something which is _____ (7) to me is how much evidence still exists of the many changes that have happened to it over the years. For example, _____ (8) you are travelling on the Central Line _____ (9) Holborn, have a look through the window. You will notice a station which used to be called 'British Museum'. No passengers have _____ (10) off here since 1932, but the station is still there.

There are about forty of these _____ (11) stations – or 'ghost stations' – on the Underground network along its entire 408 km of track. Some have vanished without trace whereas others are almost intact – _____ (12) time capsules of a past era.

1 a spreading	b stretching	c sprawling	d crawling
2 a amused	b intrigued	c stunned	d flabbergasted
3 a trips	b voyages	c travels	d treks
4 a entertained	b dazed	c amazed	d confused
5 a As	b When	c While	d Finally
6 a happiness	b desirability	c excitement	d affection
7 a embarrassing	b fascinating	c stunning	d misleading
8 a while	b then	c after	d during
9 a for	b forwards	c towards	d backwards
10 a got	b gone	c walked	d tripped
11 a run-down	b bustling	c abandoned	d isolated
12 a desirable	b quaint	c fashionable	d upmarket

5 Complete the text with one word in each gap.

I'll never forget the first time I went to a football match. It was so different from watching a match on TV. From an early age, I used _____ (1) love playing football in the park with my friends and I _____ (2) always asking my dad to take me to a real match. I remember it was a freezing cold day _____ (3) the middle of winter when he came home from work with two tickets. I couldn't believe it! We _____ (4) to get up early on the day of the match because the stadium was quite far away. As _____ (5) as we got off the train, I was amazed to see huge crowds of fans walking _____ (6) the stadium. I hadn't imagined that there would be so many people. They _____ (7) already making an incredible noise and that was even before the match had started! The crowd went really wild _____ (8) our team scored. That was the highlight of the day for me! Unfortunately, we lost the match _____ (9) the end, but it didn't matter really. The whole experience had been far more exciting _____ (10) I had imagined and I had enjoyed _____ (11) so much. That first match with my dad remains one of the _____ (12) special memories of my childhood.

6 Use the word given at the end of some of the lines of this text to form a word that fits in the gap *in the same line*.

Alfred Adler was a pioneer in the study of birth order. He suggested that social *relationships*, (0) especially among siblings and between children and parents, had a significant impact on the _____ (1) of children later in their lives.	relation personal
_____ (2), studies have linked first-born children with higher academic _____ (3) when compared to later-born children. In general, first-born children have been found to be _____ (4), assertive and task-oriented, often rising to _____ (5) positions as adults.	tradition achieve response leader
Second-borns and middle children often feel inferior to older children because they do not have their advanced _____ (6). Middle children have been found to _____ (7) in team sports, and both they and last-borns have been found to be more _____ (8) adjusted if they come from large families.	able success social
The _____ (9) of social skills is often strongest in last-borns from large families. As a group, they have been found to be the most _____ (10) in relating to others.	develop success

7 Complete the second sentence so that it has a similar meaning to the first sentence, using the word given. Do not change the word given. You must use between two and five words, including the word given.

I don't want to lose contact with all my old school friends.
touch

I want to stay **in touch with** all my old school friends.

a I'm not nearly as good at tennis as Debbie.
  far
  Debbie plays tennis _____.
b You're supposed to phone the school if you're going to be late.
  ought
  You _____ phone the school if you're going to be late.
c When I was a child, I went on holiday to Ireland every year.
  used
  When I was a child, I _____ on holiday to Ireland every year.
d I'm quite tired so I think I'll go to bed early tonight.
  bit
  I'm _____ tired so I think I'll go to bed early tonight.

e The living room has a door which leads directly to the garden.
  opens
  The living room has a door which _____ the garden.
f It's essential not to write more than 150 words in your report.
  must
  You _____ more than 150 words in your report.
g I am familiar with life in this town now and it doesn't feel strange.
  used
  I _____ in this town now and it doesn't feel strange.
h My younger brother and I are the same height.
  as
  My younger brother _____ me.

Chapter 6: Ages and stages

Getting started...

1 Work with a partner and describe what you think is happening in the pictures.

2 Work with a partner. Look at the 'stages of life' in the box and discuss the questions.

> a teenager   an adult   a baby
> middle-aged   elderly/old   a child

- What do you think the approximate age range is for each stage of life?

- Which stages do you think are the happiest/most difficult? Why?

3 R.14 ▶ Listen and answer these questions about Britain.

  a Between what ages are you legally required to go to school?

  b At what age do people typically have a 'coming-of-age' party?

  c At what age can you legally learn to drive?

  d What is the minimum legal age for getting married?

  e At what age do people typically retire?

4 Work with a partner. Ask and answer the questions in Exercise 3 about your country. Do you think that any of the ages in your answers should be changed? Discuss your ideas with your partner.

Exam hint

Exercise 3 is a practice task for Part 1 of the Reading and Writing Paper.

📖 Reading

1 Work with a partner and describe what you can see in the pictures.

2 You are going to read a magazine article on pages 78–79 about people at different stages of life. Skim the text quickly and match each part to the correct picture. Try to do this in one minute.

'It's their age ...'

A Thomas Robert Daley was born on the 21st May 1994. He is an English diver who specialises in the 10 metre platform event and is currently the FINA World Champion. He started diving at the age of seven and has made an impact in national and international competition at an early age. He represented Great Britain at the 2008 Summer Olympics, where he was Britain's youngest competitor, the youngest competitor of any nationality outside the sport of swimming, and the youngest to participate in a final. He lives in England with father Robert, mother Debbie and two brothers, William and Ben. He won two gold medals at the 2010 Commonwealth Games, in the 10 metre synchro diving event (with Max Brick) and the 10 metre individual platform competition.

B Kishan is only ten. Starting at the age of four, he has already acted in twenty-four feature films and has starred in 1,000 episodes of a hit soap opera on television in India. Now he's directing a full-length feature film about a child who lives on the streets. 'When I was six years old, I saw children selling newspapers at the traffic lights and my dad said they do not have parents. I thought I must do something for them,' Kishan told the BBC. Now he juggles school and filming, and although he misses out on playing with his friends, he has no regrets. He has his critics, however, who believe that he is having to become an adult too quickly, which is ironic, considering the subject matter of his film.

C Leona Louise Lewis was born on the 3rd April 1985. She is a British pop singer and songwriter. She auditioned for The X Factor in 2006 and after being announced the winner, received a £1 million recording contract. Leona has released two albums to date, Spirit and Echo, in 2007 and 2009 respectively. Spirit became the fastest-selling debut album and the biggest seller of 2007 in both the United Kingdom and Ireland. It has sold over 6.5 million copies worldwide. Leona's debut single 'A Moment Like This' became the fastest selling UK single after being downloaded over 50,000 times within 30 minutes of its release. Her second single, 'Bleeding Love', reached number one positions in over thirty singles charts around the world.

D Rabbit Kekai is a top international surfer. He comes from Hawaii and started surfing at the age of four. There are many top surfers from Hawaii, and many of them start young. Not many of them, however, continue surfing and competing in tournaments around the world as long as Rabbit, who is now an incredible eighty-three years old. He and his wife Lynn live in an apartment which is just 200 metres from Waikiki beach, and he gets up at 5.00 a.m. every single day of the year and goes straight down to the beach. He earns his living by teaching surfing and making commercials, but says, 'I still prefer to compete. I had six or seven first places last year. To be honest, I surf to keep alive.'

3 Read the text again and complete the tasks that follow on page 80.

Read the text again and complete the tasks that follow on page 80.

> ### Vocabulary hint
>
> FINA World Championships = World Championships for aquatic (water) sports
> synchro diving = two divers who attempt to perform identical or mirrored dives

Questions

1–3

Choose **A**, **B**, **C** or **D** for each question.

Which section

1   mentions someone's brothers? _____

2   makes reference to the Internet? _____

3   talks about making sacrifices? _____

4–6

Answer these questions using no more than **three words** or **a number**.

4   From an early age, Tom has competed at both a _____ level.

5   At the Summer Olympics 2008, Tom was _____ in the British team.

6   He and his partner won a gold medal in _____ at the 2010 Commonwealth Games.

7–9

Choose **one** correct answer for each question.

7   Kishan Shinkanth is unusual because he has

   a   directed 24 feature films.

   b   appeared in a soap opera.

   c   made a film about himself.

8   When Kishan was six years old he

   a   sold newspapers in town.

   b   did not live with his parents.

   c   decided to help street children.

9   Some people feel that Kishan

   a   should spend more time studying.

   b   is growing up faster than he should.

   c   needs to find a new topic for his film.

10–12

Answer these questions using no more than **three words** or **a number**.

10   Leona was given a recording contract after being successful in _____.

11   _____ is Leona's first album and has been a global success.

12   The single _____ outsold other singles around the world.

13–15

Choose **three** correct answers.

Rabbit Kekai

   a   helps others to learn how to surf.

   b   is a judge for surfing competitions.

   c   surfs in the morning with his wife.

   d   surfed from an unusually early age.

   e   outperforms others in competitions.

   f   is the oldest known competitive surfer.

   g   goes surfing every day all year round.

Exam hint

Exercise 1 is a practice task for Part 1 of the Speaking Paper.

🗣 Speaking

1   Work with a partner and decide who is going to answer the Student A questions and who is going to answer the Student B questions. Student A needs to answer all four questions, taking no more than 3 minutes. Repeat the process for the Student B questions.

Student A
Let's talk about age
What is the best thing about being a teenager? (Why is that?)
What is the worst thing about being a teenager? (Why is that?)
Which do you think is the best age to be? (Tell me about that.)
Which age are you not looking forward to? (Why is that?)

Student B
Let's talk about age
What are you going to do after your GCSEs? (Tell me about that.)
Why have you chosen to _____ (*answer from previous question*)? (Tell me about that.)
At what age are you planning to learn how to drive? (Why is that?)
What are the benefits of learning how to drive? (Tell me about that.)

Grammar: *so/such*; *too/enough*

Grammar reference: see page 236

1 Match sentences a–d with the correct grammar rule i–iv. Complete the gaps using *so* or *such*.

a I wish he wouldn't speak **so** *quickly*.

b She is **so** *kind* to all the children.

c I've got **so** *little* time left.

d We had **such** *good weather*.

i We use _____ with adjectives.

ii We use _____ with adverbs.

iii We use _____ with adjective + noun.

iv We use _____ with quantifiers (*much, many, few, little*).

2 Complete these sentences with *so, such* or *such a/an*. Look at the words in italics to help you.

a Steve Williams was _____ *fed up* with his daughter's bedroom that he put some photos on the Internet.

b I tidy up my bedroom _____ *rarely* that it's often a complete mess.

c There were _____ *many people* waiting to vote that I had to queue.

d It's not right for _____ *young child* to do an adult job like being a film director.

e I'm _____ *excited* about my wedding next week that I can hardly wait!

f There's _____ *little time* left before my exam that I have to study every evening.

g They planned the party _____ *carefully* that it went really well.

h This is _____ *interesting survey* about the attitudes of young people!

3 Work with a partner and discuss the difference in meaning between these pairs of sentences.

a i *We arrived at the party very late.*

ii *We arrived at the party too late.*

b i *I haven't got fresh enough vegetables.*

ii *I haven't got enough fresh vegetables.*

4 There is a mistake in each of these sentences. Find the mistakes and correct them.

a These trousers are too much small for me.

b There's much too salt in this soup.

c This food is too spicy for me to eat it.

d Too people tried to board the train and the doors wouldn't close.

e I'm not enough old to vote.

f Have you got enough of milk?

g It's an enough early train to get me there on time.

h This suitcase is too heavy to me to carry.

5 Complete the second sentence so that it has a similar meaning to the first sentence, using the word given. Do not change the word given. You must use between two and five words, including the word given.

a I couldn't reach the shelf because it was too high.

 me

 The shelf was _____ reach.

b I haven't seen a film as good as that for ages.

 such

 It's ages since I've seen _____ .

c This room is too hot to do gymnastics in.

 cool

 This room _____ to do gymnastics in.

d I was surprised there wasn't more cheese in the fridge.

 so

 I didn't think there was _____ in the fridge.

e The flight was overbooked.

 people

 There were _____ booked onto the flight.

f I can't believe you've bought a camera as expensive as this one.

 an

 I can't believe you've bought _____ .

g Her exam grades were too low for a place at university.

 high

 Her exam grades weren't _____ her to go to university.

h The camera instructions were too complicated for me to understand.

 that

 The camera instructions were _____ I couldn't understand them.

6 Work with a partner. Do you agree or disagree with these sentences? Discuss them with your partner and give details to justify your answers.

● My last holiday was full of so many exciting experiences!

● I never have enough time to see my friends.

● My last birthday was such a memorable day that I'll never forget it.

● I often find that I spend too much when I go shopping for clothes.

Vocabulary: prepositions

1 Match the sentence halves a–l with i–xii to make complete sentences.

a She was ashamed ...

b She was depressed ...

c You should be responsible ...

d He's famous ...

e I'm interested ...

f I'm proud ...

g Her dad complained ...

h I succeeded ...

i We are preparing ...

j I've decided to apply ...

k I'm not sure if I believe ...

l It depends ...

i ... in taking up surfing.

ii ... of the state of her bedroom.

iii ... for your actions by the time you're twenty.

iv ... about the results of the test.

v ... of passing my exam with an A grade.

vi ... for being the oldest surfer competing internationally.

vii ... in astrology or not.

viii ... about her messy bedroom all the time.

ix ... on the weather if we play tennis or not.

x ... for that job I told you about.

xi ... for my eighteenth birthday party at the moment.

xii ... in passing my driving test the second time I took it.

Grammar hint

Verbs following prepositions

Which of these sentences is correct? What is the general rule for the verb form that follows a preposition?

1 *I'm interested in* **learn** *to ski.*

2 *I'm interested in* **to learn** *to ski.*

3 *I'm interested in* **learning** *to ski.*

2 Complete these questions with the correct prepositions.

a What's the most difficult exam or test you've ever prepared _____?

b Have you succeeded _____ doing something difficult recently?

c Have you ever done anything that you feel particularly proud _____?

d Do you believe _____ the saying 'Every cloud has a silver lining'?

e Are you interested _____ taking part in traditional ceremonies and rituals?

f Would you ever consider applying _____ a job as a driving instructor?

g If you could be famous, what would you like to be famous _____?

h When you were a child, did you often complain _____ the food you had to eat?

3 Choose four of the questions to ask and answer with a partner. Encourage your partner to give more details by asking more questions.

◁))) Listening

1 Work with a partner and discuss these questions:

● At what age do you think you become an adult?

● Do you have any ceremonies in your country to celebrate becoming an adult?

● Do you think these types of ceremonies are important?

2 R.15 ▶ Listen to a radio interview about the coming-of-age ceremony in Japan and answer the questions on page 84.

Exam hint

Exercise 2 is a practice task for Part 3 of the Listening Paper.

Questions

1–5

Choose **one** correct answer.

1   How much does the interviewer know about this ceremony?

   a   absolutely nothing

   b   hardly anything at all

   c   quite a lot about the history

2   Traditionally, those taking part in the coming-of-age ceremony

   a   were only teenage boys.

   b   received some new clothes.

   c   were from the lower classes.

3   Why is the interviewer surprised about the age of the people involved in this ceremony?

   a   Because he expected them to be younger.

   b   Because it happens at a later age for boys than girls.

   c   Because they can already vote before the ceremony takes place.

4   On which day is the modern-day celebration of adulthood held?

   a   any Monday in January

   b   the second of January

   c   the second Monday of January

5   In the modern coming-of-age ceremony girls 'kimonos',

   a   are short-sleeved.

   b   have colourful sleeves.

   c   are of a formal type.

6–10

Complete these sentences using no more than **three words** or **a number**.

6   The _____ of the kimono is the belt or obi.

7   For the ceremony most of the boys dress in _____.

8   During the ceremony the young people have to _____ and they also receive some money.

9   Archers shoot arrows to ask the gods _____ the young people.

10   After the coming-of-age ceremony, the young people spend time with _____.

3   R.15 ▶ Listen again and check your answers.

 Speaking

1   Work with a partner and each choose one of the topics below. Prepare to time your partner – give them 1 minute to prepare and then ask them to start speaking. Tell them to stop speaking after 2 minutes. Did your partner answer the question on the card?

Exam hint

Exercise 1 is a practice task for Part 2 of the Speaking Paper.

Student A

You are going to talk about **different stages in life**. You can use some or all of the ideas listed below in your talk but <u>you must answer this question</u>:

Which birthday is most memorable for you and why?
You must talk for 1 to 2 minutes. You have 1 minute to think and make notes before your talk begins.

Here are some ideas to help you:
· Age
· People
· Location
· Activity

Student B

You are going to talk about **different stages in life**. You can use some or all of the ideas listed below in your talk but <u>you must answer this question</u>:

Which recent gathering (e.g. *a wedding*) was enjoyable for you and why?
You must talk for 1 to 2 minutes. You have 1 minute to think and make notes before your talk begins.

Here are some ideas to help you:
• Occasion
• People
• Location
• Food

2 Work with a partner and take it in turns to ask and answer the following questions. Remember to give as much information as possible and try to keep talking for at least 5 minutes.

Exam hint

Exercise 2 is a practice task for Part 3 of the Speaking Paper.

Part 3

We have been talking about **different stages in life** and I would like to ask you some more questions on this topic.
• At what age do you think that young people should be encouraged to get a part-time job? (Why is that?)
• What values can be learned from working part-time from an early age? (Tell me about that.)
• How can young people learn the value of money? (Tell me about that.)

• What do you think is a good age to get married and settle down? (Why is that?)
• What are the advantages of having children when you are young? (e.g. *25 years of age*) (Why is that?)
• What are the advantages of having children when you are older? (e.g. *40 years of age*) (Why is that?)

• Now that people are living longer, what are the consequences for society? (Tell me about that.)
• Do you think that people should be forced to retire at a certain age? (Why is that?)
• How does it benefit companies to take on younger employees? (Tell me about that.)

Grammar: present perfect simple and continuous

1 Work with a partner and discuss these questions.

a Which of these is correct?

   i ***Have you ever been*** *to Japan?*

   ii ***Have ever you been*** *to Japan?*

b Which of these is correct? What's the rule?

   i *I've lived here* ***for three months***.

   ii *I've lived here* ***since three months***.

c Work with a partner and write one statement and one question with each of the words below. Remember to use the present perfect simple.

   i *just*   ii *yet*   iii *already*

   What does each word mean, and what is its usual position in a statement (at the beginning, at the end or before the main verb)? What is its usual position in a question?

Grammar reference: see page 236

2 Choose the correct alternative.

a I first *went/have* been on an aeroplane when I was ten.

b I've been at this school *for/since* more than a year.

c Have you *yet packed your bag/packed your bag yet*?

d You'll never guess what *I've just done/I just have done*!

e He's passed his driving test *yet/already*.

f This is the first time I *have/'ve had* a place of my own.

g You're one of the kindest people I *ever met/'ve ever met*.

h When I *last saw/'ve last seen* Sonia, she was just about to get married.

3 Answer the questions about these pairs of sentences. They use the present perfect simple and the present perfect continuous.

a Which sentence is focusing on the finished action and which on the activity itself?

   i I've read a book about unusual weddings.

   ii I've been reading a book about unusual weddings.

b Match **Sentences 1** and **2** with the attitude each speaker is expressing in i and ii.

Sentence 1

I've lived in this flat for two months.

Sentence 2

I've been living in this flat for two months.

   i I still live here but it's probably temporary.

   ii I still live here and I probably won't move.

4 Read the e-mail quickly and answer these questions.

a What has the writer (Sonia) been doing?

b What does she want Emily to help her with?

Dear Emily

Just writing to tell you how the wedding plans are going! I've been working (1) so hard to get everything done! It's the first big thing like this that I do (2) and I can tell you, it's the most complicated thing I ever organised (3), for sure! I can't believe that I am thinking (4) about all the arrangements for over three months already … and there's loads more still to do.

I'm pleased though, because one thing I have sorted (5) out is the dress! I loved it the moment I've seen (6) it. I just have tried (7) it on and it's really gorgeous! I'm not going to say more than that because I want it to be a surprise. I didn't decide (8) on the dresses for the two bridesmaids yet. I've been thinking (9) about two different designs and I can't make up my mind. Are you free next week to come up and have a look with me?

By the way, have you received the photos I yet sent you (10)?

I'll write again soon.

Sonia xxx

5 Look at the highlighted phrases in the e-mail. There are mistakes in seven of them. Find the mistakes and correct them.

6 Look at these topics. Think of one key word that, for you, relates to each of them.

- Something you feel proud you've done
- Something important that has changed in your life in the last five years
- Something special you've had since you were a child
- A hobby you've been doing for more than a month
- Something exciting you want to do but you haven't done yet
- One of the most memorable places you've visited

7 Work with a partner and compare your key words. Choose four of your partner's key words and ask him/her to talk about the related topics. Ask questions to encourage your partner to give more details.

 Writing

1 Read the advertisement and task below. Are these statements true or false?

a The advertisement is for driving courses.

b There are three bullets which you need to write about.

c You don't need to include all the bullet points in your letter.

d You should write a maximum of 150 words.

e You should write your address at the top of the letter.

Learn to drive in a week!

Learn to drive at the Learner Driver Centre with highly-trained, professional instructors. You can pass your test in just one week – or take one of the other options. One-to-one practical tuition with all cars and equipment provided. No experience necessary – beginners welcome.

Discounts available in off-peak periods.

Come today and learn an invaluable skill for life!

Writing task

You have seen the above advertisement in a newspaper. You are interested in going, but you would like more information.

Read the advertisement carefully and then write a letter to the *Learner Driver Centre*.

In your letter you should:

- ask for more information about the one week course and other options
- ask for details about off peak discounts
- ask how you book a place at the Centre.

Write your letter using between 100 and 150 words.

Exam hint

If you are asked to write a letter for Part 5 of the Reading and Writing Paper remember you do not have to write a postal address.

2 Read the two letters written by different students and answer the questions for each one.

a Are there any language mistakes?

b Has the student covered all the bullet points in the task?

A

Dear Sir/Madam,

With reference to your advertisement in *The Times*, I am writing to ask for more information about driving courses at the Learner Driver Centre.

First of all, I'd like to know what times the course starts and finishes each day. Could you also tell me what other possibilities there are, for example, part-time courses? I would be grateful if you could tell me if there is a minimum age for your courses. I will be seventeen next month and i have never driven a car before.

Lastly, could you give me some more information about the available discounts? I'd like to know when the off-peak periods are and how much the courses cost at these times.

I look forward to hearing from you.

Yours faithfully,

Manuel Mendes
Manuel Mendes

B

Dear Sir/Madam,

With reference to your advertisement in *The Times*, I am writing to ask for more information about driving courses at the Learner Driver Centre.

First of all things, I'd like to know what times do the classes starts and finishes every day. Could you also say me if you are opened every day? I would be like other options so I would be grateful if you could tell me there are part-time courses, etc. Also I would like to know what is the minimum age for your courses.

Could you give me some more information about the different prices? I'd like to know when the off-peak periods is and how much the courses costs.

Finally, could you tell me if it is necessary to book or we can just arrive on the day?

I look forward to hearing from you.

Yours faithfully,

Jagoda Rosinska
Jagoda Rosinska

3 Look at these phrases and match them with the best part of the letter in the paragraph plan below.

a I'd like to know ...

b Could you tell me ...?

c With reference to your advertisement ...

d I look forward to hearing from you.

e I would be grateful if you could tell me ...

f I am writing to ask for more information about ...

g Could you give me some more information about ...?

Paragraph 1: Introduction (where advert seen/reason for writing)

Paragraphs 2, 3 and 4: Asking for specific information (based on the bullet points in the task)

Paragraph 5: Finishing the letter (asking for a reply)

4 Read the task and advertisement and make a note of the key points you must include in your e-mail.

The Job Station

The Job Station will start you on the right track!

Applying for your first job can be a daunting experience. Our courses can help you whatever job you're interested in.

• Completely personalised service – tailored for your specific needs.

• Expert advice on writing a CV which will get you noticed for the right reasons.

• Practical and realistic help with interview techniques.

Day and weekend courses to suit all. Discounts available when you take more than one course.

Writing task

You have seen the above advertisement in a newspaper. You are interested in going, but you would like more information.

Read the advertisement carefully and then write an e-mail to The Job Station.

In your e-mail you should:

• ask for more information about course content

• find out if there are computers and printers you can use

• ask about course times and costs.

Write your e-mail using between 100 and 150 words.

5 Write your e-mail using the paragraph plan and at least four of the phrases in Exercise 3.

6 Read your e-mail and answer these questions:

● Have you included all the points from the task?

● Have you organised your paragraphs appropriately?

● Have you used opening and closing paragraphs?

● Can you find any mistakes with grammar and spelling?

Exam hint

Exercise 5 is a practice task for Part 5 of the Reading and Writing Paper.

7 Now rewrite your e-mail, using your answers to the questions in Exercise 6 to improve it.

Summarising

Exam hint

Exercise 1 is a practice task for Part 6 of the Reading and Writing Paper.

1 Read the article about newly qualified teenage drivers and write a summary for your teacher.

In your summary you should:

● give two reasons why newly qualified drivers pay higher insurance premiums

● give two reasons why young drivers are more likely to have accidents

● give two ways in which newly qualified drivers can reduce their risk of accidents.

Write your summary using between 100 and 150 words.

Newly qualified teenage drivers

It is felt by some that the number one road safety priority for Britain should be reducing accidents involving young drivers. Research carried out by the insurance industry shows that teenage drivers are ten times more likely to have accidents while driving than motorists in their 40s. And, while road deaths and serious accidents are falling on average for the majority, they went up for young people, by a shocking 12% last year.

Young drivers are expected to pay higher insurance premiums than older drivers as they are seen as being high-risk drivers. Unfortunately, statistics prove that young drivers, especially males, are more likely to claim on their insurance, and these claims are likely to be more expensive.

Accidents involving young drivers have different characteristics from those that involve other drivers. Young, usually male, drivers were found to be more likely to have accidents driving at speed or around bends on weekend nights without any other cars being involved, but while carrying passengers. Young males were found to be more frequently at fault for their accidents than either females or older drivers. In order to reduce the

risk of young drivers being involved in accidents, there are a number of areas that need to be addressed.

Young drivers tend to have good vehicle control skills because they have had driving lessons more recently than older drivers; also their reaction times are faster. However, it's more likely to be peer pressure or carelessness that causes accidents in this area. Young drivers should not feel pressured or pushed into driving faster than they are comfortable with and shouldn't carry out dangerous manoeuvres because they are being 'egged' on by their friends.

Young drivers do not have the road knowledge or experience that older drivers do. Many accidents involving younger people happen during bad weather, which suggests they are not able to adapt their

driving style appropriately to the conditions. Time should always be taken to 'read the road' properly; experience can only come with time. Having an accident can dent your confidence and set you back months, even years, not to mention increasing your insurance premium.

Young drivers are suddenly propelled into a position of power when they pass their test, and they are likely to drive for pleasure and thrills until the novelty wears off. When surveyed, young drivers viewed breaking the speed limit as a less important factor in causing road accidents than older drivers did.

The most effective way for young drivers to reduce their chances of being involved in an accident and bring down their motoring costs is to drive safely. Insurers can only base their estimates of future risk in part upon your past driving experiences. If you've had an accident-free few years, you'll see your no claims bonus start to climb and then you'll start to see a difference. In four or more years, it's not unusual to get a 60% reduction on your premium with some companies offering 75% discounts for the 'safest drivers'.

Vocabulary

1   Complete each sentence with the best word from the box. Four of the words cannot be used.

> off   ceremony   flatmate   partner   engaged   graduated   retired   primary   child   teenager

a   We got _____ about eighteen months before we finally got married.
b   I've loved dancing ever since I was a _____, aged about six.
c   In some countries, the coming-of-age _____ is one of the biggest events in a young person's life.
d   My grandfather was bored when he _____ because he liked working and didn't really want to stop.
e   Being a _____ is a very interesting stage in life as you are no longer a child and not yet an adult.
f   I owed the bank a lot of money by the time I _____ from university.

2   Read the text and choose which answer, a, b, c or d, best fits each gap.

Bus cleaner retires at 100

A Los Angeles man has just retired from his job at the age of 100. Arthur Winston is proud _____ (1) the fact that he worked cleaning buses for over seventy-six years. He was so dedicated to his job that he only had one day off – when his wife died in 1988. And in 1996, he succeeded _____ (2) picking up an award for his hard work and commitment.

Mr Winston's first job was picking cotton at the age of ten. Then after a few years, in 1924, he applied _____ (3) his first job cleaning the 'buses', which were horses and carts in those days! In recent years, Mr Winston has been responsible _____ (4) a team of eleven workers, washing dozens of buses every day.

'Some people think I should've retired earlier and enjoyed my old age!' he says. 'But it depends _____ (5) how you see things. I've never complained _____ (6) my work. I'd rather be working than lying around the house.' He is now preparing _____ (7) a different kind of life, but he still wants to work. He is interested _____ (8) finding some kind of job working with senior citizens.

1	a	in	b	of	c	with	d	to
2	a	to	b	by	c	in	d	with
3	a	for	b	to	c	at	d	with
4	a	to	b	about	c	on	d	for
5	a	of	b	on	c	in	d	at
6	a	about	b	with	c	for	d	to
7	a	to	b	about	c	for	d	by
8	a	in	b	with	c	to	d	of

Grammar

3   Choose the correct alternatives.

Is seventeen the perfect age?

I really think seventeen is *such/so*[1] a perfect age! I love being seventeen. I have *so much/too much*[2] freedom – my parents let me do anything I want. I'm still studying at school but I don't have *too many/too much*[3] to do really. Next year will be harder, I think.

I'm *enough old/old enough*[4] to learn to drive now, which is really cool. I haven't had lessons yet, though, because I haven't got *enough money/money enough*[5] at the moment. But as soon as I have, I will!

Another thing which is great about being seventeen is that you have *such/so much*[6] to look forward to. There are *such/so*[7] great places to see and *so many/too many*[8] things to do. It's really exciting.

One thing that is a bit frustrating about being seventeen is that you feel *enough responsible/responsible enough*[9] to be an adult but some people treat you like a child. It's *so/such*[10] annoying!

4   Complete the sentences by writing the verb/phrase in brackets in the correct tense.

a   _____ (you/ever/break) your arm or leg?
b   I _____ (know) my best friend since I was five.
c   Tom _____ (phone) me three times yesterday.
d   Oh no! What _____ (you/do) to your hair!
e   She's very upset. She _____ (cry) all morning.
f   It's one of the best songs I _____ (ever/hear).
g   This is the second time he _____ (ask) me to help him.
h   _____ (she/take) her exams yet?
i   I _____ (work) here since May, but I hope to get a better job soon.
j   A lot _____ (happen) in the last couple of weeks.

Exam tips

Paper 1: Reading and Writing

 Part 5: Writing (20 marks)

This section requires you to produce an informal piece of writing.

You are asked to produce an appropriate and relevant short piece of writing (between 100 and 150 words) in response to, e.g. a given situation, a letter, an advert or a short article. Don't worry – the description of the situation or the content of the letter, etc. will always be in accessible language so you should easily understand what you are being asked to respond to.

Your piece of writing could take the form of a:

- a letter
- a fax
- an e-mail

You may be asked to do two things: to provide information and to ask for required information. You should try to respond imaginatively to these situations, drawing on your own experiences wherever possible.

Remember, your piece of writing will be marked according to four criteria. These are:

- **Communicative quality:** how successfully and relevantly you have completed the task. Make sure you address all aspects within the word count and check you have used the correct tone and register for the audience.

- **Lexical accuracy and range:** the range of vocabulary you use and how appropriate it is to the task. This assessment grid also assesses how accurately you use the vocabulary.

- **Grammatical accuracy and range:** the range of grammatical structures you use and how effectively and accurately you use them.

- **Effective organisation:** how well you have organised your response in terms of paragraphing, cohesion and coherence. This grid also assesses how easy it is for the reader to understand and follow what you have written.

Cohesion means that your writing appears as a single piece, rather than a random sequence of thoughts or sentences. To achieve this, you should use cohesive devices. These are the links that hold a text together; they make the sentences, ideas and details fit together clearly and smoothly, which means that readers can follow your writing easily.

Conjunctives are one of the most useful cohesive devices. They are words (or short phrases) that show how ideas are connected and they can join sentences. Here are some examples of high frequency conjunctives: *firstly, secondly, so, therefore, moreover, however, nevertheless, yet, in conclusion, by contrast, on the other hand, in addition, also, but, in addition, as far as … is concerned.* Try to use a variety of these in your writing.

Let's look at this question in the Edexcel International GCSE ESL paper in November 2009:

Together with a classmate, you are doing a project on a famous person. You receive this e-mail from your classmate.

To...	Lee@netnet.com
Cc...	
Bcc...	
Subject:	Project

We need to get started on our project, 'A Famous Person', as it has to be handed in next month.

Do you have any suggestions on who we should choose? Don't forget that we have to cover three main areas of his or her life.

We will need to get organised, so tell me which areas you want me to do.

I think we should get together to work on it. Any suggestions? I'm free all of next week.

Reply to this e-mail, answering all the points raised.

*You should write between **100 and 150 words**.*

It is important to read all the information given. It tells you to:

- write an e-mail to a friend – this confirms to you the format for your piece of writing, the tone and register needed – you will write informally to a friend and you should use appropriate language to suit this.

- make at least one suggestion of a famous person for your project. This could be anybody you like from Barack Obama to Miley Cyrus. It might be better to choose someone you know something about because of the next part of the task.

- state which areas of this famous person's life you would like your friend to deal with: three main aspects of this person's life have to be covered – so you might want to list those three before suggesting which one(s) your friend should deal with.

- make suggestions of when (and possibly where) you can meet your friend to work on this project.

You must deal with each aspect of the task to be able to access the full range of marks. Remember to use a variety of conjunctives to make your piece of writing more cohesive, rather than just a sequence of points.

Chapter 7: Technology rules

Getting started...

1 Look at the pictures. What do you think they show? Use these words to help you.

> discover invention technology
> experiment analysis

2 `R.16` ▶ You are going to listen to four people discussing important inventions. Write down the inventions that they discuss.

3 Work in small groups. Make a list of the three most important inventions you know. (Be prepared to justify your choices.) Decide on one invention you wish had never been invented.

4 Explain your choices to the rest of the class. As a class, vote on the three most important inventions and the one thing you wish had never been invented.

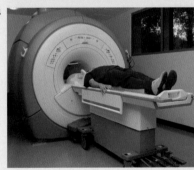

👄 Speaking

Exam hint

Exercise 1 is a practice task for Part 1 of the Speaking Paper.

1 Work with a partner and decide who is going to answer the Student A questions and who is going to answer the Student B questions. Student A needs to answer all four questions, taking no more than 3 minutes. Repeat the process for the Student B questions.

Student A
Let's talk about technology
How often do you use a computer? (Tell me about that.)
What do you use it for? (Tell me about that.)
Which piece of technology is most important to you? (Why is that?)
Which piece of technology could you live without? (Why is that?)

Student B
Let's talk about technology
At what age did you get a mobile phone? (Tell me about that.)
What do you mainly use your phone for? (Tell me about that.)
Could you live without your phone? (Why is that?)
Could you live without technology? (Why is that?)

Reading

1 Work with a partner and discuss these questions:

- Do you enjoy gaming?

- If yes, why do you enjoy it? What type of games do you enjoy playing?

- If no, why don't you enjoy it? What do you prefer to do?

2 Read the list of computer games and match each of the statements that follow to one of the games. You must choose answers based on the information given below. You should only use each game once. One of the games will not be used.

Exam hint

Exercise 2 is a practice task for Part 1 of the Reading and Writing Paper.

Games

A   Athletics

Modern 3D environments and three difficulty settings. Compete in 28 disciplines with world athletes, fight for medals, progress through a complete career of a custom made athlete and get ready for a unique Championship Mode. Challenge your friends in split screen or hot seat multiplayer mode and create your own competitions.

B   Skateboarding

The city is stretched over massive districts with tons of challenges to complete. Players can skate any way they want, using eighty skate tricks. Create a customised skating world that can be shared with friends. Challenge your friends, online or local split-screen. Rank yourself against players from across the world.

C   World Ruler

Players strive to become ruler of the world by establishing and leading a civilisation from the dawn of man into the space age, waging war, conducting diplomacy, discovering new technologies, going head-to-head with some of history's greatest leaders and building the most powerful empire the world has ever known.

D   Football Crazy

Real life personalities of your favourite footballers. Accuracy with the control pad dictates pass accuracy. Customised chants for every team and league, and play your own music from the hard drive. Create yourself in game and play as yourself. Grow your player attributes and take your Virtual Pro online to become a global superstar.

E   The Orient

Exploring a fascinating island world, players get to know the culture and technology of the ancient Orient while learning the tricks of local trade, diplomacy and economy in order to build their own city. Bigger islands and worlds provide players with endless opportunities to express creative vision, making all cities truly unique.

F   Formula 1

Complete with official drivers, teams and circuits. Nineteen realistic tracks. Fully dynamic weather affects your strategy and performance. Build a career by working up from the bottom and switch teams. Extensive online multiplayer options allowing players to take on their friends and the rest of the world in a range of race modes.

G   Sports Active

Customise workouts with seventy exercises and activities and receive guidance from your own personal trainer. Heart rate monitor (sits on left arm) provides constant on-screen monitoring, allowing users to capture intensity and optimise performance over time. Track your fitness data and share workout data with others. Nine week total body conditioning programme available.

H   Dance Fitness

One-of-a-kind dance fitness workout set to high-energy international music. An instructor guides you through thirty routines that will work you into a sweat and make you forget you're even exercising. Featuring exclusive music and choreography. See yourself on screen. An ultra fun interactive fitness party that's focused on the joy of movement.

I   Totally Fit

Comprehensive and energetic workout programme. More than a hundred exercises spanning from aerobics to fitbox and cardio. Supports a wide range of fitness accessories, like fitball, resistance band, ankle and wrist weights and step. Moreover, it includes a nutritional programme with one hundred and forty recipes tailored for the user's preferences.

J   Test Drive

Hundreds of miles of off-road tracks. New terrain types, architecture and vistas. Dynamic weather, day/night and motion blur. Tailor your car with custom paint jobs and trims. All-new single player story mode with character progression. Whole new out-of-car mode which means you can walk around shared spaces and interact with other players.

K   Speed King

Exhilarating extreme off-road racing experience, including mountain tracks and cliff edges. Dramatic race locations over three continents and a variety of racing events. Packed with the most powerful race cars, new and classic. Rally Cross events, switching between dirt and road racing, where competition is tight, fast and collisions with opponents inevitable.

	Statements	Games										
		A	B	C	D	E	F	G	H	I	J	K
1	This game makes use of music from around the globe.											
2	You are certain to have accidents by crashing into others in this game.											
3	You can change the time of day in this game.											
4	This game also includes tips on healthy eating.											
5	You can make use of your own fitness coach in this game.											
6	In this game you can include your own music.											
7	This game allows you to design your own contests.											
8	Create your own island city in this game.											
9	There is a choice of eighty different moves in this game.											
10	In this game you can move from one team to another.											

Vocabulary: alternatives to *very*

1 Replace all the examples of *very* in this book review with more interesting words from the box. Make sure the word you choose is a word that is usually used with the adjective.

notoriously   blissfully   breathtakingly   bitterly
hilariously   exceedingly   utterly   fabulously

Book Reviews

Looking for a book for the beach? Melanie Watson reviews the pick of the paperbacks.

Michael Hodges' latest title is a science fiction thriller set in the 22nd century. Climate conditions have become quite extreme and most of the action is set in a *very*[1] cold New York City, where temperatures are below freezing for most of the year. Living conditions for most people are *very*[2] harsh as many of the Earth's natural resources have run out.

The story is built around an ex-cop called Krycic and his side-kick, Tnyr, who isn't especially bright but is *very*[3] devoted to Krycic. Krycic has been called back into service by his old boss, Commander Yzeem, after some renegade robots have gone on the run.

Krycic's search takes him all over the galaxy, and some of the descriptions of the landscape that he sees when he goes to nearby planets are *very*[4] beautiful, almost poetic.

While Krycic is looking for the renegade robots, he is *very*[5] unaware of the fact that he is also being hunted by agents of the *very*[6] wealthy corporation that made the robots and doesn't want them destroyed.

As well as being an exciting page-turner, this novel is also *very*[7] funny in places. While it is *very*[8] difficult for science fiction titles to come high up in the bestseller lists, I have no doubt that this will do extremely well. A definite must for holiday reading lists!

Grammar reference: see page 237

Grammar: *like* versus *as*

1 Read the grammar rules about *like* and *as* on page 237 of the Grammar reference. Match each of these examples with *like* or *as* to one of the rules.

a *As* he sat watching TV, she was listening to music on her iPod.

b She bought a new laptop *like* the one her friend had.

c *As* he proved with his exam results, hard work does pay.

d Some of the technology that we use *like* chat rooms gives rise to safety issues.

e It was *as* if there had never been life without computers.

f He worked *as* an assistant in the technology department for three years.

g He ran *like* the wind to get his assignment in on time.

h *As* you know, advances in technology have created many new communication options for people.

2 Complete each of these sentences with *like* or *as*.

a My grandfather looks a bit _____ Albert Einstein!

b I'm not as good at technology _____ my friend, Jules.

c _____ I was waiting to take my maths exam, I tried to remember all the important formulae.

d Some of the world's greatest scientists, _____ Marie Curie, have died because of their research.

e _____ I understand it, we still need two main speakers for the conference.

f _____ we agreed, we will increase funding for new computers and printers in the library.

g Everyone said she sang _____ an angel at the concert.

h If you use that knife _____ a screwdriver, you'll break it.

3 Are any of these statements true for you? Change the ones that are not to make them true.

● I am more like my mother than my father.

● I don't think I am as creative as my best friend.

● I'd be quite interested in working as a tour guide for a couple of months.

● I am very keen to visit parts of east Africa like Kenya.

4 Work with a partner and share your sentences. Explain in what way they are true for you.

 Speaking

1 Work with a partner and each choose one of the topics below. Prepare to time your partner – give them 1 minute to prepare and then ask them to start speaking. Tell them to stop speaking after 2 minutes. Did your partner answer the question on the card?

Exam hint

Exercise 1 is a practice task for Part 2 of the Speaking Paper.

Student A

You are going to talk about **technology**. You can use some or all of the ideas listed below in your talk but <u>you must answer this question</u>:

How does using digital technology make school lessons more interesting?

You must talk for 1 to 2 minutes. You have 1 minute to think and make notes before your talk begins.

Here are some ideas to help you:
- Information
- Computer skills
- Active learning
- Independence

Student B

You are going to talk about **technology**. You can use some or all of the ideas listed below in your talk but <u>you must answer this question</u>:

What role does digital technology play in your free time?

You must talk for 1 to 2 minutes. You have 1 minute to think and make notes before your talk begins.

Here are some ideas to help you:
- Socialising
- Communication
- Information
- Homework

2 Work with a partner and take it in turns to ask and answer the following questions. Remember to give as much information as possible and try to keep talking for at least 5 minutes.

> ### Exam hint
>
> Exercise 2 is a practice task for Part 3 of the Speaking Paper.

Part 3

We have been talking about **technology** and I would like to ask you some more questions on this topic.

- How do you keep in touch with your friends? (Tell me about that.)
- What are the benefits of using social networking sites? (Tell me about that.)
- What are the negative points of using social networking sites? (Tell me about that.)

- Do you think that young people feel that they have to own the latest technological devices? (Why is that?)
- Do you think that some technological devices that appeal to young people are too expensive? (Tell me about that.)
- Do you think that parents should encourage their children to keep up with the latest technological devices? (Tell me about that.)

- Do you think that some people spend too much time on social networking sites? (Why is that?)
- Do you think that the use of social networking sites is impacting on our face-to-face social skills? (Why is that?)
- Do you think that social networking sites will become more popular or be replaced by something else in the future? (Why is that?)

Listening

1 Work with a partner. What major changes do you think there will be to our lives in the next fifty years? (Think about entertainment, transport, holidays, communication, medicine, etc.) Discuss your ideas.

2 R.17 ▶ Now listen to part of a radio programme about one man's vision of the future and answer these questions.

Exam hint

Exercise 2 is a practice task for Part 3 of the Listening Paper.

Questions

1–5

Answer these questions using no more than **three words** or **a number**.

1 Which field has Ian Pearson worked in for the last two decades?

....

2 Why has Ian been in the public eye lately?

....

3 What does Ian hope to be able to put on a machine by 2050?

....

4 Which machine does 75 trillion calculations per second?

....

5 What is the main problem with designing a conscious computer?

....

6–10

Complete these sentences using no more than **three words** or **a number**.

6 As well as being highly intelligent, conscious computers would also have _____.

7 By applying the new technology to a call centre, it would be possible to increase the number of _____.

8 Ian feels that there should be _____ on technology and how best we use it.

9 Ian also predicts that part of our normal everyday lives will be spent in _____ communicating with others.

10 It will feel as though you are actually with the person you are speaking to because of connections made to their _____.

3 R.17 ▶ Listen again and check your answers.

4 Work in a small group and discuss these questions:

● Make a list of the main predictions that Ian Pearson makes about the future. Were any of them similar to your predictions in Exercise 1?

● Which word from the box best describes how you feel about each of Ian Pearson's predictions?

> interesting   exciting   worrying   depressing   unbelievable

Grammar: overview of future forms

1 Look at these extracts from three e-mail messages. What is the main point of each extract?

a

Just wondering if you've started your packing yet? I can't decide what to take … the weather forecast says it's going to rain for the first few days and then clear up. It's never been really cold there – in fact, I think it'll be quite warm. Have you packed any summer clothes?

b

Jan and I are taking the kids to the new Information Technology Museum exhibition on Saturday. It's all about great inventions and we were wondering if Toby would like to come, too. David has just told me he'll join us for some of the day, but I know he's going to visit his mother in the afternoon. Let me know if you're interested.

c

Bet you didn't know this, but on Friday, next week, Mr Brown, who teaches us science, will have been here at the school for exactly twenty-five years. We'll be celebrating with him on Friday (15th) at a surprise party at Le Polidor restaurant in Ship Street. Please let me know by e-mail if you can come. (The party starts at 6pm.)

> ## Grammar hint
>
> *time clauses*
>
> What do you notice about each of the verbs in *italics*? What is strange about this?
> 1 Tell me when the post *arrives*.
> 2 Before you *go*, remember to shut all the windows.
> 3 I want you to go to bed as soon as the film *finishes*.
>
> Grammar reference: see page 238

2 Read the messages again and find examples of these future forms:
   a *will* (two examples)
   b *going to* (two examples)
   c present continuous (one example)
   d present simple (one example)
   e future perfect (one example)
   f future continuous (one example)

3 Work with a partner and discuss when we use each form to talk about the future.
*We can use '**will**' to talk about making predictions based on what we know or believe.*

4 Work with a partner and look at the predictions. For each one decide which alternative is more likely and explain why.
   a I don't feel very well. I'm going to *be/'ll* be sick.
   b What on earth is that man doing up there? He's going to *fall/falling*.
   c This time next year, I'*ll be working/'ll work* in New York.
   d She's *finishing/'ll have finished* her essay by Friday.

5 Work with a partner. Choose one of the sentences in Exercise 4, think about a possible context and make a short dialogue which includes it.

A: *What's the matter? You look terrible.*

B: ***I don't feel very well. I'm going to be sick.***

A: *Maybe it was those prawns you had at lunchtime?*

B: *Don't remind me about the prawns! Go and get me some water ... please!*

6 R.18 ▶ You will hear someone talking about their future plans. Listen and take notes.

7 R.19 ▶ Listen again, section by section, and write down exactly what you hear. You will hear each section twice.

8 R.19 ▶ Listen one final time and check what you have written. In particular, check that your grammar and spelling are correct.

9 Complete the following sentences to make plans/intentions that are true for you.

a This evening I'm definitely ...

b This weekend I'm probably going to ...

c By this time next year I hope I will have ...

d At this time on New Year's Day I will be ...

10 Find out how other students have completed the sentences. Which student's sentences are most similar to yours?

 Writing

1 This article is based on the interview with Ian Pearson. Read the article and answer these two questions.

a What is the main area *not* referred to that was discussed in the interview?

b Do you think the journalist views Pearson as: slightly mad, a misunderstood visionary, a serious scientist with thought-provoking ideas or a potential danger to society?

Grammar hint

due to/about to

Which of the following sentences is *not* correct? Why?

1 The match is due to start in two hours' time.

2 The match is about to start in two hours' time.

'Never-say-die' technology!

Head of the 'futurology unit' at British Telecom, Ian Pearson, is well-known for some of his controversial views, but his latest predictions have caused a lot of interest in the scientific community. People take notice of his ideas, partly because his CV is obviously so impressive – including many years in the fields of theoretical physics, missile design and, more recently, cybernetics. I met him last week to try to find out what all the fuss was about.

Pearson is a mild-mannered individual, which seems at odds with the sometimes mind-blowing projections he is making about our future world. To begin with, he is suggesting that by 2050, physical death will not mean the end for an individual person. Basically, he predicts that by then we will have the technological ability to download human minds into machines. So, the individual in us can live on – perhaps indefinitely.

The next area with potentially massive implications is the development of 'conscious' computers. Pearson says this

will be possible by 2020, given the way computer speeds are accelerating. The problem seems to be defining exactly what 'consciousness' is, but Pearson seems sure that computers will have some kind of emotional reactions soon. So, for example, a plane would actually be 'afraid' of crashing into the ground.

'Virtual reality' is something that he believes is just round the corner, too. In practice, he envisages that we will be able to touch and interact with life-size 3D images of people wherever they might actually be in the real world and this will soon be the normal way of communicating with people.

Pearson is certainly not oblivious to the need for public debate about what all these developments may mean. But, at the same time, he has a very clear sense of the way in which technological advances are currently heading. And, if even one-tenth of what he predicts happens, then the world we are going to be living in, in the not-too-distant future, is going to be quite a different one to the one we know now.

2 Think about the article in Exercise 1 and decide which of the following statements are true about a well-written article.

   a It should have an eye-catching title.

   b It should engage and interest the reader.

   c Each paragraph must have a sub-title.

   d It can 'talk' directly to the reader.

   e It should have specific examples to help bring the points to life.

   f It should be divided into paragraphs, each with a different main focus.

   g It must use formal language.

   h You should make a comment or give your opinion at the end of the article.

3 Check your ideas in the Writing reference on page 252.

4 You are going to write an article on one of these topics. First choose the most interesting topic:

- a clever invention

- a problem that the world will face in the future

5 Decide what invention or what future problem your article is going to be about. Before you plan your paragraphs, brainstorm ideas.

- Think of *any* points and examples you might include in your article. Note down all your ideas. At this stage, include *anything* you can think of.

- Show your ideas to other students and ask them if they have other ideas. Again, include *anything* they can think of.

- Now choose your best ideas and group them into possible paragraphs.

6 Plan your opening and closing paragraphs. How are you going to introduce your article? What comment or opinions are you going to express at the end?

7 Think of a short, eye-catching title. Show it to other students. Ask them if it would make them interested in reading your article.

8 Write your article using between 100 and 150 words. The article is for your technology teacher. When you have finished, read it through. Check that:

- you have included all your best ideas

- it is divided into paragraphs each paragraph with a different focus

- the language you use is varied and interesting

- you have avoided basic grammar and spelling mistakes.

Exam hint

Exercise 8 is a practice task for Part 4 of the Reading and Writing Paper.

Summarising

1 Read the article about a new gaming technology *Kinect* and write a summary for your technology teacher.

In your summary you should:

● give two benefits of *Kinect*

● give two potential problems with *Kinect*

● say how *Kinect* is competing with the Wii.

Write your summary using between 100 and 150 words.

Kinect

Technology is moving so fast within the video games industry that you now don't need to rely on a hand held control or have to press any buttons to interact with what is happening on the screen. The new Kinect gaming system uses your actual body movements to control what you are doing onscreen. This is done via a camera, which is also able to distinguish between players. The Kinect system also allows you to use your voice to navigate the menu and control the console. This technology adds a new dimension to gaming

Microsoft's Kinect is used with an Xbox 360 console. It is able to pick up gestures and player movement through an infrared emitter. The Kinect bar, which houses the emitter, should be placed either directly on the television or beneath it. Infrared light is bounced off 48 different points on players and this allows the system to accurately detect where gamers are and what they are doing. It is important for the bar to be placed in the correct position and gamers will also need to make sure that they are using the system in a large enough room.

Despite the obvious positives of the technology, some drawbacks have also been noted. The system response time could be seen as being slower as, for example, it takes longer to process information from a camera than from pressing a button. Although this technology allows gamers to interact directly with the screen, it has been recognised that some types of games are less suited to this new technology than others, for example driving games.

Analysts believe that the initial success of Kinect will be based on the software available. The launch titles are similar to those that people are already familiar with through using the Wii, and include fitness, party and dance software. For continued success, it is thought that the hardware will have to be further investigated and its strengths exploited to expose new gaming possibilities. One concept which could be further investigated is Kinectimals (virtual pet simulation). If the strengths of the new technology can be realised by developers, it is thought that the Kinect will put Microsoft in a position which rivals Nintendo in the gaming market.

Up to now, the Wii has remained unchallenged in the mainstream gaming market, but this may be about to change. By introducing Kinect and related software, Microsoft is now moving into the same market as the Wii, appealing to those looking for fun and party type games. If Kinect does prove successful, there is the added advantage for Microsoft that the Xbox 360 will not need updating until 2015. Even though Kinect costs as much as a Wii, based on the number of orders received and interest from retailers to date, Microsoft are confident of making more sales than they originally anticipated. There has been an extremely positive response to this technology and it will be interesting to see how this technology develops.

Grammar

1 Correct the sentences using *like* rather than as, where necessary.

  a Simon was late for the technology lecture as usual.
  b Her brother is a physics teacher as me.
  c I hate this flat. It's as living in a shoe box.
  d As you know, Sheila and I are thinking of getting married in the spring.
  e We're using the spare room as Mike's office until the extension is finished.
  f Some of our neighbours, as the people at number seven, want to organise a street party.
  g My feet are freezing. They're as blocks of ice.
  h Paris is great as a place to visit but not to live.

2 There is a mistake with the future form in five of these sentences. Find the mistake and correct it.

  a What time does this train arrive in Cardiff?
  b Do you think Brazil are winning the next World Cup?
  c We'll be thinking of you at this time tomorrow.
  d What will we have had for dinner this evening?
  e We're going to move to the country next year.
  f It looks like it rains soon.
  g He says he will have finished the report by Friday.
  h If you wait a minute, I'm helping you to the car with those boxes.
  i How long will you have learnt English by the end of this year?

Vocabulary

3 Complete these sentences with the correct word. You have been given the beginning of each word.

  a Is it ever right to do ex_____ on animals?
  b He realised that someone had used his computer without his kn_____.
  c What's the name of the in_____ of the clockwork radio?
  d Our research team are carrying out a detailed an_____ of the test results.
  e Th_____, the crime rate should decrease as employment increases, but that's not always the case.
  f Driving through the mountains, the scenery was br_____ beautiful.
  g Put on your gloves. It's bi_____ cold outside.
  h The book was so hi_____ funny that she laughed until she cried.

4 Complete the sentences with the words in the box.

> scientific   discover   invention   technology   knowledgeable   experiment   analysis   theoretically

  a Scientists are still trying to _____ why dinosaurs became extinct.
  b She's very _____ on the subject of astronomy. You can ask her anything and she'll know the answer!
  c I think it's wrong for scientists to _____ on animals, whatever the circumstances.
  d _____, there's no reason why you can't clone humans, but there are lots of ethical issues to consider.
  e They took some blood samples and sent them to the laboratory for _____.
  f Of course, books had to be written by hand before the _____ of printing.
  g We do keep some records but I'm afraid we're not very _____ about it.
  h Despite advances in modern _____, people don't seem to be any happier.

Exam tips

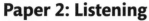

Paper 2: Listening

🔊 Part 2: Listening (10 marks)

Text type

In this part, you will listen to a longer recording. You need to demonstrate your ability to understand a discussion, an argument or a conversation between two or more speakers in which information is being negotiated and exchanged.

Skills

You will have to show that you can distinguish between facts, ideas and opinions. In particular, you need to be able to identify a speaker's viewpoint and attitude – whether this is stated openly or just implied. Therefore, you will be determining exactly what a speaker means by what she/he says.

Task types

There are 10 marks available in this part and there will be 10 questions, each worth one mark.

Task types in this section include:

- **Notes and sentence completion:** you will need to write your answers out in words for this task type. The prompts show clearly what parts of speech you should use in your answer. The answers are all words heard in the recording, and you should not change the form of the words you hear. The answer required will be either a number or one, two or three words (check the instruction for the exact number).

- **Multiple-choice questions:** you have to decide which option is the correct answer to the question, or which option best fills a gap in a sentence. There are generally three options for each question.

- **Short-answer questions:** you need to write your answers out in words for this task type, which is usually used for direct, factual information. The answers are all words you will hear in the recording, and you must not change the form of the words you hear. The required answer will be either a number or one, two or three words – this will be made clear in the instruction.

Let's look at this extract from the Edexcel IGCSE ESL Listening Paper in November 2008:

> In this section, you will hear two students, Mark and Amy, discussing plans to set up a support group for students in the school.

> Mark: Well, let's start with what support the group will offer.
>
> Amy: I think we should provide an opportunity for students to chat about problems at school such as making friends or if they are feeling low. And what about helping students if they are having problems with their school work?
>
> Mark: Well, we could, but I think we should really direct them to the School Advisors. They are the ones to talk to about that. Plus, there's a new reading support group starting so I think that kind of thing is already covered.
>
> Amy: OK then.

Here you have listened to them negotiating the kind of support the group will offer and then you have to choose the correct answer to the question:

> What kind of support do they decide to provide?
> a Emotional
> b Educational
> c Both

Amy thinks the support group should be for any emotional difficulties the students are having as well as for any difficulties connected with their schoolwork, but Mark feels the schoolwork aspect is covered by the School Advisors. They agree to focus the support they will offer on emotional problems – so the answer is option *a*. You have to follow the conversation carefully – but remember, you will hear this a second time and you will be able to confirm your choice.

A bit later in their conversation, you hear this:

> Amy: What about the temporary classrooms?
>
> Mark: They are a bit far from everything. We need to be somewhere closer to the centre of the school.
>
> Amy: But we don't want it to be too public.
>
> Mark: Good point. A more out-of-the-way place would be better.

Here you have heard them exchanging opinions on the use of the temporary classrooms as their base for the support group and have to answer this question:

> What is the advantage of the temporary classrooms?
> a They are central.
> b They are quiet.
> c They are remote.

They negotiate the suitability of the temporary classrooms – at first it seems that the fact these classrooms are a bit far from everything else is a disadvantage, but, eventually, it turns out that this is in fact a distinct advantage – and so the correct answer is *c They are remote.*

Getting started...

1 Look at the pictures. Say what each one makes you think about and why.

2 Work with a partner. Read these sentences and make sure you understand the words/phrases in *italics*. Then ask and answer the questions with your partner:

- How often do you have *fizzy drinks*? Which is your favourite?

- How do you feel about *junk food*? How often do you have it? What, if any, is your favourite?

- What is your favourite thing for a *quick snack*? Why?

- Have you ever had *food poisoning*? What happened?

- When was the last time you had a *slap-up meal*? What was the occasion?

- How often do you get *a takeaway*? Why? What kind?

 Speaking

1 Work with a partner and decide who is going to answer the Student A questions and who is going to answer the Student B questions. Student A needs to answer all four questions, taking no more than 3 minutes. Repeat the process for the Student B questions.

> ### Exam hint
>
> Exercise 1 is a practice task for Part 1 of the Speaking Paper.

Student A
Let's talk about food
Who does the cooking in your house? (Why is that?)
What sort of food does your family eat? (Tell me about that.)
How often do you eat at restaurants? (Tell me about that.)
Is there any type of food you don't like? (Tell me about that.)

Student B
Let's talk about food
How well can you cook? (Tell me about that.)
How important is it for you to be able to cook? (Why is that?)
Would you say you had a healthy diet? (Tell me about that.)
How could you make it healthier? (Tell me about that.)

Reading

1 You are going to read about two restaurants: The Carnivore in Nairobi, Kenya and Encounter in Los Angeles, USA. What do you think makes each of these restaurants special or different?

2 Work in two groups, A and B.

Group A Read the text about The Carnivore.

Group B Read the text on page 228 about Encounter.

Read your text quickly and check your ideas from Exercise 1.

The Carnivore

A GREAT PLACE FOR BOTH TOURISTS AND LOCALS, THE CARNIVORE – VOTED ONE OF THE TOP FIFTY RESTAURANTS IN THE WORLD – IS AN EXPERIENCE FOR ALL THE SENSES. As you enter the restaurant, the smell of charred meat and fragrant smoke greets you. When you get inside, the first thing you see is a board with a list of what appears to be every African wild animal you can think of. This is your menu. The next thing you see, and hear, is the huge circular stone Masai barbecue with countless spits of roasting meat.

The Masai people of Kenya and Tanzania are a nomadic tribe and are reputed to have the best cattle in the world. Their staple diet is cow blood mixed with milk. Considering that the cow is the very lifeblood of the Masai, you would expect that they know how to cook it superbly – and they do. On the barbecue there are huge joints of meat on Masai spears roasting gently over burning coals. If you look closely, you will see over twenty varieties of meat sizzling away.

The food at The Carnivore changes on a daily basis, but the following are among the meats you can expect to try: Crocodile is juicy and well-flavoured. Giraffe is like succulent pork and tastes better if slightly pink. Top of my list was waterbuck which is generally very tender. The smell alone will make your mouth water and you certainly won't be disappointed by the taste, either. Zebra, on the other hand, is slightly tough. Hartebeest, too, requires a substantial amount of chewing that will give you jaw ache for about five minutes. It's tasty but not really worth the effort.

Not only is the food unusual, but the service at The Carnivore is, too. When you take your seat, you will be given a plate, napkin, knife and fork, and a flag. The flag is very important. When you are ready to eat, you put your flag upright and the waiters know that you are ready

to be served. They come to your table waving huge Masai spears with hunks of meat spilling their juices on the floor and tables. Your waiter will plonk the end of the spear on your cast iron plate and carve away. When you have eaten your fill, simply lower your flag and the waiter will leave you alone. If, after a pause, you are ready to eat again, simply raise your flag and your waiter will reappear.

The Carnivore is an eat-as-much-as-you-can restaurant, with starters, dessert and coffee, as well as the meat, of course, all included in one price. Also included are an amazingly lively atmosphere, wonderful music and friendly, helpful staff. In my opinion, it really is an experience-as-much-as-you-can restaurant! You won't be disappointed (unless you're a vegetarian, that is).

Nairobi, Kenya

3 Read your text again and make notes about your restaurant.

		The Carnivore	Encounter
1	Decor and atmosphere		
2	Main feature of the restaurant		
3	Main type of food on the menu		
4	What food is recommended		
5	Waiters and service		
6	Writer's overall opinion of the restaurant		

4 Prepare to tell another student about the restaurant you read about. Look again at the text and the notes you made in Exercise 3. Add any other points you think are interesting.

5 Work with a partner (one of you will be from Group A and the other from Group B) and tell each other about your restaurant.

6 Work with a partner and discuss these questions:

● Would you be interested in eating in either (or both) of the restaurants described in the texts? Why/Why not?

● What kind of restaurant would you normally choose to eat out in? Why?

Summarising

1 Using the notes you made about the restaurant in Exercise 3, write a summary for your school magazine.

Your summary should include:

● the main feature of the restaurant

● **two** details about decor and atmosphere

● **two** details about the food and service.

Write your summary using between 100 and 150 words.

Exam hint

Exercise 1 is a practice task for Part 6 of the Reading and Writing Paper.

Vocabulary: food

1 Work with a partner. Put the words in the box into two groups: *Ways of describing food* and *Ways of preparing food*. Use a dictionary to help you.

> tasty   roast   slice   tough   succulent   whisk   juicy
> mix   tender   mouth-watering   boil   chop   raw
> spicy   well-done   bake   sweet   stir   sour   fry   bitter
> grill   grate   scramble   crunchy   rare   creamy

Ways of describing food	Ways of preparing food
tasty	roast

Vocabulary hint

cook/cooker

Choose the correct alternative in each sentence:

1 I've applied for a job to be a cook/cooker in an Italian restaurant.

2 We need to buy a new cook/cooker because the old one doesn't work properly.

2 Choose the correct alternatives.

a I've never eaten *rare/raw/well-done* fish. I prefer things cooked.

b This coffee has a distinctive *succulent/sour/bitter* taste.

c *Chop/Slice/Mix* the onion into pieces about 1 cm square.

d You need to *roast/boil/bake* the pasta for about ten minutes in very hot water.

e This meat has been overcooked and is very *mouth-watering/tender/tough*.

f *Stir/Whisk/Scramble* all the dry ingredients together slowly with a wooden spoon.

g Please don't cook the carrots for too long. I prefer them a bit *crunchy/creamy/juicy*.

h You can either *fry/grill/grate* the cheese or cut it into very small pieces.

3 Look at the <u>underlined</u> sounds in each of the words in A, B and C. Put the words in the correct columns in the tables.

A

cr<u>u</u>nchy   ch<u>o</u>p   r<u>oa</u>st   t<u>ou</u>gh   c<u>oo</u>k   well-d<u>o</u>ne   s<u>u</u>cculent   c<u>oo</u>ker

1 l<u>u</u>nch	2 l<u>oo</u>k	3 n<u>o</u>t	4 n<u>o</u>te
crunchy			

B

b<u>a</u>ke   st<u>ir</u>   t<u>a</u>sty   r<u>aw</u>   gr<u>a</u>te   r<u>are</u>

1 m<u>a</u>ke	2 b<u>ir</u>d	3 f<u>our</u>	4 h<u>air</u>
bake			

C

fr<u>y</u>   gr<u>i</u>ll   wh<u>i</u>sk   j<u>ui</u>cy   b<u>i</u>tter   b<u>oi</u>l   sl<u>i</u>ce   m<u>i</u>x   sp<u>i</u>cy

1 l<u>ie</u>	2 b<u>i</u>t	3 b<u>oo</u>t	4 t<u>oy</u>
fry			

4 R.20 ▶ Listen and check your answers. Then repeat saying the words.

5 Work with a partner and discuss these questions:

● How often do you eat meat? What is your favourite kind of meat? How do you like it cooked?

● How often do you eat eggs? What is your favourite way of cooking them?

● Think of a meal you have eaten and/or cooked in the last seven days. What was it? How was it cooked?

Grammar: countable and uncountable nouns

1 R21 ▶ Listen to three short conversations and write down the phrases you hear.

  a a plate   some plate

  b an information   some information

  c a chocolate   some chocolate

2 Work with a partner. Which of the phrases in Exercise 1 are not possible? Explain why.

> **Grammar reference:** see page 238

3 There is a mistake in each of these sentences. Find the mistakes and correct them.

  a I usually have a bread for breakfast.

  b Being a waiter is often a very hard work.

  c Cutting down on sweet things is a good advice.

  d Drinking coffee always gives me terrible headache.

  e I've taken your blood pressure and I'm afraid the news aren't good.

  f I would like a sandwich with a chicken and mayonnaise in it, please.

  g We didn't have any furnitures, so we ate dinner sitting on the floor.

4 Put these words in the correct columns.

> plate headache furniture information chicken
> news chocolate bread advice work

A Countable nouns	B Uncountable nouns	C Nouns which can be both countable and uncountable
plate		

5 Add three more words to each column, then compare your words with a partner. Look at the Grammar reference on page 238 if necessary.

6 Work with a partner and look again at the nouns in group C in Exercise 4. These can be both countable and uncountable (e.g. *chocolate/a chocolate*). What is the difference in meaning between each pair?

7 Read the information on modifying countable and uncountable nouns on page 238 and then choose the correct alternatives in the text.

My first experience of The Blind Cow in Zurich was when I was taken there by a few/a *little*[1] friends for a meal to celebrate passing our exams. *A large amount of/ Several*[2] people had read good reviews about it and we were all keen to experience this unusual place for ourselves. I must admit, however, that I approached the evening with a few/a *little*[3] nervousness. Why? Well, The Blind Cow isn't like *any/ many*[4] other restaurant I know, since you eat your meal in pitch black!

We met in the bar area and spent little/a *little*[5] time getting used to the darkness. I had thought that there would at least be a few/a small amount *of*[6] light somewhere, but there wasn't! There weren't *many/much*[7] other people in the bar, but I still kept thinking I wouldbump but I still kept thinking I would

Grammar hint

few/a few and little/a little

What is the difference in meaning between the words/phrases in *italics* in each pair?
1 I've got a *few* biscuits. Would you like one? There are *few* people who I trust as much as you.
2 I'll just have a *little* milk in my coffee, please. He's got *little* time now, but he can see you later.

bump into someone. But it's amazing how quickly it gets easier as you start using your other senses. After *few/a few* [8] drinks in the bar, we went down to the actual restaurant, where already the *plenty of/lack of* [9] light wasn't really bothering me anymore. In fact, I was beginning to enjoy it. There are *a great deal of/a lot of* [10] waiters and other staff there to help you and I must say, it is one of the most enjoyable meals I've had for *many/a large amount of* [11] years. And also one of the tastiest – somehow because I couldn't see *none/any* [12] of the food, the taste became all the more delicious.

8 How do you think you would feel if you went to The Blind Cow restaurant? Why?

9 R22 ▶ Listen to two people playing 'the shopping trolley memory game' and answer these questions.
1 What are the two rules?
2 What mistake does the man make?

10 Play 'the shopping trolley memory game' in pairs or small groups. Which group got furthest in the alphabet, without making a mistake and naming a type of food for each letter?

 Speaking

1 Work with a partner and each choose one of the topics below. Prepare to time your partner – give them 1 minute to prepare and then ask them to start speaking. Tell them to stop speaking after 2 minutes. Did your partner answer the question on the card?

Exam hint
Exercise 1 is a practice task for Part 2 of the Speaking Paper.

Language hint
Organising your ideas
Firstly, ...
First of all, I'd like to say ...
The first point is ...
Secondly, ...
What's more, ...
Another important point is ...
Finally, ...
Last but not least, ...
Then, there is the point about ...

Student A
You are going to talk about **cooking**. You can use some or all of the ideas listed below in your talk but <u>you must answer this question</u>:

Should secondary schools provide students with cookery lessons?
You must talk for 1 to 2 minutes. You have 1 minute to think and make notes before your talk begins.

Here are some ideas to help you:
· Life skill
· Health
· Nutrition
· Learn at home

Student B
You are going to talk about **healthy eating**. You can use some or all of the ideas listed below in your talk but <u>you must answer this question</u>:

Why do so many young people go to fast food restaurants?
You must talk for 1 to 2 minutes. You have 1 minute to think and make notes before your talk begins.

Here are some ideas to help you:
· Convenience
· Atmosphere
· Price
· Choice

2 Work with a partner and take it in turns to ask and answer the following questions. Remember to give as much information as possible and try to keep talking for at least 5 minutes.

Exam hint

Exercise 2 is a practice task for Part 3 of the Speaking Paper.

Part 3
We have been talking about **cooking and healthy eating** and I would like to ask you some more questions on this topic.

- Do you think that all young people should learn how to cook? (Why is that?)
- Who is responsible for teaching young people to cook? (Why is that?)
- Do you think that learning how to cook is as important as learning academic subjects? (Why is that?)

- Which age group(s) do you think is/are most likely to use fast food restaurants? (Why is that?)
- Do you think that fast food restaurants serve unhealthy food? (Tell me about that.)
- Do you think that there are too many fast food restaurants in city centres? (Why is that?)

- How does bad diet affect people's health? (Tell me about that.)
- What could the government do to encourage people to eat more healthily? (Tell me about that.)
- Do you think it is the government's responsibility to make people eat more healthily? (Why is that?)

 Writing

1 Work with a partner and discuss these questions:

- What times are meals in your country?

- What is a typical breakfast in your country?

- Is there any food that you really don't like or that you are allergic to?

- Have you ever eaten food from any of these countries? What are typical dishes/ingredients from these countries?

| India | Mexico | Japan | China | Thailand | England | France | Turkey |

2 Read the task and letter on page 114 and write down the things which are mentioned.

a Meal times

b Breakfast

c Learning to cook

d Trying new restaurants

e Picnics and barbecues

f Food preferences and allergies

Thank you for your letter telling me when you will be arriving in September. I'm looking forward to having you come and stay with me.

I'd really like to make your stay with us as comfortable and happy as possible. Firstly, could you let me know what kinds of food you like and, of course, what you really don't like! It would also be very useful to know if you are allergic to any kind of food.

You will probably find that eating habits and times are a bit different in Britain from what you're used to. What times do people have their meals in your country? And what do you usually have for breakfast? Do you go out to restaurants very much? Where I live, there are quite a few restaurants with lots of different types of food. I wonder if there is a particular kind of food you would like to try.

Writing task

An English friend, Alex, has recently invited you to stay and has just sent you a letter. Read Alex's letter and then write a suitable letter to Alex.

In your letter you should:
- describe your food preferences and allergies
- say how meal times/food are different in your country
- say what kind of restaurants you like.

Write your letter using between 100 and 150 words.

---

3 The sentence in *italics* in this paragraph is a topic sentence. What is the purpose of a topic sentence?

My friends and I had a really fantastic picnic last week. We were celebrating my friend Sam's birthday and there were about eight of us altogether. The day before it had been raining, but in the end we were really lucky with the weather – it was warm and sunny all day. I took a football and we ended up playing with that all afternoon. It was really good fun.

4 Look again at the letter in Exercise 2. What are the three topic sentences?

5 Write a topic sentence for this paragraph.

_____ . I've never really learned how to cook properly so I can only cook very basic things – not very well! Then I saw an advert in the library for some cookery classes. They are every Thursday evening and they are held in the local school. So, don't be surprised if I invite you round for dinner in a few weeks.

6 Look at this paragraph plan for the task in Exercise 2 and write a topic sentence for paragraphs 2, 3 and 4.

Paragraph 1 Thanks for letter

Paragraph 2 Describe your food preferences and allergies

Paragraph 3 Say how meal times/food are different in your country

Paragraph 4 Say what kind of restaurants you like

Paragraph 5 Ending

7 Write your letter using the paragraph plan and topic sentences in Exercise 6 to help you. (You could also look at the Writing reference on page 254.)

8 Read through your letter and answer these questions.

a Have you included all the points from the task?

b Have you organised it clearly with topic sentences?

c Have you used an informal style with friendly opening and closing paragraphs?

d Can you find any mistakes with grammar and spelling?

9 Now rewrite your letter, using your answers to the questions to improve it.

Exam hint

Exercise 7 is a practice task for Part 5 of the Reading and Writing Paper.

◁))) Listening

1 Work with a partner and discuss these questions:

● Do you chew chewing gum? Why/Why not?

● Which brands of chewing gum do you know?

● How do you think the problem of chewing gum litter on pavements could be solved?

Exam hint

Exercise 2 is a practice task for Part 1 of the Listening Paper.

2 ▮R23▮ ▶ Listen to five short reports giving information about chewing gum and complete these notes using no more than **three words** or **a number**.

Report 1
- Ancient Greeks were the first to chew gum
- Modern chewing gum first appeared in _____ (1) in the 1860s
- William Wrigley gave it a minty taste and (2)_____
- In today's market _____ (3) of chewing gum is made by Wrigley

Report 2
- In the UK in the previous year _____ (4) on chewing gum
- A rise of 40% in last 5 years
- 75% of the total market is _____ (5)
- Chewing gum now has a two-in-one function
- Two main functions: a sweet and _____ (6)

Report 3
- Britney Spears is _____ (7) onto the pavement
- It was picked it up and then sold in an _____ (8)
- There were a high number of bidders and it was bought for _____ (9)

Report 4
- In the UK every year three and a half billion pieces of gum thrown away
- On Oxford Street pavements in London there are _____ (10) used pieces of gum
- Fine enforcement and now boards for people to _____ (11)
- Long-term answer to the problem is _____ (12)

Report 5
- Ben Wilson enjoys _____ (13) chewing gum found on pavements
- He uses _____ (14) to dry it when he has finished
- Does animals, flowers and landscapes
- He has been _____ (15) for his work

Grammar: articles

1 Find the <u>underlined</u> examples of articles in audioscript R.42 on page 226 and match them to the uses in the box.

> **The indefinite article *a/an* is used:**
> With singular countable nouns (mentioned for the first time or when it doesn't matter which one), e.g. _____ (1)
> With jobs, e.g. _____ (2)
>
> **The definite article *the* is used:**
> With previously mentioned nouns, e.g. _____ (3)
> With superlatives, e.g. _____ (4)
> With particular nouns when it is clear what we are referring to, e.g. _____ (5)
> With national groups (when described as a whole nation), e.g. _____ (6)
> With inventions and species of animal, e.g. *the computer, the polar bear*
> When there is only one of something, e.g. *the moon, the equator*
> With rivers, oceans, seas, e.g. *the River Thames, the Atlantic Ocean*
>
> **No article (the zero article) is used:**
> With uncountable, plural and abstract nouns used in their general sense, e.g.
> _____ (7), _____ (8) and _____ (9)
> With most streets, villages, towns, cities, countries, lakes, mountains, e.g.
> _____ (10), _____ (11) and _____ (12) (For countries and groups of islands in the plural, we use *the*, e.g. _____ (13).)

2 Complete the texts using *a*, *an*, *the* or Ø (zero article) as appropriate.

THE ORIGINAL SANDWICH

Selling sandwiches is __Ø__ (1) big business, thought to be worth $50 billion a year globally and growing fast. _____ (2) Americans are _____ (3) biggest consumers of sandwiches in _____ (4) world, including such favourites as the peanut butter and jelly sandwich, as well as _____ (5) hamburgers of course.

Its origins are not in the States, however. _____ (6) sandwich is said to have been invented in _____ (7) England in the 18th century by the 4th Earl of Sandwich. The story goes that he didn't have _____ (8) time to eat _____ (9) proper meal so he asked for _____ (10) meat and cheese to be served between two slices of bread.

THE MOST EXPENSIVE SANDWICH

In Selfridges department store in London you can buy _____ (11) sandwich which costs £85. That almost certainly makes it the most expensive sandwich in London, or maybe anywhere. _____ (12) gigantic sandwich weighs 600g, contains 2,500 calories and is made of _____ (13) long list of specialised ingredients, including _____ (14) Japanese beef, red pepper and paté de foie gras. _____ (15) bread is freshly-baked every morning from _____ (16) original recipe specially created for the sandwich.

Vocabulary: compound adjectives

1 Complete these sentences with the compound adjectives in the box.

> sugar-free   never-ending   mass-produced

Vocabulary hint
A compound adjective is made up of two or more words put together.

a   William Wrigley started making the first _____ gum in 1892.

b   _____ brands are now the most popular.

c   Biodegradable gum may solve the _____ litter problem.

2 Match these words to make compound adjectives.

a ice-   i   air
b deep-   ii made
c home-   iii minute
d world-   iv famous
e open-   v   fried
f last-   vi cold

3 Complete each sentence with the best compound adjective from Exercise 2.

a All the cakes are _____ in the kitchen behind the shop.

b We were lucky to get a _____ booking. It's a very popular restaurant.

c I don't think Jamie Oliver is a _____ cook but he's certainly very well-known in Britain.

d One of my favourite things is fresh prawns, _____ in very hot oil.

e I love going to the Mosaica restaurant in warm weather when you can sit in the _____ area at the back.

f There's nothing like an _____ drink at the end of a hot, busy day.

Language recap

Grammar

1 Choose the alternative which is *not* possible.

a   Would you like *some/a piece of/a* toast?
b   There are *plenty of/several/much* tickets still available.
c   Have you got *a few/a small amount of/any* good books I could borrow?
d   I saved *a piece of/a few/a little* cake for you.
e   I haven't got *much/a great deal of/a lack of* money left.
f   We saved *a huge amount of/a little/several* time by leaving very early in the morning.
g   Let me give you *a bit of/some/an* advice.
h   It's OK. We've got *a little/little/a bit of* time before we have to go.
i   There are quite *a lot of/a little/a few* plates that need washing up.
j   The show was cancelled because there was *few/not much/a lack of* interest.

2 Choose the correct alternatives (Ø = zero article).

Choose **one** of these **desserts** and see what the psychiatrists say about **you!**

- **Chocolate cake**
- **Ice cream**
- **Carrot cake**
- **Lemon pie**

If you chose chocolate cake, you are *a/an*[1] adventurous type with *Ø/a*[2] clever sense of humour. *The/Ø*[3] people often choose you to be *a/the*[4] leader of *a/the*[5] group as you are usually *Ø/the*[6] best person for the job.

If you chose carrot cake, you are a fun-loving person who likes *the/Ø*[7] laughter. You often choose *a/the*[8] company of people from warmer places like *the/Ø*[9] South America.

If you chose ice cream, you are active and love *the/Ø*[10] sports. *The/Ø*[11] sports you are most interested in are usually competitive ones. You would like nothing better than to sail round *a/the*[12] world as fast as possible.

If you chose lemon pie, you are articulate and intelligent. You are *the/an*[13] excellent speaker and would make *Ø/a*[14] very good teacher. You are also ambitious and have *the/Ø*[15] high standards.

Vocabulary

3 Complete the gaps in the recipe using the words from the box.

tasty   stir   boil   sweet   grill   bitter   fry   slice   chop

Pasta with spinach, red peppers and halloumi cheese

This is a _____, colourful pasta dish with a creamy sauce combining the _____ taste of red peppers with the slightly _____ taste of spinach. The deep-fried haloumi cheese adds extra interest.

● Wash the red peppers and _____ them until the skins are blackened. Then _____ them into thin strips.

● _____ the halloumi into small cubes and then _____ in very hot oil, turning once until golden.

● Fry the onion, garlic and chilli in a frying pan for a couple of minutes.

● Wash the spinach and then _____ briefly in very little hot water.

● Cook the pasta in boiling water for about ten minutes.

● Add cream and yoghurt to the onion mixture. Then add the red peppers, halloumi and spinach. Then slowly _____ in the pasta with a wooden spoon.

4 Add the best compound adjective from the box in the correct place in each sentence.

open-air   last-minute   never-ending
ice-cold   sugar-free   home-made   deep-fried

a   I think what we all need are some drinks.
b   I've decided to go on a diet for the next month.
c   I'm not going to eat chicken anymore. I'll grill it instead.
d   He seems to have a lot of complaints at the moment.
e   Do you want to come to the concert next weekend?
f   I'm going to do some revision tonight before my food technology exam tomorrow.
g   My grandmother makes the most delicious apple pie I've ever tasted.

Paper 3: Speaking

Remember, the speaking examination is in three parts and lasts about 12 minutes in total. You will be interviewed by an interlocutor – most probably a teacher within your centre. Your speaking exam will be recorded and then sent to an Edexcel examiner to be assessed.

 Part 2: Speaking: Student talk (1-minute preparation, plus a talk of 1 to 2 minutes)

The interlocutor indicates the end of Part 1 and introduces Part 2.

In Part 2 you have to give a single, uninterrupted talk of at least 1 minute but no longer than 2 minutes. The interlocutor will hand you a task card provided by Edexcel which gives you a topic (e.g. learning a language, the shopping facilities in your town, studying at university, life in towns and cities), some bullet points to stimulate your ideas, and a question relating to the topic. The topics are ones which are familiar to you and you will be able to call on your own experience, knowledge or ideas in your talk. You do not need to address all the bullet points on the card (they are more like suggestions), but you must address the specific question on the task card within the 2 minutes. You will also have some paper and a pen to make notes if you wish.

You have 1 minute to prepare for the talk, and, during this minute, you may make notes which you can refer to throughout your talk and which will be collected by the interlocutor at the end of the test. These notes are not assessed. The interlocutor will tell you when your 1-minute preparation time has finished and then ask you to talk for no more than 2 minutes about the given topic.

This part of the test is timed by the interlocutor who will interrupt you if you speak for longer than 2 minutes. The interlocutor brings this part of the test to a close and introduces Part 3.

If you have a question regarding the task you have been given, you may ask the interlocutor, but remember she/he may explain the occasional word but is not allowed to give you a detailed explanation nor able to paraphrase the question for you.

The assessment includes an evaluation of how you organised your talk and how well you were able to cope with the topic and the specified question.

Your oral is assessed as a whole – all three parts together. Your overall performance is marked for:

- **Communicative ability and content:** your ability to express opinions and information, to initiate and to respond to questions appropriately.

- **Pronunciation and fluency:** your ability to produce clear and understandable language.

- **Lexical accuracy and range:** how accurately and appropriately you use vocabulary to communicate, and how well you cope with any vocabulary problems, e.g. if you forget a word during the test.

- **Grammatical accuracy and range:** range and accuracy of the grammatical structures you use.

Let's have a look at this Part 2 Student's card from the Edexcel International GCSE ESL Speaking Paper in November 2009:

PART TWO

STUDENT'S CARD 1

*You are going to talk about **visiting your country**.*

You can use some or all of the ideas listed below in your talk, but you must answer this question:

What things should people know if they want to visit your country?

You must talk for 1 to 2 minutes. You have 1 minute to think and make notes before your talk begins.

Here are some ideas to help you:

- *Clothes*
- *Behaviour*
- *Customs and traditions*
- *Weather*
- *Other*

This topic of people visiting your country is likely to be of interest to you and is most probably a topic on which you have plenty of views and opinions. The bullet points give you the opportunity to offer both information and opinions and allow you to use a wide range of structures, e.g. present tense, conditional tense, passive, modal verbs, superlatives, relative clauses, other subordinate clauses – as well as a large range of vocabulary as you mention the different aspects. Remember, although you do not have to mention all the aspects raised in the bullet points, you do have to answer the question in bold: *What things should people know if they want to visit your country?*

Chapter 9: The natural world

Getting started...

1 Work with a partner and answer these questions:

- What can you see in the pictures?
- What thoughts or feelings do you have about each picture?

2 Work with a partner and match the words in the box to the categories.

- Environmental problems
- Geographical features
- Natural disasters
- Animals

> lion   jungle   earthquake   pollution
> elephant   flood   beach   cliff   mountain
> volcano   drought   buffalo   forest
> greenhouse effect   stream   leopard
> famine   ocean   ozone layer   coast
> river   global warming   rhino

Exam hint

Exercise 1 is a practice task for Part 1 of the Speaking Paper.

Speaking

1 Work with a partner and decide who is going to answer the Student A questions and who is going to answer the Student B questions. Student A needs to answer all four questions, taking no more than 3 minutes. Repeat the process for the Student B questions.

Student A
Let's talk about pets

Do you have any family pets? If not, why not? If yes, what do you have?

Would you like to have a/any more pet(s)? (Tell me about that.)

How do you feel about keeping reptiles as pets (e.g. *snakes and lizards*)? (Tell me about that.)

What are the benefits of keeping pets? (Tell me about that.)

Student B
Let's talk about holidays

Does your family prefer to spend their free time near the sea or in the countryside? (Why is that?)

What do you enjoy doing near the sea/in the countryside? (Tell me about that.)

Do you go to the same place or different places for your family holidays? (Tell me about that.)

Is there anywhere new you would like to go for a family holiday? (Why is that?)

Reading

1 Work in a small group and discuss these questions:

- What can you see in the picture?

- What is commercial logging?

- What is selective logging?

- What are the environmental consequences of logging?

2 Read the article and answer the questions on page 122.

Exam hint

Exercise 2 is a practice task for Part 3 of the Reading and Writing Paper.

Logging

Over the past 40 years commercial logging in central Africa has spread from accessible coastal regions to the Congo River Basin's interior rainforests. There are now hundreds of logging concessions in the region. A study conducted confirms environmentalists' concerns that logging can push more hunting of wild animals and the over-harvest of

commercially valuable timber. Yet the researchers also say logging companies can help to conserve vulnerable regions of rainforest, provided they operate in an environmentally sustainable way.

Central Africa has the world's second largest area of rain-forest after South America's Amazon Basin. The Democratic Republic of Congo alone has 1.2 million square kilometres of tropical forest, an area three times the size of California. Of central Africa's remaining intact forest, around 40 per cent now falls within commercial logging concessions granted by govern-ments to companies and individuals.

While the study found that loggers target 35 tree species, just two, gaboon mahogany and sapele mahogany, account for over half of all logged timber. Four other species compose another 25 per cent. Operational costs based on distance to port and markets drive this selectivity. Logging in the Central African Republic necessitates the need to transport timber by road over more than a thousand kilometres. As a result, companies only log commercially valuable tree species, which recuperate the cost of harvest and transportation.

Selective harvesting doesn't threaten the survival of these trees, according to the study. However, the practice does mean loggers need to operate over a much larger area of rainforest. This increases penetration inside the forest and opens new, previously untouched forests. As access to once remote forests grows, so does the risk of greater "bush meat" hunting, or the hunting of wild animals for food. Bush-meat hunters kill not only forest antelopes, wild pigs and primates, but also endangered mammals such as gorillas and forest elephants. The study also reports that many logging concessions lack adequate management plans. The researchers found that among all concessions with shorter-term logging leases, with terms under ten years, none had management plans in place.

Despite these findings, the study suggests central Africa can sustain more logging and that timber concessions could actually help advance conservation goals. Logging activity on the studied concessions was relatively light, according to the researchers. On average, only two to three trees per hectare were harvested. Companies could log a wider range of trees species, which in turn should reduce pressure to extend harvesting into virgin rainforest. Concessionaires will be likely to harvest more species if they can sell them at a profit.

The best way to intensify the harvest locally would be to put in place incentives, for instance, lower taxes for the less valuable species. About eight per cent of central Africa's low-access tropical forest is protected by parks and reserves. Properly managed logging concessions can help to preserve rainforest biodiversity in other areas. Most logging companies do not like to see their name associated with hunting, as they do not generate income from it and get only bad press, so they are willing to cooperate with non-governmental organisations to tackle the problem.

Forestry is becoming increasingly important to the central African economy. In Cameroon, for example, tropical timber products generate around 20 per cent of the country's export revenue. Elsewhere, the Democratic Republic of Congo is trying to kick-start its economy after years of civil war. The country is currently opening up previously untouched areas of its vast rainforests to logging companies, a move that has attracted fierce criticism from environmentalists.

Logging will continue, like it or not. The only course of action is to make sure that it's as well managed as possible. A properly managed timber concession is most likely to be the best bet in terms of biodiversity conservation outside protected areas. Environmental organisations, however, are currently campaigning against plans to expand industrial logging in the Democratic Republic of Congo. The country holds by far the largest area of pristine rainforest in central Africa. Greenpeace claims that instead of helping to alleviate poverty, increased logging will fuel corruption, social conflict and environmental destruction. Experience from other countries in the Congo Basin, such as Cameroon, clearly shows that it is extremely difficult to control the multiple negative impacts of logging, such as the illegal bush-meat trade, illegal timber trade and social conflicts. Even when multilateral agencies such as the World Bank put serious conditions in place for the forestry sector, they often turn a blind eye when implementation proves to be poor.

Questions

1–5

Choose **one** correct answer.

1 In central Africa, commercial logging operations are

   a discouraging hunting.

   b penetrating inland.

   c decreasing in number.

2 The central African rainforest is

   a the third largest in the world.

   b covers the same area as California.

   c in some parts open to logging.

3 Commercial loggers in this area usually

   a harvest equally thirty five types of tree.

   b have low harvest and transport costs.

   c cover costs with selective harvesting.

4 Selective harvesting

   a is a threat to tree species survival.

   b disturbs untouched areas of forest.

   c does not adversely affect animals.

5 The research conducted suggests that

   a logging has now reached maximum levels.

   b a low number of trees were logged per hectare.

   c logging more tree species will use more land.

6–10

Choose **true**, **false** or **not given** for each statement.

		True	False	Not given
6	Logging areas could be reduced by lowering taxes.	☐	☐	☐
7	Logging concessions can contribute to preservation.	☐	☐	☐
8	Logging companies are not willing to challenge hunting.	☐	☐	☐
9	Central Africa relies heavily on its forestry income.	☐	☐	☐
10	Trade in bananas and coffee is also being expanded.	☐	☐	☐

11–15

Answer these questions using no more than **three words** or **a number**.

11 What will a well managed timber concession contribute to?

....

12 Who is against logging proposals in central Africa?

....

13 What positive outcome is hoped for by increasing logging?

....

14 According to findings, what is hard to manage with logging?

....

15 What is the World Bank being criticised for ignoring?

....

Grammar: participle phrases

1 Complete the text with the participles from the box. There are more participles than you need.

Grammar reference: see page 240

looking named starting behaving taken wanting
finding given being having separated

_____ (1) from his mother after a recent flood, a baby hippo in Kenya was close to death. _____ (2) the one-year-old hippo alone and dehydrated, rangers took him to a sanctuary in Mombasa. _____ (3) 'Owen' by the staff at the sanctuary, he quickly became a firm favourite, despite _____ (4) quite nervous and shy at first.

After a few days, _____ (5) to get his confidence back, Owen tried to make friends with a 100-year-old tortoise called 'Mzee' (meaning 'Old Man'). Despite _____ (6) in quite an unfriendly way to begin with, Mzee now refuses to be apart from Owen.

2 Look at the participle phrases in *italics*. How could you express the sentences with additional words to show the same meaning?

Well looked after and exercised, pets can be very rewarding to keep.
If they are *well looked after and exercised*, pets can be very rewarding to keep.

a *Wanting to enjoy the sunny weather*, she worked in the garden.

b *Having been on a long country walk*, they fell asleep after lunch.

c *Working late that evening*, he didn't get home until 9pm.

d *Hearing the door bell ring*, the dog barked loudly.

e *Given the choice of two holiday destinations*, the children chose to holiday by the sea.

Vocabulary: weather

1 Look at these extracts from postcards about the weather. Put the words/phrases in **bold** in the correct column in the table.

a I can't believe it – it's been **pouring with rain** all week long!

b Most days it's been fairly **cloudy** with a **light drizzle** – I wish it would decide if it's going to rain properly or not!

c Yesterday there was a **strong wind**, which was great for windsurfing.

d It's quite **warm** and **humid** during the day, but it can get **freezing cold** at night.

e When we went outside the tent this morning, there was **frost** on the ground and a **thick fog** – we could hardly see the other tents!

f   The weather's been lovely – blue skies and **unbroken sunshine** but with a **gentle breeze** to keep us cool!

g   Last night there was the most amazing storm with some really dramatic **thunder and lightning**.

h   It's been quite **chilly** for September and we've had quite a few **showers**, too, which hasn't been great.

rain	wind	temperature	snow/ice	other
pouring with rain	strong wind			

2   Work with a partner. Look again at the types of weather in Exercise 1 and answer these questions:

● Which do you hate?

● Which do you not mind?

● Which do you love?

● Which have you never experienced?

3   Read the story. Complete each gap with one of the words from the box. There are three extra words that you do not need to use.

> warmth   chilly   shone   shady   cloud   breeze   power
> hot   shivered   harder   poured   blew   icy   stronger

The Wind and the Sun were arguing about their strength.

'I have the strongest _____ (1) that ever was,' said the Sun. 'Nothing can stand against me.'

'Nothing except me,' said the Wind. 'I am far _____ (2) than you.'

'We shall find out,' said the Sun. 'I know a way to settle the argument. Do you see that man coming down the road? Well, whichever one of us makes him take off his coat, he must be considered the strongest. You try first.'

The Sun hid himself behind a _____ (3) while the Wind began. The Wind _____ (4). The man bent his head. The Wind whistled. The man _____ (5). The Wind roared and raged and sent _____ (6) blasts against the man. But the_____ (7) the Wind blew, the closer the man wrapped his coat about him.

'My turn now,' said the Sun as it came out from behind the cloud.

At first the Sun _____ (8) gently, and the man unbuttoned his coat and let it hang loosely from his shoulders. Then the Sun covered the whole Earth with _____ (9). Within a few minutes the man was so _____ (10) he was glad to take off his coat and find a _____ (11) place.

4 Work with a partner and discuss these questions:

- What do you think the moral of the story is? (The original moral is given on page 228.)

- Do you agree with it?

🔊 Listening

1 Work with a partner and discuss these questions:

- Do you ever watch wildlife programmes on TV? Why do you like/dislike them?

- What do you know about Emperor penguins?

- Have you seen the film *March of the Penguins*?

- If not, have you heard of it? What do you know about it?

2 R24 ▶ Listen to an interview with a film critic talking about the film *March of the Penguins* and answer the questions.

Exam hint

Exercise 2 is a practice task for Part 3 of the Listening Paper.

Questions

1–5

Complete the sentences using no more than **three words** or **a number**.

1 Some people have been _____ from showings of *March of the Penguins* due to its popularity.

2 *March of the Penguins* is directed by Luc Jacquet who works as a _____.

3 The penguins travel approximately _____ to reach their mating grounds.

4 Until the chicks are independent, the parents _____ travelling from the feeding to the mating grounds.

5 Steven Jacobs describes the camera-work as _____.

6–10

Complete these notes using no more than **three words** or **a number**.

Reactions to the film – the audience
● The audience was gripped by the film.
● There were giggles at funny parts, _____ (6) at sad parts and eyes were covered when there was danger.
Reactions to the film – the director
● The director is surprised at the reaction to the film because it is only a _____ (7) production.
● He thinks people's love of penguins and people's curiosity about _____ (8) have contributed to the success of the film.
● The director was touched by the story of the penguins and his aim was _____ (9) with other people.
● He praises his production team for their dedication.
● After being caught in a blizzard, one of his cameramen nearly lost _____ (10).

3 R24 ▶ Now listen again and check your answers.

Writing reference: see page 260

✏️ Writing

1 Read the review about the film *March of the Penguins*. What is the one negative point that the writer mentions about the film?

March of the Penguins

Made in 2005, *March of the Penguins* is now firmly established as a wildlife classic, thanks to the amazing efforts of French filmmaker Luc Jacquet and his devoted team. Together they endured a year of extreme conditions in Antarctica to track the extraordinary life cycle of Emperor penguins on film.

The film is remarkable in its story, which is beautifully narrated by Morgan Freeman. But even more incredible is its photography. Hundreds of penguins are seen returning, in a single-file march of seventy miles or more, to their frozen breeding ground. At times dramatic and at times just plain funny, the film follows their treacherous task of protecting eggs and hatchlings in temperatures as low as 128 degrees below zero. This unique film perfectly balances fascinating scientific information with highly entertaining visuals.

A story of love and survival, *March of the Penguins* is an eye-opening and educational experience. Although some will criticise it for being sentimental at times, it certainly is a must for anyone interested in wildlife.

(Released: 30ᵗʰ March 2005, Cert PG, Wildlife based animal adventure story)

2 To write effective reviews that will interest the reader, it is important to use a good range of vocabulary. Put the words in the box in the correct columns in the table, according to their meaning.

> extraordinary amusing fascinating gripping unbelievable
> dull hilarious intriguing nail-biting tedious

funny	exciting	interesting	surprising	boring

3 Choose the correct alternative in these sentences.

a Last night's party was incredibly *gripping/tedious/amazing*. I didn't know anybody and they were all talking about the weather.

b Your brother is absolutely *hilarious/nail-biting/exciting*. His story about his boss made me laugh until I cried!

c There was a *dull/funny/fascinating* programme on TV last night about global warming. It made me want to find out a lot more about the subject.

d Did Sarah tell you the *extraordinary/boring/dull* story about how her dog saved her from drowning?

e The end of the race was absolutely *nail-biting/amusing/tedious*, but in the end Pierre won by half a second.

4 Your principal has asked you to recommend a book to share with others in the book club at school. Write a letter to your principal recommending a book.

In your letter you should:

● give two pieces of information about the book

● give two reasons why you enjoyed it so much

● give any negative points about the book.

Write your article using between 100 and 150 words.

Exam hint

Exercise 4 is a practice task for Part 5 of the Reading and Writing Paper.

 # Speaking

1 Work with a partner and each choose one of the topics below. Prepare to time your partner – give them 1 minute to prepare and then ask them to start speaking. Tell them to stop speaking after 2 minutes. Did your partner answer the question on the card?

Exam hint

Exercise 1 is a practice task for Part 2 of the Speaking Paper.

Student A

You are going to talk about **the natural world**. You can use some or all of the ideas listed below in your talk but <u>you must answer this question</u>:

Why is it good for young people to keep pets?

You must talk for 1 to 2 minutes. You have 1 minute to think and make notes before your talk begins.

Here are some ideas to help you:
· Friendship
· Responsibility
· Education
· Exercise

Student B

You are going to talk about **the natural world**. You can use some or all of the ideas listed below in your talk but <u>you must answer this question</u>:

What is your favourite time of year and why?

You must talk for 1 to 2 minutes. You have 1 minute to think and make notes before your talk begins.

Here are some ideas to help you:
· Weather
· Activities
· Celebrations
· Holidays

2 Work with a partner and take it in turns to ask and answer the following questions. Remember to give as much information as possible and try to keep talking for at least 5 minutes.

Part 3

We have been talking about **the natural world** and I would like to ask you some more questions on this topic.

- Do you think that zoos are still as popular as they were in the past? (Why is that?)
- How are modern zoos different to traditional zoos in the past? (Tell me about that.)
- Do you think we should have zoos? (Why is that?)

- Is it important to protect animals that are in danger of extinction? (Why is that?)
- What is the best way to protect animals without taking them from their home environment? (Tell me about that.)
- Do you think that giving money to animal charities or sponsoring endangered animals is a good idea? (Why is that?)

- What environmental dangers does the world currently face? (Tell me about that.)
- How can ordinary people help to protect the environment? (Tell me about that.)
- How can governments help to protect the environment? (Tell me about that.)

Vocabulary: animals

1 R25 ▶ Listen to three people playing the 'Animal alphabet' game and answer these questions.

a How do you play the game?

b Why does one person say *Challenge!*?

2 Work in groups of three. Play the 'Animal alphabet' game. Which group got furthest in the alphabet without making a mistake?

3 In your groups, look at the pictures. Can you name the different parts of each animal? Which group can name the most parts?

4 In your groups, discuss which animals are often considered to be:

a loyal. d intelligent.

b cunning. e hard-working.

c brave. f independent.

5 In your groups, discuss this question:

● If you were an animal, what would you choose to be and why?

 **Listening**

1 Work with a partner and answer these questions:

● Why do people become vegetarians?

● How do you feel about zoos?

● What is the purpose of animal conservation areas?

2 R26 ▶ Listen to Charlotte talking about animal issues and answer the questions.

Questions

1–5

Complete these sentences using no more than **three words** or **a number**.

1 Charlotte grew up _____ in the company of animals.

2 Her family were surprised when she _____ at an early age.

3 For a short time _____ made fun of her for not eating meat.

4 As we are to blame for harming the enviornment, Charlotte believes it is our job to _____.

5 She feels that it is the duty of every country to provide places for animals to _____ in safety.

6–10

Complete these notes using no more than **three words** or **a number**.

Charlotte has:
● provided material for her _____ (6).

● written to her local Member of Parliament.

● tried to _____ (7) of the plight of animals and birds.

Charlotte disagrees with:
● the existence of _____ (8).

● the view that zoos are _____ (9).

● keeping animals in cages as they have _____ (10).

3 R26 ▶ Listen again and check your answers.

Grammar: expressing purpose

1 Choose the best alternative in these sentences.

a It's important to get plenty of publicity *in case/so as to* put pressure on the government to change the law.

b Showing children animals in zoos *so that/in order to* teach them about life in the wild doesn't make sense.

c I think I'll make a vegetable curry *in case/so that* either of them are vegetarians.

Grammar hint

infinitive of purpose

Which of the following sentences are not grammatically correct?
1 She stopped to admire the view.
2 He went to the information desk for to find out the time of the next train.
3 I left some soup for them to have when they got home from the match.
4 I got up early for packing for my holiday.
5 She moved to a new flat so as be near her new job.

Grammar reference: see page 240

d We need to be more active in the community *to/so that* ordinary people understand the kinds of tests that some of these drug companies are carrying out on animals.

e We're making this advertisement *in case/in order to* remind people that when they buy an animal as a pet, it is a responsibility for life.

2 For questions a–e, complete the second sentence so that it has a similar meaning to the first sentence, using the word given. Do not change the word given. You must use between two and five words, including the word given.

a I'd like to save the discussion about zoos until next week so as to be able to finish the meeting by 5.00 p.m.

order

I'd like to save the discussion about zoos until next week _____ be able to finish the meeting by 5.00 p.m.

b You should read this book in order to know how to look after your pet rabbit.

so

You should read this book _____ know how to look after your pet rabbit.

c Suki decided to work late because she wanted to finish her monthly report.

as

Suki decided to work late _____ finish her monthly report.

d Could you arrive early to help us organise the banners for the demonstration?

that

Could you arrive early _____ help us organise the banners for the demonstration?

e Take this compass to help you if you get lost.

in

Take this compass to help you _____ get lost.

3 Write sentences using each of the phrases in the box. Make sentences which are true or meaningful for you.

> so that   in order to   in case   so as not to

I'm learning English **so that** *I'll be able to apply for a place to study veterinary science at an Australian university.*

4 Work with a partner and share your sentences. Give more details about your sentences.

Summarising

1 You are doing a geography project on logging and its effects. Read the article below and write a summary for your geography teacher.

In your summary you should:

- state what selective logging is
- say why organisations log in this way
- state two negative points about selective logging.

Write your summary using between 100 and 150 words.

Exam hint

Exercise 1 is a practice task for Part 6 of the Reading and Writing Paper.

Logging

Over the past 40 years commercial logging in central Africa has spread from accessible coastal regions to the Congo River Basin's interior rainforests. There are now hundreds of logging concessions in the region. A study conducted confirms environmentalists' concerns that logging can push more hunting of wild animals and the over-harvest of commercially valuable timber. Yet the researchers also say logging companies can help to conserve vulnerable regions of rainforest, provided they operate in an environmentally sustainable way.

Central Africa has the world's second largest area of rainforest after South America's Amazon Basin. The Democratic Republic of Congo alone has 1.2 million square kilometres of tropical forest, an area three times the size of California. Of central Africa's remaining intact forest, around 40 per cent now falls within commercial logging concessions granted by governments to companies and individuals.

While the study found that loggers target 35 tree species, just two, gaboon mahogany and sapele mahogany, account for over half of all logged timber. Four other species comprise another 25 per cent. Operational costs based on distance to port and markets drive this selectivity. Logging in the Central African Republic necessitates the need to transport timber by road over more than a thousand kilometres. As a result, companies only log commercially valuable tree species, which recuperate the cost of harvest and transportation.

Selective harvesting doesn't threaten the survival of these trees, according to the study. However, the practice does mean loggers need to operate over a much larger area of rainforest. This increases penetration inside the forest and opens new, previously untouched forests. As access to once remote forests grows, so does the risk of greater "bush meat" hunting, or the hunting of wild animals for food. Bush-meat hunters kill not only forest antelopes, wild pigs and primates, but also endangered mammals such as gorillas and forest elephants. The study also reports that many logging concessions lack adequate management plans. The researchers found that among all concessions with shorter-term logging leases, with terms under ten years, none had management plans in place.

Despite these findings, the study suggests central Africa can sustain more logging and that timber concessions could actually help advance conservation goals. Logging activity on the studied concessions was relatively light, according to the researchers. On average, only two to three trees per hectare were harvested. Companies could log a wider range of trees species, which in turn should reduce pressure to extend harvesting into virgin rainforest. Concessionaires will be likely to harvest more species if they can sell them at a profit.

The best way to intensify the harvest locally would be to put in place incentives, for instance, lower taxes for the less valuable species. About eight per cent of central Africa's low-access tropical forest is protected by parks and reserves. Properly managed logging concessions can help to preserve rainforest biodiversity in other areas. Most logging companies do not like to see their name associated with hunting, as they do not generate income from it and get only bad press, so they are willing to cooperate with non-governmental organisations to tackle the problem.

Language recap

Grammar

1 There are mistakes in six of these sentences. Find the mistakes and correct them.

  a Remembering it was Sally's birthday, he decided to give her a call.

  b Anyone arrived after the performance starts will not be permitted to take their seats until the interval.

  c Not have a garden of his own, he likes to go and sit in the park nearby.

  d Because being from a large family, he enjoyed big meals with lots of talk and laughter.

  e He just sat on the sofa, watching TV.

  f Smiled to herself, she put the Sunday newspaper on Simon's desk.

  g Knowing how much she liked flowers, he bought her a large bunch of white roses.

  h When noticing that the front door was open, he went inside to investigate.

  i Having so much money didn't always make him particularly happy.

  j As soon as realising he had left his umbrella at home, he decided to go back and get it.

2 Combine these pairs of sentences into one sentence using the expression in brackets.

  a I'd like to take a map of the area. I don't want to get lost. (so that)

  b We should take a first-aid kit. It's possible someone might have an accident. (in case)

  c We need to start packing this evening. This will mean we can leave by 9.00 a.m. tomorrow. (in order to)

  d We must keep very quiet. We don't want to disturb any of the animals. (so as not to)

  e Shall I pick you up from the airport? Then you won't need to worry about getting a taxi. (so that)

  f Let me give you my mobile number. You could call me if there are any problems. (in case)

  g He made this film. He wanted people to know that these animals are nearly extinct. (to)

  h We took a taxi. We wanted to be sure we arrived on time. (so as to)

  i I think I'll take a book. It's possible that I will have to wait a long time for a doctor to see me. (in case)

  j It's important that we look at alternative forms of energy. We must protect the environment in the future. (in order to)

Vocabulary

3 Choose the correct alternatives in these sentences.

  a You don't really need an umbrella – it's just a light *drizzle/storm/rain*.

  b I wish it wasn't so *humid/chilly/cloudy* today. I can't stop shivering.

  c There's a really *strong/heavy/rough* wind. We should go and fly our kite.

  d The *fog/cloud/frost* was so bad we couldn't find the car for ages.

  e I got caught in a heavy *shower/sunshine/lightning* on the way home and got soaked to the skin!

  f Apparently, this little thing on my penknife is for getting stones out of horses' *hooves/feet/claws*.

  g I think that little bird has broken its *fin/wing/arm*. It doesn't seem to be able to fly.

4 Complete these sentences with the correct word. You have been given the beginning of each word and the exact number of missing letters.

  a I saw a h_ _ _ _ _ _ _ _ comedy film on TV last night about a dog that could talk.

  b There's an i_ _ _ _ _ _ _ _ _ story behind the strange disappearance of Agatha Christie in 1926. Nobody seems to know the real truth.

  c Long parts of the book are very t_ _ _ _ _ _ with nothing much of interest, but the final chapter is excellent.

  d Simon made us all smile last night when he told us quite a f_ _ _ _ story about how he got his first job.

  e There's a n _ _ _-_ _ _ _ _ _ end to the film. Honestly, I was on the edge of my seat with excitement.

  f The traffic was u_ _ _ _ _ _ _ _ _ _ last night. It took me four hours to get home!

  g I don't find his jokes at all a_ _ _ _ _ _.

  h She could never understand how he could find geology to be such a f_ _ _ _ _ _ _ _ _ subject.

  i This book I am reading about outer space is absolutely g_ _ _ _ _ _. I really don't want to put it down!

  j Her boyfriend is so d_ _ _. All he ever wants to talk about is cars and computers!

Paper 3: Speaking

🗣 **Part 2 Speaking: Student talk (1minute preparation, plus a talk of 1 to 2 minutes)**

Remember, in this part you will give an uninterrupted presentation of between 1 and 2 minutes on a topic provided by Edexcel. On the test card, there are some bullet point suggestions to give you ideas and a question relating to the topic which you **must** answer during your talk. You will also have some paper and a pen to make notes during the 1minute preparation time.

You might want to consider creating your notes as a mind map. A mind map is a diagram which represents words, ideas and concepts linked to a central theme. It helps you to:

● brainstorm information and ideas

● organise the information and ideas

● answer the set question

● plan your presentation

● give the necessary information.

Let's have a look at this task in the Edexcel International GCSE ESL Speaking Paper in November 2009:

*You are going to talk about **visiting your country**.
You can use some or all of the ideas listed below in your talk, but you must answer this question:*

What things should people know if they want to visit your country?
Here are some ideas to help you.

- *Clothes*
- *Behaviour*
- *Customs and traditions*
- *Weather*
- *Other*

To create your mind map for this task, write the idea you want to develop – ***visiting your country*** – in the middle of the blank piece of paper. (It will be easier if you use the page in landscape orientation.) Then write the related subtopics around this central idea, connecting each of them to the centre with a line. You should then add more ideas which are linked to the subtopics. You can underline the information which you think people should know if they visit your country. Let's look at an example:

A mind map will give you lots of prompts about what to say in your presentation. You can develop some things and leave other things out - but you will not run out of things to say. It is always good practice to try to write down as many ideas as you can in the time given for preparation.

Getting started...

1 What can you see in each picture? What do they have in common?

2 Work with a partner. Check you understand the phrases in *italics*, then answer the questions.

- How do you feel about *making small talk* in English?
- How much experience of *public speaking* do you have? How do you feel about it? Why?
- What do you think of TV *chat shows*? Do you have any favourites?
- Do you have experience of any *English-speaking* countries? What did you think of them?

3 R.27 ▶ All the numbers, dates and times in the box refer to facts about text messaging. Listen and say what each one refers to.

fcts abt txts
1992   85%   10   10.30 p.m.   11 p.m.
New Year's Day 2006   43.2 seconds

1

2

3

4

Exam hint

Exercise 1 is a practice task for Part 1 of the Speaking Paper.

🗣 Speaking

1 Work with a partner and decide who is going to answer the Student A questions and who is going to answer the Student B questions. Student A needs to answer all four questions, taking no more than 3 minutes. Repeat the process for the Student B questions.

Student A
Let's talk about texting
How often do you send text messages? (Why is that?)
How fast are you at writing texts? (Why is that?)
Who do you usually send texts to? (Tell me about that.)
What are they usually about? (Tell me about that.)

Student B
Let's talk about social networking sites
How do you usually keep in contact with friends? (Tell me about that.)
How often do you use social networking sites? (Why is that?)
What do you like about social networking sites? (Tell me about that.)
Is there anything you don't like about them? (Tell me about that.)

Vocabulary: phrasal verbs (speaking)

1 **R.28** ▶ Listen to eight dialogues and match each one with the correct phrasal verb.

   a   to get through (to someone)

   b   to get (your point/message) across

   c   to speak up

   d   to speak out (about something)

   e   to talk down (to someone)

   f   to pick up (a new language)

   g   to pass on (a message/greetings/congratulations/etc.)

   h   to bring up (a point/the subject)

2 Look at the audioscript on page 226. Rewrite the <u>underlined</u> parts using the correct phrasal verb.

   It's a big room so you'll need to <u>speak loudly</u>. ⟶ *It's a big room so you'll need to speak up.*

3 **R.29** ▶ Listen and check your answers to Exercise 2.

4 Work in a small group and discuss these questions:

   ● Do you find it more difficult getting your message across in English on the phone than in person? Why/Why not?

   ● Generally, do you prefer speaking to people face-to-face or on the phone? Why?

   ● How do you feel when you get through to a company's electronic answering system (e.g. when you hear 'Press 1 for …' and/or music while you wait to be connected)?

   ● What kinds of issues have you spoken out/might you speak out about in lessons, school meetings or when you are with friends?

   ● How long do you think you need to live in a country before you pick up the language? Do you think it's important to have lessons as well? Why/Why not?

   ● How do you feel about bringing up the subject of money with your friends (e.g. when deciding who pays for something or borrowing/lending money)?

Writing

1 Read the task and answer the questions a–e. Refer to the Writing reference on page 250 if necessary.

> **Writing task**
>
> Your school has been given a large sum of money to spend on either a new computer area in the library or a new garden area. You have been asked to write a report for the school principal.
>
> In your report you should:
>
> • give **two** advantages of a computer area
>
> • give **two** advantages of a garden area
>
> • give your opinion and make a recommendation.
>
> Write your report using between 100 and 150 words.

a Which of these would be most appropriate to include in your introductory paragraph?

   i State the purpose of the report.

   ii Give your personal opinion about which option is best.

   iii Recommend your preferred option.

b What will the two main paragraphs be about?

c Which of these would be most appropriate to include in your concluding paragraph?

   i State the purpose of the report.

   ii Give your personal opinion about which option is best.

   iii Recommend your preferred option.

d What four subheadings could you use?

e Who are you writing the report for? What does that tell you about the style of your writing?

2 Complete these sentences about advantages and recommendations with the words in the box.

> benefit   benefits   beneficial   valuable   points
> difference   recommend   offer   appeal

a More webcams would be extremely _beneficial_ as the present facilities are too limited.

b A new computer area would offer many _____ to the school.

c There are a number of good _____ about the existing computer suite.

d A new garden area would be a _____ addition to the existing outdoor area.

e Spending the money on networking the computers would _____ the school in two main ways.

f   A DVD player in every classroom would _____ to many students.

g   A larger covered patio area would _____ the following advantages.

h   A new computer area would make a big _____ to the school.

i   I would strongly _____ spending the money on a new computer area.

3 Now write your report using some of the language from Exercise 2 as appropriate.

4 Read your report and answer these questions:

● Have you organised your report clearly, using paragraphs and subheadings?

● Have you used an appropriate style?

● Have you used a range of appropriate vocabulary to talk about advantages?

● Have you made any mistakes with grammar?

5 Make changes to your report as necessary.

Exam hint

Exercise 3 is a practice task for Part 4 of the Reading and Writing Paper.

Writing reference: see page 250

 Reading

1 Work with a partner and discuss these questions:

● How many computers and games consoles does your family have?

● Do you sit in separate rooms when using technology?

● How much time do your parents spend using a computer or the games console?

● Do you think your parents fully understand the technology that you use?

Exam hint

Exercise 2 is a practice task for Part 3 of the Reading and Writing Paper.

2 Read the article and complete the tasks that follow.

Twitter, e-mail, texts: we don't talk any more!

Gone are the days when we tripped over each other in the kitchen or slumped happily against each other on the sofa to watch a family film. I should thank my lucky stars we had our children before the age of cheap laptops and mobile phones for primary school children, otherwise we might never have known those times. Fast forward to 2010 and, with four computers in the house, it's usual to find all five family members in five separate rooms, clicking or bashing away on the PlayStation. Also, when you're chatting by e-mail to friends in New Zealand, it seems reasonable to slip in a message to your child, sitting in front of his own computer a few yards away on the other side of the bedroom wall.

With laptops before breakfast, mobiles left switched on by bedsides and iPods stuck in ears as they fall asleep, I do worry my sons will soon lose the power of speech entirely. When I was a child, I would spend hours gossiping with my mates. My children are happier to stay in their rooms and converse by keyboard. Should I resist the inevitable march of progress? After all, I know I'm a hypocrite when it comes to the lure of the laptop. I used to start every day gazing at my children; these days I open my Mac before I open their doors.

As soon as I wake up I crack open my laptop and take a crafty peek at my e-mail. E-mails checked, I click on to my social networking site, in case I'm missing anything. That's when I notice my 13-year-old son is online with his friend and doing exactly the same thing. Then there are the crucial messages I need to pass on to my eldest such as when I am working late or when his rugby training has been cancelled. All these messages are sent by e-mail because they have more chance of reaching his brain than actual, face-to-face human-being exchanges. I've suddenly realised these kids have sucked me into their hi-tech way of doing things. Now I'm communicating with them via message boards, phones and computers, just like their friends.

Research has uncovered that if a child is exposed to a relentless diet of TV and computer games and deprived of interaction at home, this can be very damaging to their social development. This information is falling on deaf ears in our house. The more gadgets that appear, the less we have to do with one another. The other night our street was plunged into darkness by a power cut and the boys were truly shocked. Once the excitement of candles and no showers had waned, the horror of the situation sank in and they slunk off to bed. Nothing better to do, you see.

The way they plan their social life has changed, too. Everything is left to the last minute because everyone can be reached immediately, no matter where they are. Hours of no visible or audible signs of communication with their friends are suddenly followed by a slammed front door as they react to an urgent message or e-mail. I text them to find out what time they are coming back as they disappear up the road. I leave my phone next to my pillow as I try to sleep, comforted only by a bleep-bleep of a response and an eventual key in the door.

Then there's social networking. My youngest tolerates me as a friend, but he has nothing to hide ... yet. My eldest two won't let me near them, though I'm sure I could easily hang around unnoticed among the thousands of friends they have somehow collected. Interestingly, some of their peers have added me as a friend and I often spy on my children from a distance.

It's not just speech that is disappearing in our house. The handwritten word is an endangered species, too. My boys rarely trouble a ballpoint pen and homework is always produced on the computer; handwritten notes left for me are therefore no more than a scribble. I think back to my own school days, of aching fingers and 90-minute essay exams, and wonder how on earth these children manage when they are not used to holding a pen.

The way we communicate is changing and families can't live in a bubble and ignore technology. However, children learn how to communicate from their parents and we lose all sorts of things, crucial body language for example, by not talking face to face. Families should make use of the new communication methods, but make sure they take time to talk about things other than the daily routine.

Questions

1–5

Choose **true**, **false** or **not given** for each statement.

	True	False	Not given
1 The author did not enjoy watching films with the family.	☐	☐	☐
2 The author is grateful that technology was not as invasive when the children were young.	☐	☐	☐
3 Even when everybody is at home, they tend to do their own thing.	☐	☐	☐
4 The children still prefer to meet up with their friends to talk.	☐	☐	☐
5 The author does not acknowledge that times are different now.	☐	☐	☐

6–10

Answer these questions using no more than **three words** or **a number**.

6 What does the author do first thing in the morning?

....

7 How does the author give her eldest son important messages?

....

8 According to research, what should children use in moderation?

....

9 Why could the children not take a shower?

....

10 How does the author find out what time her children are returning home?

....

11–15

Complete these notes using no more than **three words** or **a number**.

- On social networking sites, the author is _____ (11) to her youngest child, but not the older two.

- Using social networking sites, she is able to _____ (12) on the older two children indirectly.

- The author wonders how her children cope in _____ (13) as everything for school is now done on a computer.

- Ways of communicating are changing and we must accept technology.

- Still need face-to-face communication to learn skills such as _____ (14)

- Need a balance between _____ (15) and families conversing on topics beyond those necessary for the home to function

Grammar: adverbs

Grammar reference: see page 240

1 Look at these sentences. What makes the second one more interesting?

　a He spoke to me.

　b Surprisingly, he spoke to me quite rudely.

Grammar hint

adverbs with two forms

Some adverbs have two different forms with different meanings.

a Complete these pairs of sentences with the correct adverb. (The meanings of the adverbs are in brackets.)

fine/finely

   i First, add some _____ chopped onions. (= small, carefully-done)

   ii He's doing _____ in all his subjects at school. (= well)

high/highly

   i She can jump incredibly _____. (= referring to height)

   ii This restaurant is _____ recommended. (= very much)

late/lately

   i The train's _____ arrival caused chaos. (= not on time)

   ii He's been working very hard _____ . (= recently)

b Can you think of three more examples of adverbs like this?

---

2 Complete the table using the adverbs from the box.

> these days   unfortunately   completely   quickly
> definitely   finally   intensely   never   here

Adverbs of manner	*politely, rudely, angrily, well, in a friendly way,* _____ (1)
Adverbs of place	*at the bus stop, in the corner, there,* _____ (2)
Adverbs of time	*today, afterwards, in May,* _____ (3)
Adverbs of frequency	*usually, sometimes, ever, always, rarely, once a week,* _____ (4)
Adverbs of certainty	*perhaps, probably, certainly,* _____ (5)
Adverbs of completeness	*practically, nearly, quite, rather,* _____ (6)
Emphasising adverbs	*very, extremely, terribly,* _____ (7)
Connecting adverbs	*then, next, suddenly, however, anyway,* _____ (8)
Comment adverbs	*surprisingly, stupidly,* _____ (9)

3 There are eight mistakes in these sentences. Find the mistakes and correct them.

  a He asked me if politely he could borrow £10.

  b The shop assistant spoke to me friendlily.

  c I waited at home all morning patiently.

  d I'll easyly finish reading this book by Friday.

  e Always I say hello to shop assistants.

  f She sang beautifully the whole song.

  g I'd rather you didn't drive so fastly.

  h I think he is a truely great singer.

  i At the bus stop I've been waiting for thirty minutes.

  j He always does his homework very carefuly.

4 Work with a partner and write the adverbs from these adjectives, paying attention to correct spelling. Check in a dictionary if necessary.

> slow   secret   happy   nervous   angry   loving   gentle
> violent   quick   shy   careful   automatic   silly   noisy   excited

Vocabulary: ways of speaking

1 Match the verb phrases a–h with the definitions i–viii.

  a boast about something

  b exaggerate about something

  c grumble about something

  d moan about something

  e mumble about something

  f mutter about something

  g insist on something

  h object to something

  i   to say that you do not like or approve of something

  ii   to say that you are not satisfied with or not happy about something

  iii   to say something very quietly and in a way that is difficult to understand

  iv   to say something quietly, especially because you are annoyed or do not want someone to hear

  v   to talk too much about your own abilities and achievements in a way that annoys other people

  vi   to demand that something should happen

  vii to complain about something in an annoying way

  viii to make something seem better, larger, worse, etc. than it really is

2 Choose the correct alternative in each sentence.

  a I *object to/boast about* holding the door open for people when they don't even say 'thank you'.

  b My mother *insisted on/objected to* good manners when I was a child. We always had to say 'please', 'thank you' and 'excuse me'.

  c Nobody will hear you if you *moan/mumble* like that. You'll have to speak louder and more clearly.

  d I couldn't hear what he said because he *grumbled/muttered* under his breath, but he was clearly angry.

  e My flatmate is never satisfied. It's so annoying because she *moans/exaggerates* about absolutely everything.

  f My brother's so full-of-himself. He's always *boasting/mumbling* about how clever he is and what good marks he gets in his exams.

  g I heard someone on the bus *mumbling/grumbling* about the weather. She said it was too cold and wet.

  h I'm sure he's *insisting on/exaggerating* about his illness. He's really not very ill – he's only got a bit of a cold.

3 Work with a partner. Tell each other about two situations similar to those in Exercise 2. For each situation, use one of the verb phrases from Exercise 1.

  A good friend of mine is always exaggerating about things. Recently he told me about an accident he'd had and ...

◁») Listening

1 Work with a partner and discuss these questions:

  ● Do you ever read blogs on the Internet? Why/Why not?

  ● Do you write a blog (or a diary)? Would you consider starting one? Why/Why not?

> **Vocabulary Hint**
>
> Blog – the word 'blog' comes from 'web log' and is like a diary on a webpage. People write their thoughts and opinions and other people can add to them.

Exam hint

Exercise 2 is a practice task for Part 3 of the Listening Paper.

2 R30 ▶ You are now going to listen to part of a radio interview with a woman who is doing research into blogging. Listen to the interview and answer the questions.

Questions

1–5

Answer these questions using no more than **three words** and/or **number**.

1 What does Ros Hargreaves currently do?

....

2 According to Ros, what do people write in their blogs?

....

3 According to statistics, how many blogs are there on the web?

....

4 How would some critics describe blogs?

....

5 What does Ros think that blogs will influence?

....

6–15

Complete these notes using no more than **three words** or **a number**.

Two-way blogs

● Two-way blogs are the best.

● People swap _____ (6)

● A good example being the BBC news blog 'The Editors'

● It's basically a _____ (7) about what is happening in the news.

● A good way for _____ (8) to participate

● In the past _____ (9) did not have much scope.

● Now the writer and the reader can converse.

● Another benefit is the large _____ (10) that can get involved.

Personal blogs

● Anya Peters was homeless.

● Her blog is about _____ (11).

● By writing her blog, she was trying to stay in touch with _____ (12).

● A publisher saw her blog and offered her _____ (13).

● She managed to escape homelessness.

Recognised form of literature

● Now a literary prize for blogging

● The first prize winner is from _____ (14).

● She wrote a blog about _____ (15).

---

3 R30 ▶ Listen again and check your answers.

 **Speaking**

1 **R31** ▶ Listen to two pairs of students. Which two questions are they talking about?

- Which, if any, of the three blogs mentioned in the listening above would you like to read?

- Do you ever read blogs on the Internet?

- Do you write a blog (or a diary)? Would you consider starting one?

- Do you enjoy reading the diaries of famous people?

- What, if anything, do you mainly use the Internet for?

2 **R31** ▶ Listen again. How do you think they could make what they are saying sound more interesting?

3 Look at the audioscript and replace the words in brackets with more interesting and varied words or phrases.

A: Well, I'm not sure but I think the one about that woman is (interesting) _____[1] because it would be (interesting) _____[2] to hear about her life. I want to know about her and why she was living in a car. What do you think? Which one are you interested in?

B: Well, I'd like to look at the news one actually, because I think that sounds (interesting) _____[3]. Sometimes I hear something on the news and I want to give my opinion.

C: I can't understand why people write blogs. I think it's very strange for people to write about normal things and put it on the Internet for other people to read. And why do people read these blogs? It's (strange) _____[4]. Do you agree?

D: I suppose you're right. And also it's (strange) _____[5] that people write things like this and they don't know who will read it. I certainly wouldn't write one.

4 Work in pairs. Choose two questions from Exercise 1 to discuss. Before you start talking, make notes about a range of words and phrases you could use.

5 Discuss the two questions you chose, making sure you use a range of interesting vocabulary.

Exam hint

Exercise 1 is a practice task for Part 2 of the Speaking Paper.

6 Work with a partner and each choose one of the topics below. Prepare to time your partner – give them 1 minute to prepare and then ask them to start speaking. Tell them to stop speaking after 2 minutes. Did your partner answer the question on the card?

Student A

You are going to talk about **communication**. You can use some or all of the ideas listed below in your talk but you must answer this question:

Which types of communication do you use for different situations and why?
You must talk for 1 to 2 minutes. You have 1 minute to think and make notes before your talk begins.

Here are some ideas to help you:
- E-mail/texts
- Letters/cards
- Twitter/blogs
- Telephone

Student B

You are going to talk about **communication**. You can use some or all of the ideas listed below in your talk but you must answer this question:

When did you last receive a letter/card that was special to you and why was it special?
You must talk for 1 to 2 minutes. You have 1 minute to think and make notes before your talk begins.

Here are some ideas to help you:
- Birthday
- Festival
- Family
- Friend

Exam hint

Exercise 2 is a practice task for Part 3 of the Speaking Paper.

7 Work with a partner and take it in turns to ask and answer the following questions. Remember to give as much information as possible and try to keep talking for at least 5 minutes.

Part 3

We have been talking about **communication** and I would like to ask you some more questions on this topic.

- What are the advantages of instant communication? (e.g. *texting*) (Tell me about that.)
- What are the disadvantages of instant communication? (Tell me about that.)
- Do today's communication methods put pressure on people to respond immediately? (Why is that?)

- Do you think that chat shows are popular forms of entertainment? (Why is that?)
- Do you think they are the same form of entertainment as reading blogs and tweets? (Why is that?)
- Why do you think that people are so interested in the lives of others? (Tell me about that.)

- Do you think that traditional methods of communication are being replaced by other forms? (Tell me about that.)
- Do you think they should be replaced? (Why is that?)
- How do you think that communication methods will develop in the future? (Tell me about that.)

Grammar: causative *have* and *get*

1 R32 ▶ Listen to a short phone message. What was the problem? What was the solution?

Grammar reference: see page 242

2 Look at these pairs of sentences. What are the differences in form and in meaning?

   a i *I repaired my computer.*

      ii *I had my computer repaired.*

   b i *I had my computer repaired.*

      ii *I got my computer repaired.*

3 Match the words in *italics* in a–d with the correct uses i–iv.

   a She *got/had her bag stolen* last week.

   b She is trying to *get the computer to work.*

   c I'll *get my essay done* and then I can meet you.

   d He *gets/has his eyes tested every year.*

   i   to talk about when somebody else does something for you (often when you arrange and pay them to do so)

   ii to talk about an experience or something that happens to you (often something you have no control over)

   iii to talk about completing work on something

   iv to talk about when you make somebody/something do something (often with the idea of difficulty)

4 Look at the words in *italics* in Exercise 3 again and answer these questions.

   a Which three uses have this form: *have/get* + object + past participle?

   b Which one has this form: *get* + object + *to*-infinitive?

5 Read the text and answer the questions.

a Where do you think you might read this text?

b How would you summarise the writer's attitude to his trip to the hairdresser: irritated, embarrassed, amused or surprised?

| HOME | ABOUT ME | PICTURES | RECENT ENTRIES | ARCHIVE |

16th January …

<u>CUT THE CHAT</u>

This is a picture of me – I (just / my hair / cut) _____ (1). My entry today is about (your hair / cut) _____ (2) in a trendy ladies' salon – alien territory for a man like me. The cut is fine … it's the chat I object to. My usual barber has gone, so when I went along to this salon, I wasn't quite sure what to expect.

I was greeted by a stylist, Debbie, who (me / put on) _____ (3) a robe and sit in front of the mirror. I then had to try to explain what I wanted, which is not something I'm used to doing and I felt terribly awkward. Then, I (my hair / wash) _____ (4) and the real chatting started. I really feel that talking to someone who is behind you, while (your head / massage) _____ (5) and with your neck at a funny angle, is not all that pleasant. But I tried to listen and mumble some sort of polite reply.

Then the proper hair cutting started. And the chatting stepped up a gear, too.

I thought perhaps I could (her / stop) _____ (6) asking me questions by closing my eyes – but no, that didn't stop her. Debbie seemed to continue quite happily with a rather one-sided conversation, however. She told me about (a new kitchen / fit) _____ (7), grumbled about her noisy neighbours and talked about (her wallet / steal) _____ (8) on the bus last week. I got all the details.

And although she clearly didn't really expect much response from me, I still felt guilty for not wanting to join in. Far from just relaxing, all I could think about was (the whole thing / finish) _____ (9) and escaping. Is it just me? Or does everyone feel like this?

<u>Comments</u> [2]

6 Complete the text in the blog using the prompts. In some cases, it is correct to use a form of *have* or *get*.

7 Work with a partner and correct the mistakes in *italics* in questions a–e, then discuss the questions with your partner.

a How do you feel about *having cut your hair*? Do you like chatting to the hairdresser? Why/Why not?

b How do you feel if you *can't get a machine worked* (e.g. your computer, your TV, your phone, etc.)? What do you usually do?

c If you won a lot of money, what (if anything) *would you have do* to the place you live in?

d When was the last time *you taken your photo*? What was it for?

e *Have you ever had stolen* anything? What was it? What happened?

Summarising

1 Read the article on communication in a typical household and write a summary for your teacher.

In your summary you should:

- state what the children use technology for
- state what the author uses technology for
- state what worries the author has about technology.

Write your summary using between 100 and 150 words.

Exam hint

Exercise 1 is a practice task for Part 6 of the Reading and Writing Paper.

Twitter, e-mail, texts: we don't talk any more!

With laptops before breakfast, mobiles left switched on by bedsides and iPods stuck in ears as they fall asleep, I do worry my sons will soon lose the power of speech entirely. When I was a child, I would spend hours gossiping with my mates. My children are happier to stay in their rooms and converse by keyboard. Should I resist the inevitable march of progress? After all, I know I'm a hypocrite when it comes to the lure of the laptop. I used to start every day gazing at my children; these days I open my Mac before I open their doors.

As soon as I wake up I crack open my laptop and take a crafty peek at my e-mail. E-mails checked, I click on to my social networking site, in case I'm missing anything. That's when I notice my 13-year-old son is online with his friend and doing exactly the same thing. Then there are the crucial messages I need to pass on to my eldest such as when I am working late or when his rugby training has been cancelled. All these messages are sent by e-mail because they have more chance of reaching his brain than actual, face-to-face human-being exchanges. I've suddenly realised these kids have sucked me into their hi-tech way of doing things. Now I'm communicating with them via message boards, phones and computers, just like their friends.

The way they plan their social life has changed, too. Everything is left to the last minute because everyone can be reached immediately, no matter where they are. Hours of no visible or audible signs of communication with their friends are suddenly followed by a slammed front door as they react to an urgent message or e-mail. I text them to find out what time they are coming back as they disappear up the road. I leave my phone next to my pillow as I try to sleep, comforted only by a bleep-bleep of a response and an eventual key in the door.

It's not just speech that is disappearing in our house. The handwritten word is an endangered species, too. My boys rarely trouble a ballpoint pen and homework is always produced on the computer; handwritten notes left for me are therefore no more than a scribble. I think back to my own school days, of aching fingers and 90-minute essay exams, and wonder how on earth these children manage when they are not used to holding a pen.

The way we communicate is changing and families can't live in a bubble and ignore technology. However, children learn how to communicate from their parents and we lose all sorts of things, crucial body language for example, by not talking face to face. Families should make use of new methods of communicating but make sure they take time to talk about things other than the daily routine.

Language recap

Grammar

1 Write the adverbs/adverbial phrases in brackets in the best place in each sentence. (Sometimes there may be more than one correct answer.)

    a I watch chat shows on TV. (never)
    b I'm bad at making small talk at parties. (really)
    c We go to Spanish conversation classes. (every week)
    d I'll meet you at the library later. (probably)
    e She's finished the whole book. (nearly)
    f He started shouting at me. (suddenly)
    g I've been waiting for over half an hour. (here)
    h I couldn't remember how to say 'thank you' in French. (unfortunately)

2 Put the words in the correct order to form sentences.

    a i Hey! Your hair looks lovely.
        ii Oh, thanks. _____
           (had morning cut it I this)
    b i Oh dear. You look upset. What's happened?
        ii _____
           (just my had stolen think purse I've I)

    c i Why are you angry with Monica?
        ii _____
           (can't her to I anything do ask I get)
    d i Why haven't you got your car today?
        ii _____
           (broke repaired and having It it down I'm)
    e i Why don't you come out with us tonight?
        ii _____
           (get and I'll I'll done first then my you join homework)
    f i What's the matter with your eyes?
        ii _____
           (headaches I I to get getting them because keep tested need)
    g i Why isn't the TV working?
        ii _____
           (can't work not but I'm I sure get the switch to volume)
    h i Oh dear. I've spilt coffee on your jacket.
        ii _____
           (doesn't It I can it later have matter drycleaned because)

Vocabulary

3 Complete the second sentence so that it has a similar meaning to the first sentence, using the word given. Do not change the word given. You must use between two and five words, including the word given.

    a You'll have to talk more loudly because she's a bit deaf.
        up
        You'll have to _____ because she's a bit deaf.
    b I've been trying to contact her about the job.
        get
        I've been trying to _____ her about the job.
    c I'm hoping to learn a bit of Chinese when I go there.
        up
        I'm hoping to _____ a bit of Chinese when I go there.
    d Will you give my best wishes to Maria when you see her?
        pass
        Will you _____ my best wishes to Maria when you see her?
    e I'm not sure how to make people understand my point.
        across
        I'm not sure how to _____ to people.
    f I admire her for saying what she feels in public about testing on animals.
        speaking
        I admire her for _____ about testing on animals.

    g My flatmate really annoys me when he talks to me as if I'm stupid all the time.
        down
        My flatmate really annoys me when he _____ all the time.
    h I'd like to start discussing my university prospects.
        up
        I'd like to _____ my university prospects.

4 There is a mistake in each of these sentences. Find the mistakes and correct them.

    a She told me she's got hundreds of pairs of shoes, but I'm sure she's examining about it.
    b He's intruding on not coming with us and I can't persuade him to change his mind.
    c He spends all his time saying how great he is and boosting about his achievements.
    d It's not that I obsess to what he's saying; it's just the way he says it.
    e I wish she wasn't so negative. Nothing is ever right with her; she mows about absolutely everything.
    f My son muffles about things all the time and I can't understand a word he says.

Paper 1: Reading and Writing

 Part 3: Reading (15 marks)

Text types

The texts in this part are longer (typically 800 words) and they could be a report or an article. They could come from an academic source but will be on a topic of general interest, e.g. VSO (Voluntary Services Overseas), laughter, life on the moon.

Skills

This part of the paper requires you to show your ability to:

1 read for **gist** and **detail**. So, you need to grasp the main points first and then focus on the finer detail.

2 follow a **line of argument** or **discussion** to its logical conclusion. This means you need to see the development of ideas – how one part or step of an argument or idea follows on from the previous one.

3 identify **attitudes** and **opinions** – whether openly stated or implied (i.e. you might need to 'read between the lines'). Here you have to show, firstly, that you understand exactly what the writer means – her/his attitudes and opinions – from the way she/he presents information in the text; and, secondly, that you can distinguish between facts, ideas and opinions. So, you need to evaluate whether the information – what is being presented – is an undisputed fact or more of an opinion. The writer might have written the text to persuade, to warn or to inform the reader, etc.

Let's take an example from the Edexcel IGCSE ESL paper in May 2010. You read this extract:

> *However, Manchester United's manager fined Beckham £50,000 for babysitting their sick child because Victoria was seen at a London Fashion Week event on the same day. Ferguson claimed that Beckham would have been able to train if his wife had stayed at home that day. Beckham's growing celebrity status caused serious tension between the two men ....*

and have to answer this question:

> *Sir Alex Ferguson believed that David should have been able to .... with the team.*

The correct answer here is **train**. The writer has a positive attitude towards David Beckham. In the text, you read Ferguson **claimed** Beckham could have trained with the team, i.e. the writer wants you to know that this was not necessarily correct – it was in the opinion of Ferguson. The

word **believed** is used in the question to indicate that there is some doubt over this statement – that it is just Ferguson's opinion.

Task types

To answer the questions successfully you must recognise and understand paraphrasing – it is highly unlikely that the same words will be used in both the questions and the texts. Don't forget the questions follow the order of information presented in the texts and that you will find all the answers in the text.

Task types in this part include:

- **Multiple-choice:** you choose which option is the correct answer to a question, or which option best fills a gap in a sentence. There could be three or four options – the number of options will always be the same within the task, but only one will be correct.

- **Short-answer questions:** the instruction states exactly how many words you need to write to answer the question – usually between one and three – and you must stick to the number allowed. You will find the words for your answers in the text and you should copy these words, unchanged, directly from the text. Don't copy out whole sentences – you will not gain the mark even if the correct answer is somewhere within the sentence you have copied. Make sure you spell the words correctly, as this is an important part of completing the task successfully.

- **True/False/Not given:** you have to decide if the information given in each statement is True, False or Not Given according to the text. Remember, *Not Given* means there is no information within the text as to whether the statement is true or false.

- **Notes completion, sentence completion:** you write your answers out in words in this task type. You can complete the notes or sentences with just a few words – the exact number is specified in the instruction. The answers are words in the text which you must copy unchanged. The prompts give you grammatical cues so it should be clear what part of speech is required in the gaps. The notes or sentences to be completed will paraphrase information in the text. Again, you should avoid copying whole sentences from the text.

- **Diagram completion:** you will write your answers out in words for this task type, taking words from the text to label a diagram or other graphic. It may represent an object, a process or a set of data described in the text.

1 Complete the sentences with the correct word. The first two letters have been given to help you.

a I'm not keen on sc _____ eggs, but I do like them fr _____.

b I wish he would speak more clearly and stop mu _____ – I can't hear a thing he says.

c Many children these days live on a ne _____ -en _____ diet of TV programmes, computer games and junk food.

d I like looking down from the top of the cl _____ when you can see the sandy be _____ below and the co _____ stretching for miles.

e There was a light dr _____ in the morning, but then the skies cleared and it was warm and just a bit hu _____ in the afternoon.

f She told me that there were over a hundred people at the party but I think she was ex _____.

g She's got a very sw _____ tooth and loves all kinds of cakes, biscuits and de _____.

h My favourite dish at my local restaurant is steak, which I like cooked ra _____, with a mo _____ -wa _____ onion sauce they make to go with it.

i The change in weather patterns means that there are more dr _____ due to too little rain and also more fl _____ due to a lot of rain in a short space of time.

j It's been po _____ with rain here for so long that I decided to have a short break in Spain. I managed to get a really good last-mi _____ deal.

2 There are mistakes with six of the verbs in these dialogues. Find the mistakes and correct them.

a i Why isn't Tina here today?
  ii She'll go to the dentist this afternoon.

b i Is Pete coming to the party?
  ii I'm not sure. I'll ask him as soon as I'm going to see him.

c i I'm so worried about my driving test tomorrow.
  ii It's OK – you'll be fine. You've done lots of practice.

d i I don't feel like cooking at all tonight. I'm too tired.
  ii Oh, don't worry. In that case, I'm making you something.

e i Have you decided what to do on your eighteenth birthday?
  ii Yes definitely. I have a big party, but I'm not sure exactly when yet.

f i What time is your train tomorrow?
  ii I'd like to catch the one that leaving at 9.25 a.m.

g i What time shall I phone you tonight?
  ii After 9 o'clock, because I'll be watching the football until then.

h i How long have you lived here?
  ii Well, by the end of this year, I live here for six years.

3 Read the text and decide which answer, a, b, c or d, best fits each gap.

> **Ray Mears – survivalist**
>
> Over the last decade, Ray Mears has become world-famous as an authority on the subject of survival in the wilderness. _____ (1) people throughout the world have seen his television programmes in which he _____ (2) on his knowledge of survival. He has a down-to-earth approach, showing an obvious love for his subject and a _____ (3) deal of respect for the land and people he comes across.
>
> _____ (4) up in England, Ray discovered that the countryside around him was full of wildlife and he was _____ (5) drawn to learning more about it. His interest in _____ (6) survival was further inspired by a teacher, who said to Ray 'In _____ (7) to survive in the wild, you don't need equipment, you need knowledge.'
>
> So, Ray digested every _____ (8) of information relating to survival that he could find, and then started practising these ancient skills around the world. He met local people who showed him how to build shelters, hunt for food, survive in _____ (9) cold conditions. And in 1983, he founded The Woodlore School of Wilderness Bushcraft, _____ (10) that others could also learn these skills.
>
> Now, after many years of success, Ray's love of the outdoors remains the same. He is still a modest man and not someone to _____ (11) about his extensive knowledge or dwell on his fame and fortune. Instead, he prefers to roll up his _____ (12) and get his hands dirty, and show others the joys of survival outdoors.

1	a Many	b Much	c Plenty	d Lots
2	a gets	b brings	c passes	d takes
3	a big	b large	c great	d plenty
4	a Bringing	b Growing	c Getting	d Living
5	a once	b almost	c firstly	d immediately
6	a open-air	b inside-out	c out-and-about	d over-the-top
7	a case	b that	c order	d so
8	a lots	b piece	c deal	d amount
9	a chilly	b utterly	c bitterly	d notoriously
10	a so	b if	c and	d but
11	a grumble	b mumble	c moan	d boast
12	a buttons	b zips	c sleeves	d clothes

4 Choose the correct alternative.

a I'd like to complain *of/for/about* the poor service.

b She's preparing *for/with/about* her driving test.

c Please speak *out/up/across* – I can't hear you.

d Stop grumbling *for/of/about* the work and just do it.

e I've tried to get *up/over/through* to her but she won't listen.

f He succeeded *of/in/with* organising the whole trip himself.

g The school insists *on/with/for* a strict uniform policy.

h She tried very hard to get her point *through/across/out*.

5 Complete the text with one word in each gap.

My pet snake

When I was young, I loved exotic animals and wanted a pet shark. Obviously, that wasn't possible so I got interested _____ (1) snakes. I bought Sidney at a pet shop ten years ago, when I was twelve years old. I was really proud _____ (2) my new pet and determined to be responsible _____ (3) looking after him. He was about 70 cm long, very good-natured, not at all poisonous and, in my opinion, _____ (4) best pet in the world. His diet consisted of a mouse once _____ (5) week – depending _____ (6) the time of year.

One day, a _____ (7) years ago, Sidney disappeared. After several weeks I lost all hope of finding him _____ (8) these snakes are famous _____ (9) travelling many kilometres a night. Eleven months later, while I was away on holiday, my dad heard that _____ (10) black-and-yellow snake _____ (11) mine had been seen in a neighbour's garden. We knew it could only be Sidney, and three days later my brother spotted him just sitting by the garden door. He had come back to _____ (12) exact spot he had disappeared from.

6 Use the word given at the end of some of the lines to form a word that fits in the gap *in the same line*.

In 1932, Ole Kirk Christiansen from Denmark set up a business *manufacturing* (0) ladders, ironing boards and wooden toys. The company was called Lego, _____ (1) 'play well' in Danish.	manufacture mean
For the next two decades, there was a lot of _____ (2) within the company with different ways of developing Lego. They used the latest _____ (3) ideas and materials which many scientists at that time were working on, especially the _____ (4) of different plastics. In 1947, the company moved forward hugely with the _____ (5) of the first plastic bricks that fitted together. This was the start of the 'Lego System of Play', _____ (6) in 1955.	experiment technology develop invent launch
Lego _____ (7) promised that its bricks would 'develop the child's critical judgement and ability to think for himself.' _____ (8) quickly, the company's sales were further increased with the _____ (9) of Lego kits in the mid-1960s, with which children could make all sorts of buildings, trucks, planes and ships.	confident expand introduce
Over fifty years on, these plastic bricks are still a firm _____ (10) with kids, parents and teachers.	favour

7 Complete the second sentence so that it has a similar meaning to the first sentence, using the word given. Do not change the word given. You must use between two and five words, including the word given.

I can't eat my soup at the moment because it isn't cool enough.
hot
My soup is *too hot to eat* at the moment.

a Why don't you get the optician to test your eyes?
have
Why don't you _____ by the optician?

b It was a really sunny day so we took a picnic to the park.
such
It was _____ we took a picnic to the park.

c We have booked the taxi to pick us up at 10 o'clock.
due
The taxi _____ us up at 10 o'clock.

d The weather was too cold for us to stay out for long.
so
The weather was _____ we couldn't stay out for long.

e He annoys me by talking to me as if I'm stupid.
down
He annoys me by _____ me.

f Eating out in restaurants all the time is too expensive for me.
enough
I haven't got _____ out in restaurants all the time.

g You might need to phone me so I'll give you my number.
case
I'll give you my number _____ phone me.

h The strong winds last night blew part of the roof off.
got
Part of the roof _____ in the strong winds last night.

8 Choose the correct alternative.

a I *'ve had/'ve been having* my pet rabbits for over two years.

b This is the first time I *ever went/'ve ever been* to a wedding.

c He's been studying science at university *for/since* about a year and a half.

d *I've just been/I just have been* to my cousin's wedding.

e *He's sent/been sending* over ten text messages in the last ten minutes.

f She's *bought already/already bought* a really lovely new skirt for the party.

g When was the last time you *cooked/have cooked* a meal for friends?

h Have you ever *read/been reading* someone's 'blog' on the Internet?

Getting started...

1 Work with a partner and discuss these questions:

- In your country, is it common for people to give money as a present?
- On what occasions is money usually given?

2 Look at these questions. Work with a partner and check the meaning of the verbs.

Who is talking about:

a ... inheriting money?
b ... investing money?
c ... owing someone money?
d ... donating money?
e ... raising money?
f ... squandering money?
g ... haggling over the price?

3 **R33** ▶ Listen and match the people to the questions in Exercise 2.

Exam hint

Exercise 1 is a practice task for Part 1 of the Speaking Paper.

 Speaking

1 Work with a partner and decide who is going to answer the Student A questions and who is going to answer the Student B questions. Student A needs to answer all four questions, taking no more than 3 minutes. Repeat the process for the Student B questions.

Student A
Let's talk about shopping
How often do you go shopping? (Why is that?)
Who do you usually go shopping with? (Why is that?)
What do you enjoy shopping for? (Tell me about that.)
What do you spend most of your money on? (Tell me about that.)

Student B
Let's talk about money
Do you prefer to get money or presents on special occasions? (Why is that?)
Do you get pocket money from your parents or guardians? (Tell me about that.)
Are you good at saving money? (Tell me about that.)
Is there anything that you are saving up for? (Tell me about that.)

Reading

1 Look at the picture and discuss these questions.

a What can you see in the picture on the right?

b What do you think is the aim of the website discussed in the article below?

2 Now read the article on *Freecycle* and answer the questions on page 154.

Exam hint

Exercise 2 is a practice task for Part 2 of the Reading and Writing Paper.

Freecycle

The temptation to buy, buy, buy is hard to resist. A new outfit, a gadget, an item of furniture – someone is buying one right now. Now, guilty shoppers who are keen to get rid of a no-longer-needed purchase have a radical new option – simply giving it away.

Second-hand technology is notoriously difficult to offload. So, I never thought that my sluggish, ageing computer would generate much interest when I put it up for offer online. I was wrong. A bidding war quickly begins for the five-year-old machine, which is 'past its best' and a printer, which only 'probably works'. On a conventional auction site, such as eBay, I doubt there would be any takers. But I'm advertising on its philanthropic cousin, *freecycle.org*. As the name suggests, everything advertised on *Freecycle* must be free – whether it's an old sofa, unwanted CDs or even a few hours' help in the garden. Anyone who is interested simply replies by e-mail: deal done.

Freecycle is one of a number of websites that aim to reduce the amount of rubbish sent to landfill sites by encouraging one of the most efficient forms of recycling – simply giving things to people who want them. The site is the creation of Deron Beal, an environmentalist from the US, who started it in mid-2003 as an automated e-mail list. Today, *Freecycle* has 1.2 million members and is a cross between an Internet auction house and a global chain of charity shops. Mr Beal says his chief aim is to cut waste and help the environment. He recently told reporters, 'I live in the Sonora Desert in Arizona. It's a place where the landscape is absolutely stunning. And right in the middle of this desert, you've got this hideous landfill, half of which is full of perfectly good reusable stuff.'

On the London site, interest in my decrepit computer is led by Tung, who wants to get his sixty-seven-year-old mum on the net. Then there's Kate, whose son wants it for his schoolwork. There's also John, who wants it for his daughter, a nurse on a low wage. Money isn't involved, but a kind of auction is taking place to see whose situation most deserves a free PC. My inclination is to give it to someone in need, but I have to make a difficult choice between several 'bidders'. Some people may suggest that dishonest individuals could make up heart-tugging stories in order to get freebies, or even to make a profit by selling them on. But my requests seem genuine. I eventually choose Clive Brown, a project worker, who wants it for a client with learning disabilities.

Freecycle embodies some of that old charitable Internet spirit by asking that before members accept a freebie, they put something up for offer. And it's by no means all junk; there are nearly-new toys, furniture, electrical goods, even bikes and cars. That such high-quality goods are on offer does not surprise Friends of the Earth campaigner Georgina Bloomfield. She says it reflects the fact people are buying more than ever, but don't want to simply throw things away when they replace them. 'People want to feel a bit better about consuming, and so they're happy to give things away,' she says. Clive Brown, who won my auction, agrees: 'I was given a bed and didn't need the brandnew mattress, so I put it on the site and it was gone in minutes. I was delighted someone wanted it.'

Freecycle has grown rapidly around the world in countries as diverse as Mexico, Nepal, France and Romania and it seems to be on the cusp of breaking through into the mainstream. Controversially, perhaps, it has recently signed up a corporate sponsor. Mr Beal says he needs the funds to help spread the ethos even further. In the end, it would be better if people simply stopped buying so much. But realistically, until people change their ways, green groups, guilty consumers and those with an eye for the ultimate bargain seem more than happy to make the most of *Freecycle*.

Questions

1–5

Choose **true**, **false** or **not given** for each statement.

	True	False	Not given
1 It is easy to ignore the urge to make a purchase.	☐	☐	☐
2 Unwanted items can now be found a new home.	☐	☐	☐
3 Electrical items are the most popular items on the site	☐	☐	☐
4 The author's computer is not as fast as it used to be.	☐	☐	☐
5 The highest bidder wins the item on *freecycle.org*.	☐	☐	☐

6–10

Complete these sentences using no more than **three words** or **a number**.

6 Websites such as *freecycle.org* help to decrease our use of _____.

7 The man who set up *freecycle.org* works as _____.

8 _____ are currently registered with the *freecycle.org* website.

9 Near to Mr Beal's home, in _____, there is a landfill site.

10 The author gives his PC to the person who _____ it.

11–15

Answer these questions using no more than **three words** or **a number**.

11 If you are chosen to receive an item on *freecycle.org*, what should you do before taking it?

....

12 What is surprising about the condition of the items on offer?

....

13 What do people want to feel more comfortable about by passing goods on?

....

14 What did Clive Brown offer on the website?

....

15 Why does Mr Beal need sponsorship money?

....

3 Work with a partner and discuss these questions:

● What are the three main reasons for *Freecycle's* success?

● Does *Freecycle's* success surprise you? Why/Why not?

● How would you feel about using this website? Why?

Grammar: relative clauses

1 Read the grammar rules about relative clauses in the Grammar reference on page 242. Look at the sentences i–vi and answer questions a–c.

i   Clive Brown, who won my auction, agrees.

ii One of the bidders is Kate, whose son wants the computer for his schoolwork.

iii It's a place where the landscape is absolutely stunning.

Grammar hint

which versus that

In which of these sentences could you not replace *which* by *that*? Why?

1 *The computer, which I bought, was a bargain.*

2 *The computer which I bought was a bargain.*

Grammar reference: see page 242

iv *Freecycle* is a website which aims to reduce the amount of rubbish in landfill sites.

v The reason why people like *Freecycle* is it makes them feel better about consuming so much.

vi The person to whom I made the complaint was extremely unhelpful.

a Which of the sentences contain defining relative clauses and which non-defining relative clauses?

b In which sentence could you leave out the relative pronoun? Why?

c Which sentence sounds quite formal? How could you make it more informal?

2 There are seven mistakes with relative clauses in this text. Find the mistakes and correct them.

eBay

eBay is a hugely successful company, which it was founded in 1995. The person what founded eBay was a man called Pierre Omidyar. At first, it was a place which people could sell goods, particularly collectable items. Then in 1998, Pierre brought in Meg Whitman who job was to sustain eBay's success by bringing in new managers. The new vision that she created it was an image of connecting people not of selling things. The items for sale are arranged by topics, that are then sub-divided into smaller categories. People who they want to sell things on eBay pay a small fee, but it is free to buy.

3 Choose the correct relative pronoun for each of these sentences.

a One thing *what/that* makes me angry is …

b One place *which/where* I'd love to go is …

c One charity *which/what* I would like to donate to is …

d One person *who/whose* lifestyle I'd like to have is …

e One reason *what/why* I'd like to have more money is …

4 Complete each sentence to make it true for you. Work with a partner and compare your sentences.

Vocabulary: money

1 Work with a partner. Check that you understand the meaning of the verb phrases in *italics* in these sentences. Then discuss the questions.

● Have you ever *bid for something in an auction* (online or traditional)? If so, what was it? If not, would you consider doing so?

● When was the last time you *got a bargain*? Do you know anyone who is good at finding bargains?

● What's the difference between: *pay a fee, pay a fare* and *pay a fine*? What do you think of the cost of bus and train fares in your country/another country you know?

2 Work in two groups, A and B. Look at the words in your box and check their meaning and pronunciation. Use a dictionary if necessary.

A

> get a freebie   pay a deposit   pay the balance
> get a receipt   get a refund   pay rent

B

> get a discount   get paid overtime   be in debt
> pay tax   take out insurance   leave a tip

3 Now work with a partner (one of you will be from group A and one from group B). Tell each other the meaning and pronunciation of the words in your box.

4 Now choose the correct alternatives in each of these sentences.

a   You can often save money by buying a lot of things at the same time and getting a *discount/freebie*.

b   I'm working long hours at the moment so that I get paid quite a lot of *tip/overtime* – I'm saving up for my holiday.

c   If you decide not to go ahead with the booking, you will lose the £100 *balance/deposit* you've already paid.

d   I'm sorry, but we can only give you your money back if you keep the *receipt/refund* as proof of purchase.

e   You are advised to take out *tax/insurance* for all members of the family before you travel.

f   I would never borrow from friends because I never want to be in *rent/debt*.

 Writing

1 Work with a partner and discuss these questions:

● What do you think are some of the most common reasons for complaining to a department store or a shopping website?

● Have you ever complained about something you bought (either in a shop or through a website)? What weren't you happy about? What did you do? What was the response? Were you satisfied in the end?

2 Read the advert and task and answer the question.

DISCOUNT DIGITAL

We are offering 1,000s of digital cameras at bargain prices. Hurry to take advantage of this amazing offer!

We have all the major brands, including Canon, Sony, Nikon, Fuji, Olympus, Samsung and many more.

All the cameras are this year's models with all the latest, up-to-date features. They are all at discount prices, with up to 50% off on some models.

Every camera comes with all the necessary accessories (e.g. battery pack, battery charger, AV cable, AC cable, 16MB memory card, USB cable, user guide).

Guaranteed low prices if you order before 31st May. Hurry – don't miss the deadline! This is an offer you can't afford to miss.

Free post and packing on orders over £100. Guaranteed delivery within 7 working days of placing your order.

You can shop online at www.discountdigital.com or speak to one of our sales staff on 08457 464533. Our friendly customer services team are available from 8.00 a.m. to 6.30 p.m. every day to answer your queries and take your orders.

You bought a camera from the company in the advert and you were disappointed with both the product and the service you received.

Read the advert carefully and then write an e-mail to the company.

In your e-mail you should:
- make **two** complaints about your camera
- make **two** complaints about the service you received
- say what you want the company to do.

Write your e-mail using between 100 and 150 words.

Which two of the following do you need to do in your e-mail?

a suggest something

b complain about something

c request something

d give information about something

3 Which order should these paragraphs go in your e-mail?

a complaining about the two problems with the product

b saying what you want the company to do

c making two further complaints about the service

d stating the reason for your e-mail

4 Look at the phrases in list a for the opening paragraph of your e-mail and those in list b for the closing paragraph. Decide which of the phrases are appropriate and which are not. Why?

a i   I am writing to complain about ...

ii I want to say that I'm not happy about ...

iii I am writing to express my dissatisfaction with ...

iv This letter is to say how cross I am about ...

v I would like to request that ...

b vi I must insist that you refund my money immediately.

vii Please can you assure me that you will replace the ... as soon as possible.

viii I think you should give me my money back now.

ix I really think you should listen to me and give me another ...

x I would be grateful if you would give me a refund.

5 Look at these phrases for paragraphs 2 and 3 of your e-mail. Complete each one in a way which you could use.

a I was very disappointed by ...

b I would like to point out that ...

c The advertisement stated that ..., but in fact ...

d I was assured that ..., whereas actually ...

e When I received the product, to my surprise ...

f Even more worrying is the fact that ...

6 Write your e-mail using the paragraph plan in Exercise 3 and at least three of the phrases in Exercises 4 and 5 to help you.

7 Read your e-mail and check these things.

a Have you included all the bullet points from the task?

b Have you made a suggestion at the end of your e-mail?

c Have you started and finished your e-mail in an appropriate way?

d Have you written the correct number of words?

Vocabulary: numbers

1 Look again at the advert in Exercise 2 on page 157. How many numbers and dates can you find? How do you say them?

2 **R34** ▶ Listen and check your answers.

3 Match each question a–l with the correct number i–xii.

a What's your date of birth?

b What time did you get up today?

c How much did your bag cost?

d What's your phone number?

e What's the speed limit in this country?

f How much do you weigh?

g What's another way of writing 0.5?

Exam hint

Exercise 6 is a practice task for Part 5 of the Reading and Writing Paper.

Language hint

commas and full stops in numbers

How do you write each of these numbers in figures? Think carefully about the correct position of the commas and full stops.

1 Two point five

2 Six pounds twenty-five

3 One thousand five hundred

4 Five million three hundred thousand

5 Two thousand, three hundred and forty-nine pounds fifty pence

Repeat saying these numbers with a partner.

h What's another way of writing $\frac{1}{4}$?

i How far is your home from here?

j What's the interest rate at the moment?

k How much water do you drink a day?

l What's the temperature today?

i 3.2%

ii 65 kg

iii 07739 456997

iv 27°C

v 2 litres

vi 120 kph

vii 17 km

viii $\frac{1}{2}$

ix 20.05.83

x 0.25

xi £5.50

xii 7.15 a.m.

4 R35 ▶ Listen and check your answers.

5 Take turns asking and answering each question in Exercise 3 with another student. Make sure you say the numbers correctly.

6 Write down the following numbers. Make sure you know how to write and say them in English.

● An important date

● A four-digit number which is important to you

● An important phone number

7 Work with a partner and say why each number is important to you.

🔊)) **Listening**

1 Work with a partner and discuss these questions:

● The people in the pictures have decided, for different reasons, not to give their teenage children and grown-up children a lot of their money. Can you think of two reasons why this might be?

● How would you feel if they were your parents?

Exam hint

Exercise 2 is a practice task for Part 3 of the Listening Paper.

2 R36 ▶ Listen to the radio programme and answer the questions.

Questions

1–5

Complete these notes using no more than **three words** or **a number**.

Cash in Hand

● The programme is about a growing trend.

● It involves parents who are both ordinary people and _____ (1).

● Looks at their reasons for not wanting to give their children money

● Both groups have _____ (2) reasons for their decision.

Jonathan Hynde

● Gives enough money to help his children on their way

● Does not believe in children receiving money via _____ (3)

● Thinks that this has a negative effect on them

● Children need to _____ (4) and earn their own money.

● If not, lose their ambition and their way

● He came from a normal family and worked to better himself.

● Now has a better grasp on the _____ (5) and wants his children to have the same

6–10

Choose **a**, **b** or **c**.

6 More older people are 'skiing' which means they are
   a going on expensive winter holidays.
   b saving money for their offspring.
   c not prioritising leaving an inheritance.

7 The older generation today is
   a more likely to be well and mobile.
   b happy to spend their time at home.
   c not wanting to spend their savings.

8 Sarah Hewitt and her husband believe that
   a the decision they have made is not the right one.
   b they are still responsible for their grown-up children.
   c now is their time to do what they want to do.

9 Where did Sarah and her husband go last year?
   a Australia
   b New Zealand
   c Mexico

10 Sarah's son
   a thinks his parents are spending his money.
   b did not expect to be given any inheritance.
   c will have to be more careful with his finances.

3 R36 ▶ Listen again and check your answers.

Grammar: if structures

1 Complete the sentences with the correct form of *have*, *ask* or *give*.

   a If you _____ your children a lot of money, you ruin their chances of success.

   b If I _____ my parents for some money, I'm sure they'll give it to me.

   c If I _____ more money, I'd go on a skiing holiday this year.

2 Look at these pairs of sentences. In what situations would you choose to say each one?

   a i If your parents give you £500, what will you spend it on?

       ii If your parents gave you £500, what would you spend it on?

   b i What will you do if you have some free time this weekend?

       ii What would you do if you had some free time this weekend?

3 For each set of prompts, decide which type of *if* structure is best and then write the question.

   a What / you do / if you / forget / pay / something in a shop?

   b you lend / a large amount of money / a friend / if they / ask / you?

   c If you / can choose / to be / famous person / for a day / who / you choose to be?

   d If you / hear / fire alarm / during this lesson / what / you do?

   e What / you change / if you / be elected / leader of your country?

4 Work with a partner and ask each other five questions from Exercises 2 and 3.

5 Answer the questions about each of these examples.

   a *I **would have paid** by debit card if I **had** one.*

      Did I pay by debit card? Why/Why not?

   b *If I'd taken my debit card, I **would have paid** with that.*

      Did I pay by debit card? Why/Why not?

   c *If I'd brought my debit card with me, I'd pay with that now.*

      Am I going to pay by debit card now? Why/Why not?

6 Identify the verb forms in **bold** in Exercise 5.

7 There are mistakes in eight of these sentences. Find the mistakes and correct them.

   a She wouldn't have been able to buy her house if she didn't inherit so much money.

   b If I am better at maths, I would have trained to be an accountant.

   c You would have no problem exchanging the goods if you would kept the receipt.

   d If I hadn't left my old job, I'd be a lot wealthier now.

   e If I lived by the sea, I would buy a yacht a long time ago.

   f If I had had children, I would have gave them as much financial support as they wanted.

   g If I known you could donate money online, I would have done it like that.

   h You would passed many more exams if you hadn't messed around with your friends at school so much when you were younger.

   i I would have enough money to buy a new car if I hadn't been on that expensive holiday last year.

   j If I wouldn't have a family to support, I'd have taken last year off and travelled round the world.

Grammar hint

punctuation in if structures

We can use *if* structures to talk about the present and future (e.g. possibilities, hypothetical situations and general truths). We can also use if structures to talk hypothetically about the past.

Is the punctuation correct in these sentences?
1 *If I had more money, I'd travel more.*
2 *I'd travel more if I had more money.*

Grammar reference: see page 242

8 Choose the correct linking word or phrase in each of these sentences.

   a I'll lend you £20 *unless/provided that* you pay me back by Friday.

   b You can borrow some money *as long as/even if* you don't ask me every week.

   c *As long as/Unless* you pay me back by Friday, this is the last time I'll lend you any money.

   d *Even if/Provided that* you promise to pay me back by Friday, I'm afraid I'm not lending you any money.

9 Look at the phrases in *italics* in Exercise 8 and answer these questions.

   a Which two have a similar meaning?

   b Which one means '*if not*'?

   c Which one is used to emphasise the idea in the *if* clause?

10 Complete these sentences.

   If I won the jackpot on the lottery, I'd give up work immediately.

   a I'd carry on studying even if …

   b It doesn't matter how much money someone has as long as …

   c If I had had the chance, …

   d Unless people plan their studies properly, …

   e Provided that parents give children the right advice, …

   f Generally, people's salaries tend to increase over time as long as …

   g I don't think I'd give money to people begging in the street even if …

   h If I could do the last five years again, …

   i I don't mind how much I earn provided that …

   j Unless people stop throwing away so much, …

11 Work with a partner and share your sentences from Exercise 10.

 Speaking

1 Work with a partner and each choose one of the topics below. Prepare to time your partner – give them 1 minute to prepare and then ask them to start speaking. Tell them to stop speaking after 2 minutes. Did your partner answer the question on the card?

Exam hint

Exercise 1 is a practice task for Part 2 of the Speaking Paper.

> **Student A**
> You are going to talk about **money matters**. You can use some or all of the ideas listed below in your talk but <u>you must answer this question</u>:
>
> **How do you choose which shops to spend your money in?**
> You must talk for 1 to 2 minutes. You have 1 minute to think and make notes before your talk begins.
>
> Here are some ideas to help you:
> • Price
> • Items
> • Brands
> • Location

Student B

You are going to talk about **money matters**. You can use some or all of the ideas listed below in your talk but you must answer this question:

How do young people benefit from having a part-time job?

You must talk for 1 to 2 minutes. You have 1 minute to think and make notes before your talk begins.

Here are some ideas to help you:
- Money
- Confidence
- Experience
- Independence

2 Work with a partner and take it in turns to ask and answer the following questions. Remember to give as much information as possible and try to keep talking for at least 5 minutes.

Exam hint

Exercise 2 is a practice task for Part 3 of the Speaking Paper.

Part 3

We have been talking about **money matters** and I would like to ask you some more questions on this topic.

- How do you feel about lending people money? (Tell me about that.)
- How do you feel about borrowing money? (Tell me about that.)
- Is it important to have your own bank account and savings? (Why is that?)

- Do you ever shop on the Internet? (Tell me about that.)
- What are the advantages of shopping on the Internet? (Tell me about that?)
- What are the disadvantages of shopping on the Internet? (Tell me about that?)

- Do you think that people throw things away/replace things too quickly? (Why is that?)
- Why do you think that we are becoming more of a 'throw away' society? (Tell me about that.)
- What should people do with items that they no longer want or need? (Why is that?)

Summarising

1 You are doing a project for your teacher on recycling schemes. Read the article and write your summary.

In your summary you should:

● say what the aim of *Freecycle* is

● say how *Freecycle* works

● say how *Freecycle* has developed since 2003.

Write your summary using between 100 and 150 words.

Freecycle

Freecycle is one of a number of websites that aim to reduce the amount of rubbish sent to landfill sites by encouraging one of the most efficient forms of recycling – simply giving things to people who want them. As the name suggests, everything advertised on *Freecycle* must be free – whether it's an old sofa, unwanted CDs or even a few hours' help in the garden. Anyone who is interested simply replies by e-mail: deal done.

The site is the creation of Deron Beal, an environmentalist from the US who started it in mid-2003 as an automated e-mail list. Today *Freecycle* has 1.2 million members and is a cross between an Internet auction house and a global chain of charity shops. Mr Beal says his chief aim is to cut waste and help the environment. He recently told reporters, 'I live in the Sonora Desert in Arizona. It's a place where the landscape is absolutely stunning. And right in the middle of this desert, you've got this hideous landfill, half of which is full of perfectly good reusable stuff.'

On the London site, interest in a decrepit computer is led by Tung, who wants to get his sixty-seven-year-old mum on the net. Then there's Kate, whose son wants it for his schoolwork. There's also John, who wants it for his daughter, a nurse on a low wage. Money isn't involved but a kind of auction is taking place to see whose situation most deserves a free PC. The person giving it away has to make a difficult choice between several 'bidders'. Some people may suggest that dishonest individuals could make up heart-tugging stories in order to get freebies, or even to make a profit by selling them on.

Freecycle embodies some of that old charitable Internet spirit by asking that before members accept a freebie, they put something up for offer. And it's by no means all junk; there are nearly new toys, furniture, electrical goods, even bikes and cars. That such high-quality goods are on offer does not surprise Friends of the Earth campaigner Georgina Bloomfield. She says it reflects the fact that people are buying more than ever, but don't want to simply throw things away when they replace them. 'People want to feel a bit better about consuming, and so they're happy to give things away,' she says.

Freecycle has grown rapidly around the world in countries as diverse as Mexico, Nepal, France and Romania and it seems to be on the cusp of breaking through into the mainstream. Controversially, perhaps, it has recently signed up a corporate sponsor. Mr Beal says he needs the funds to help spread the ethos even further. In the end it would be better if people simply stopped buying so much. But realistically, until people change their ways, green groups, guilty consumers and those with an eye for the ultimate bargain seem more than happy to make the most of *Freecycle*.

Grammar

1 Complete the text with *who*, *whose*, *which*, *that* or *where*.

A Picasso portrait of Dora Maar has been sold for $95.2m, _____ (1) is the second highest amount ever paid for a painting at auction. The picture, _____ (2) is entitled *Dora Maar with Cat,* was sold at Sotheby's in New York in May 2006. Sotheby's said Dora's beauty and the gorgeous colours made it worth so much. 'It's the fact that the model is Dora, _____ (3) was one of Picasso's most famous subjects, and the perfection of the actual painting _____ (4) makes it so valuable,' said David Norman from Sotheby's. The most expensive picture ever sold is another Picasso, *Boy with a Pipe,* _____ (5) fetched a record $104m in 2004.

But who are the art lovers _____ (6) can afford to bid such astronomical sums? And what do they do with their multimillion-dollar purchases? Sotheby's keeps the identity of the buyers secret. But Godfrey Barker, of *Art and Auction* magazine, guesses at a likely buyer – Guido Barilla, _____ (7) pasta business Barilla has made him a billionaire. And he suspects that the Picassos will be kept in a bank vault in Switzerland, 'the one country in the world _____ (8) these things can be hidden very well'.

2 Combine these pairs of sentences to make one sentence, using a relative clause.

a   My brother's got a new friend. He works in a garage.
b   You told me about a shop. I went to the shop, but I couldn't find anything I liked.
c   I met that man in the shop last week. He's wearing a green shirt.
d   Every year we go on holiday to Cornwall. I think it is one of the most beautiful places in Britain.
e   I met Nelson Mandela. I'll never forget that time.
f   My next-door neighbour is the best neighbour I've ever had. Her house is up for sale.
g   Barcelona is a city. I've always wanted to visit it.

3 Complete each of these *if* structures with the correct form of the verbs in the box.

| catch   look after   be able to   (not) speak   (not) like   know   want   go   rain   find |

a   That car will last for years provided you _____ it properly.
b   If he _____ working with numbers, he shouldn't have trained to be an accountant.
c   If you _____ to improve your spoken English, you have to practise regularly.
d   If I hadn't had such a late night, I _____ concentrate better today.
e   I can usually understand what people say in English as long as they _____ too fast.
f   If I _____ you needed help, I'd have come round earlier.
g   If you spoke a bit more slowly, I _____ it a lot easier to understand you.
h   If I wasn't so busy all the time, I _____ to last week's conference.
i   We might have a picnic later unless it _____ .
j   If I _____ the earlier train, I'd be there already.

Vocabulary

4 Complete the sentences with a word from the box. Three of the words cannot be used.

| deposit   debt   fine   fare   fees   freebies   refund   receipt   tip   insurance   overtime   balance   bargain |

a   It's normal to pay a 10% _____ to make a booking for a holiday.
b   You should take out _____ on all your valuable possessions in case they get stolen.
c   I've never borrowed any money in my life. I'd hate to be in _____ .
d   I decided not to leave a _____ because the service was so slow and the waiter was very rude.
e   You'll get a complete _____ as long as you bring it back within twenty-eight days.
f   I should have used a better lawyer but I couldn't afford the _____ .
g   I got a really good DVD player online for a very low price. I think I got a real _____ .
h   They're giving away ten CDs as _____ when you buy one of their latest CD players.
i   I'm so annoyed. I had to pay a £50 _____ for parking on a yellow line.
j   In my new job, you can work at the weekends if you want and get paid _____ .

Paper 1: Reading and Writing

 Part 6: Writing (20 marks)

You will read one or two short texts of about 500 words in total and then produce a summary of the text(s) of between 100 and 150 words. Your summary will be for a specific purpose and reader, e.g. for students in your class, for the school magazine, for your teacher, and will be semi-formal in style.

The stimulus text will be accessible and on a topic of general interest, e.g. birds, coffee, a city, frozen food. The information may be presented in a variety of ways, including bullet points or diagrams. You will be given clear instructions on the areas you must cover in your summary.

Let's look at an example in the Edexcel IGCSE ESL Paper 1 in November 2008:

Read this information from your local council's recycling website and write a short summary for your school magazine using this information. In your summary you should include the following:

- *two reasons why recycling is important*
- *two things students can do at school*
- *two things students can do at home.*

You should write between 100 and 150 words.

You are being asked then to identify and condense the important information within a text. You have to pick out the facts that represent the main message of the text. The exact number of bullet points will vary, but there are generally two or three.

The main purpose of this summary task is not to test your reading ability, but rather your writing ability, and, therefore, you should use your own words and phrases as far as possible, rather than lifting great chunks or sentences from the stimulus text. Of course, there may well be some key words in the text that you will have to use in your summary simply because there is no synonym or paraphrase available, e.g. *recycling*.

Since you will be condensing a longer stimulus text – your summary will be just under one third the length of the original text – your language needs to be concise. However, your sentences should be logically linked so that you end up with a complete piece of writing, which is well organised, rather than just a sequence of points. It is helpful to address each bullet point in a separate paragraph.

The summary will be marked according to the same four criteria as the writing tasks in Parts 4 and 5. These are:

- **Communicative quality:** how successfully and relevantly have you completed the task? Have you addressed all the bullet points within the word count? Have you used the appropriate tone and register for the audience?

- **Lexical accuracy and range:** have you used a good range of vocabulary and how appropriate is it for the target reader? Have you used this vocabulary accurately?

- **Grammatical accuracy and range:** how wide is the range of grammatical structures you have used? To what extent have you used these structures effectively and accurately?

- **Effective organisation:** have you organised the summary effectively and linked the sentences logically? Have you used paragraphs? Have you used cohesive devices effectively to convey your message? Will the reader easily understand and follow what you have written?

Remember, you must address all the bullet points to be able to access the full range of marks.

Getting started...

1 Work with a partner and look at the pictures. Where is each picture taken? What is happening in each picture?

2 Complete the sentences using the words in the box. Use each word only once. Use a dictionary if necessary.

> interview peers residence independent
> mature university vocational college

a Sarah cannot decide whether to stay on at school to do her A levels or go to C_____ to do them.

b Marco has just finished his application forms for u_____; he wants to study Dentistry.

c Lily has been offered accommodation in halls of r_____, but she wants to rent a house with her friends instead.

d Jake was looking forward to leaving school and going to college, as he would get the chance to be more ι_____.

1

2

3

4

e Mary has been offered a place at college to study hairdressing; she is very excited about doing a __J_____ qualification.

f John's new course at college is very popular with M_____ students who are looking to get a qualification after already doing the job for a number of years.

g Doing projects and group work with your P_____ is a very rewarding and interesting learning experience.

h Amy has a formal ι_____ next week for a job; she is very nervous as she is expecting some difficult questions.

🗣 Speaking

1 Work with a partner and decide who is going to answer the Student A questions and who is going to answer the Student B questions. Student A needs to answer all four questions, taking no more than 3 minutes. Repeat the process for the Student B questions.

Student A
Let's talk about school
How do you get to school in the morning? (Tell me about that.)
What time do you usually arrive at school? (Why is that?)
What do you usually do in your breaks (e.g. *morning/afternoon/lunch*)? (Tell me about that.)
Do you stay after school to take part in any activities? (Tell me about that.)

Student B
Let's talk about exams
How do you feel about taking exams? (Tell me about that.)
How long before your exams do you start revising? (Why is that?)
How do you revise for exams? (Tell me about that.)
How do you relax when all your exams are finished? (Tell me about that.)

Exam hint

Exercise 1 is a practice task for Part 1 of the Speaking Paper.

Reading

1 Work with a partner and discuss these questions:

- What is an apprenticeship?

- What does it mean if you have a clean police record?

- What is a paper qualification?

2 Read the list of courses below and match each of the statements that follow to one of the courses. You must choose answers based on the information given. You will also need to use some courses more than once.

Exam hint

Exercise 2 is a practice task for Part 1 of the Reading and Writing Paper.

Courses

A **English Language and Literature A Level**

<u>Entry Requirements:</u>

A minimum of five Cs or above at GCSE. An A or B grade in at least one of your English subjects.

<u>Who is this course for?</u>

Anyone who wants to explore the way in which language is used both in everyday conversations and, more importantly, in all types of literary texts. Also, anyone who is interested in developing their creative writing.

B **Law A Level**

<u>Entry Requirements:</u>

Suitability for this course is determined by interview. Students will have at least five GCSEs in the A–C range. No previous knowledge of the subject is necessary.

<u>Who is this course for?</u>

Suitable for students aged over 18 who wish to study the Law A Level in one year. Useful for reading law at university and going on to a career in law.

C **Biology A Level**

<u>Entry Requirements:</u>

Five GCSE subjects at grade B or above, including science. Applicants without a Science GCSE may be considered and, if accepted, will need to do more background study to cover some topics.

<u>Who is this course for?</u>

Those who are interested in the living planet and the role that human beings play in it. The course will give you a better understanding of biological issues and prepare you for the study of biology at a higher level.

D **Hairdressing Level 3 Apprenticeship**

<u>Entry Requirements:</u>

This course is for anyone between the ages of 16 and 24 working within the hairdressing industry. You must be working full-time and have successfully completed a Level 2 Hairdressing Apprenticeship.

<u>Who is this course for?</u>

This course is for those who want to build on their Level 2 qualification and further improve on their skills and knowledge.

E **Children's Care, Learning and Development Diploma**

<u>Entry requirements:</u>

Applicants need five GCSEs at grade D or above. Mature students with fewer GCSEs (at least two) but with appropriate experience are encouraged to apply. All applicants need to have a clean police record.

<u>Who is this course for?</u>

Suitable for students wanting a broad introduction to early years and childhood education. This course can lead into employment or further studies in childcare.

F **Customer Service Certificate**

<u>Entry requirements:</u>

There are no formal entry requirements; however, you will need to be in a workplace for at least one day per week to enable you to develop your skills.

<u>Who is this course for?</u>

For those people who work with a range of customers. The course will build upon your existing knowledge and improve your competence in various customer-related situations.

G **French A Level**

<u>Entry requirements:</u>

Suitability for this course is determined by attending a group assessment day. Students should have successfully completed the GCSE Level in this subject.

<u>Who is this course for?</u>

This course will suit you if you want to mainly improve your oral communication skills in French. You must be willing to work outside of the timetabled classes for between three and five hours a week.

	Statements	A	B	C	D	E	F	G
1	Paper qualifications are not required to apply for this course.							
2	You cannot apply for this course if you are aged 25 or over.							
3	You do not have to know anything about this subject to apply for the course.							
4	For this course you need time for self study.							
5	This course will help you deal more effectively with people in your job.							
6	You and your peers will be assessed together for the course.							
7	Applicants for this course should not have been in trouble with the law.							
8	Qualifications and practical knowledge are considered for entry onto this course.							
9	You may have to do extra work for this course depending on your qualifications.							
10	Study of the written word is the main focus of this course.							

(Header spanning A–G columns: **Answers**)

◁))) Listening

1 Work with a partner and discuss these questions:

- Have you ever had a formal interview, e.g. for a course or a job?

- If yes, how did you feel?

- If no, how do you think you would feel?

- What kinds of questions do you think you would be asked in an interview for a course or a job?

2 R37 ▶ Listen to an extract from a radio programme about interviews and answer the questions.

Exam hint

Exercise 2 is a practice task for Part 2 of the Listening Paper.

Questions

1–5

Choose **a, b** or **c**.

1   In the job market today,

   a   there is a decreasing number of graduates.

   b   applying for jobs has become more difficult.

   c   interviews are becoming more challenging.

2   To find the best candidate for a job

   a   more interviews are now being conducted.

   b   a range of interview approaches is being used.

   c   companies are comparing recruitment methods.

3   In his interview, Peter Webley had to

   a   stand on the table.

   b   tell a funny story.

   c   make an animal noise.

4   Strange interview questions are used to

   a   get candidates to move around the room.

   b   see how long it takes a person to answer.

   c   check how easily a person gets embarrassed.

5   During an interview, applicants should

   a   say how good their writing skills are.

   b   talk about their hobbies and interests.

   c   focus on their academic qualifications.

6–10

Complete the notes using no more than **three words** or **a number**.

Examples of strange interviewee behaviour

- One man took out his camera and, using the (6) _____, took a picture of the interviewer. His reason was that he collected pictures of people who interviewed him.

- One woman entered the interview room wearing (7) _____. She said it wasn't a problem as she could still take part in the interview.

- One man interrupted the interview and (8) _____ after being asked a difficult question. He asked for advice on how to answer the question.

- A woman arrived wearing (9) _____. She told the interviewer that the other one had been taken while she was (10) _____ travelling to the interview.

---

3 R37 ▶ Listen again and check your answers.

Grammar: reported speech

1 Change each of the comments made by the host of the radio programme from direct speech into reported speech, making any changes you need.

Example

The host said that getting the right people for the job was crucial for all companies, large and small.

a 'Getting the right people for the job is crucial for all companies, large and small.'

b 'While the average job interview probably retains the same format it did two decades ago, there are some strange stories.'

c 'It seems that polished shoes and a bag full of qualifications are just not enough.'

d 'People are more aware of what opportunities are available.'

e 'One of the problems is that the universities are turning out more and more graduates.'

f 'Candidates at interview are increasingly being asked to go the extra mile to prove they are a cut above the rest.'

 Speaking

1 Work with a partner each choose one of the topics below. Prepare to time your partner – give them 1 minute to prepare and then ask them to start speaking. Tell them to stop speaking after 2 minutes. Did your partner answer the question on the card?

Grammar hint

Which one of these sentences is grammatically incorrect? Why?

1 Did you hear about Teri? Jon told me she lives in Lima now.

2 Jo, what are you doing here? Sarah said you are on holiday in Spain.

Grammar reference: see page 244

Student A

You are going to talk about **the role of teachers**. You can use some or all of the ideas listed below in your talk but <u>you must answer this question</u>:

What makes a good teacher?
You must talk for 1 to 2 minutes. You have 1 minute to think and make notes before your talk begins.

Here are some ideas to help you:
- Subject knowledge
- Classroom discipline
- Classroom atmosphere
- Learning activities

Student B

You are going to talk about **choosing subjects to study**. You can use some or all of the ideas listed below in your talk but <u>you must answer this question</u>:

How should you choose which subject(s) to study at college?
You must talk for 1 to 2 minutes. You have 1 minute to think and make notes before your talk begins.

Here are some ideas to help you:
- Ability
- Enjoyment
- Career prospects
- Financial rewards

2 Work with a partner and take it in turns to ask and answer the questions. Remember to give as much information as possible and try to keep talking for at least 5 minutes.

Part 3

We have been talking about **teachers and studying** and I would like to ask you some more questions on this topic.

- Do you think that there are too many exams in secondary school? (Why is that?)
- Do you think that exams are fair? (Why is that?)
- What are the advantages of continual assessment for students? (Tell me about that.)

- In what ways have teaching methods changed over the last twenty years? (Tell me about that.)
- Do you think that these changes make school more enjoyable? (Tell me about that?)
- Do you think that school discipline is now more of a problem? (Why is that?)

- Which subjects at school do you think are the most important? (Why is that?)
- Why do you think less emphasis is placed on subjects such as music and drama? (Tell me about that.)
- What would it mean for students if all subjects were given equal emphasis at school? (Tell me about that.)

Vocabulary: phrasal verbs (education)

1 Read the e-mail from Sally telling her friend about what happened when she handed her first assignment in to her tutor. Use a dictionary to check any words you are not sure of.

Hi John,

How are you getting on at college? It's so different from school, isn't it?

I recently had to *hand in* a 2,000 word essay for my psychology course and spent ages *writing* it *up*. I thought it was a really good piece of work until I got it back. Parts of my introduction had been *crossed out* and there were comments on some of the other pages about parts that the tutor felt that I should *leave out*. The only problem was I couldn't *make out* everything that the tutor had written because his handwriting is so bad.

Anyway, I met with him yesterday and we *looked over* the assignment together. It's all much clearer now and not as bad as I first thought. He has advised that I *put in* some more theories, so after sending you this e-mail, I'm going to *look up* some more information that I might be able to use.

I don't know about you, but I'm not finding it easy to *figure out* exactly what tutors expect from you when they set a piece of work. I also still need to *brush up on* how to write a bibliography. I'm not too worried though, as all the staff and other students are really helpful and they don't mind if you ask them questions.

On a happier note, I have made some really good friends and I think I'm going to enjoy college life. Write back and let me know how you're doing. Hope everything is going okay for you.

Love

Sally

2 Match the phrasal verbs in *italics* in the e-mail to the definitions.

a to include

b see/hear something well enough to understand what it means

c submit homework or an assignment

d omit/to not include

e to find information in a book, on a computer

f to write something from notes made earlier

g review/study thoroughly for a short time

h to draw a line through something because it is wrong/unnecessary

i to check or review

j to understand something after thinking about it

3 Complete the sentences with the correct forms of the phrasal verbs in Exercise 2.

a John can't _____ the submission date, now that he has spilt coffee on the assignment brief; it is either the 3rd or the 8th of next month.

b Jane is still trying to _____ how to do her mathematics homework.

c Mary had 5% taken off her final mark because she _____ her essay a week late.

d I _____ the answer yesterday; I eventually found it by using Google.

e When you are writing a formal letter, remember not to _____ your address in the top right hand corner.

f Toby was really annoyed; it took him three hours to _____ his assignment and then the computer crashed.

g Please can you _____ the last three words of the second paragraph on your handout as they should not be there.

h Sue has _____ your plan for the business studies project that you have to do and she thinks it will work really well.

i Sarah must _____ her spoken French; she is taking her oral exam in two weeks.

j Mark wants to _____ some of his own ideas and he's sure the others in the group will have comments too.

✎ Writing

1 A friend is moving to your school next term and has e-mailed asking you what the school is like. Write an e-mail back and tell your friend about your school.

In your e-mail, you should:

● give **two** details about the teachers

● give **two** details about the library

● say why your friend will like the school.

Write your e-mail using between 100 and 150 words.

Grammar hint

Phrasal verbs

All the phrasal verbs used in the sentences except for *brush up on* are separable.

When a phrasal verb is separable, it means it can be used in two ways. Have a look at this example:

I would like to *hand in* my assignment please.

OR

I would like to *hand* my assignment *in* please.

Remember that not all phrasal verbs are separable, so check in a dictionary before using them.

Exam hint

Exercise 1 is a practice task for Part 5 of the Reading and Writing Paper.

Grammar hint

suggest

Which of these patterns following *suggest* is not possible?

She suggested	going to that they go to that they should go to that they went to them to go to	the presentation that evening.

Grammar: reporting verbs

1 Complete the sentences below with any possible reporting verbs from the box.

> said   recommended   explained
> suggested   told   reminded

  a He _____ (that) we should use more paragraphs.

  b He _____ us (that) we should use more paragraphs.

  c He _____ using more paragraphs.

2 Check that you understand the meaning of the words in the box. Then use them to complete sentences a–e.

> congratulated   promised   discouraged   insisted   advised

  a She _____ on writing the whole presentation.

  b She _____ me to write the whole presentation.

  c She _____ me on writing the whole presentation.

  d She _____ to write the whole presentation.

  e She _____ me from writing the whole presentation.

3 Match these verbs to the verbs in Exercise 2 which have similar grammatical patterns.

> remind   refuse   encourage   offer   promise   threaten

4 Complete the second sentence so that it has a similar meaning to the first sentence, using the word given. You can use between two and five words including the word given.

Example

'Well done on finding out who wrote the book!'

on

He congratulated me on finding out who wrote the book.

  a 'You shouldn't try to do the assignment in one night.'

    not

    She _____ try to do the assignment in one night.

  b 'I'm not going to pay the library fine.'

    refused

    He _____ the library fine.

  c 'Don't forget to bring my pocket dictionary!'

    him

    She _____ bring her pocket dictionary.

d 'It's not true – I didn't cheat in the exam!'

   denied

   He _____ in the exam.

e 'Let's go to the library.'

   suggested

   She _____ go to the library.

f 'It was the weather that made me late for the lecture.'

   for

   He _____ him late for the lecture.

g 'It's true that I didn't ask permission to use the computer.'

   not

   She _____ asked permission to use the computer.

h 'I'll sit with you in the tutorial, if you like.'

   to

   He _____ her in the tutorial.

5 Work with a partner and tell him/her about four of these occasions:

● when you congratulated someone on something.

● when you warned someone not to do something.

● when you refused to do something.

● when you advised someone to do something.

● when you reminded someone to do something.

● when you explained to someone how to do something.

● when you offered to do something for someone.

Vocabulary: prefixes

1 Work with a partner and discuss the questions.

a What prefixes make the opposite of these words?

   i   fortunately

   ii responsible

b What prefix adds the meaning of 'again' to words like submit and take?

> **Vocabulary hint**
>
> A prefix is a group of letters added to the beginning of a word to make a new word.

2 Look at the prefixes and the examples in the table. Complete the second column, giving the meaning for each one, using the explanations in the box. You can use the explanations more than once.

> negative/opposite   wrongly/badly   again/back   too much
> too little/not enough   former   together   after   before

Prefix	Meaning	Example
un	1 negative/opposite	unfortunately
ir	2 negative/opposite	irresponsible
re	3 again/back	retake
ex	4	ex-student
il	5	illogical
in	6	inaccurate
over	7	overworked
under	8	undercook
pre	9	prejudge
post	10	postgraduate
co	11	co-worker
mis	12	misbehave
im	13	impolite
dis	14	disagree

Vocabulary hint

- The prefixes *co-* and *ex-* are often separated from what follows by *hyphens*.
- Sometimes other prefixes may also use hyphens in order to avoid strange combinations of letters (e.g. pre-arrange, re-examine).

3 Which word in each sentence should have a hyphen?

a Our company employs a lot of exoffenders.

b He handed over control of the plane to his copilot.

c Celebrities often write premarital agreements.

d He was reelected as president three times.

4 Complete each question with the word in brackets and the correct prefix.

a Do you think using mobile phones while driving should be **_illegal_**? (legal)

b Have you ever done anything slightly _____? (honest)

c What would you do if you were _____ in a restaurant and your bill was £3 too much? (charged)

d Have you got any _____ hobbies? (usual)

e Would you say that you were an _____ person? (patient)

f Are there any words you often _____? (spell)

g Do you think professional footballers are _____? (paid)

h Do you have any _____ that you keep in touch with? (schoolfriends)

i Have you got any _____ fears or phobias? (rational)

5 Work with a partner. Choose five of the questions in Exercise 4 to ask your partner.

Summarising

1 Work with a partner and discuss the questions.

   a Would you ever consider taking a gap year from your studies? Why/why not?

   b Do you think there are any benefits to taking a gap year?

2 Read the article *Taking a gap year* and write a summary for your school magazine.

   In your summary you should:

   ● say how gap year demand has changed

   ● state **two** changes in gap year trends

   ● state **two** benefits of taking a gap year.

   Write your summary using between 100 and 150 words.

Exam hint

Exercise 2 is a practice task for Part 6 of the Reading and Writing Paper.

Taking a gap year

Every summer there are students who for a myriad of reasons make a last-minute decision to take time out, but this year, gap year travel firms are reporting inquiries to the industry as a whole are up by a fifth. They have heard from a lot of students with three or four top A-levels who have just missed out on university places because the competition is so high. The squeeze on university places has sent demand for gap year schemes soaring. Students aim to ride out the recession while earning money abroad, travelling, gaining new skills or boosting exam grades, while also attacking the university entrance process with renewed vigour for university entry in the following year.

It is not just gap year numbers that are changing, trends are too. Firms report that applicants who are opting to go travelling or participate in schemes such as wildlife conservation, rather than seeking paid work, are cutting back on their spending, often by cutting the time spent abroad. Unsurprisingly, money is a major factor. It is not just students finding it harder to get paid work in the UK: parents, too, are under pressure. Instead of fleeing for six months, students are signing up for two or three months and working for the balance to pay for it.

In keeping with the economic climate and the "money factor", most gap year inquiries are for schemes that include qualifications or paying jobs. There has been a 20% increase in inquiries about paid work schemes, for example, working on farms in Australia or in Canadian ski resorts, but no change in those wanting to do voluntary work. The surge in demand means that gap year providers are filling their paid placements in record time.

A well-planned year out can not only be a lot of fun, but can be beneficial, even without a salary. It is only natural that people are very unsure about what to do in a gap year and getting employed is obviously a first choice. However, so long as school leavers keep in mind where they want to be in three years, and the skills and knowledge they need to gain in that time, their year out can still contribute to that and keep them on track with their long term goals.

Putting your studies on hold for a year can enable you to gain valuable work experience and boost chances on a second university entrance application. Even if school leavers do not originally want to do a gap year, they can use the opportunity to make sure they stand out as a candidate the following year. Doing something very different for a year could change you quite a lot as a person, make you less materialistic and more driven to do well at university.

Language recap

Vocabulary

1 There are mistakes in six of these sentences. Find the mistakes and correct them.

a Roberto handed his dissertation in yesterday after working on it for three long months.
b Yuka records lectures so she can catch all the main points; she then wrote up her lecture notes when she gets home.
c Please can you cross your name out on this list if you have already received a student handbook.
d The tutor felt that Andreas had leaved the most important part of the essay out.
e As Sam was sitting at the back of the lecture hall, he couldn't always making out what the speaker was saying.
f After over looking the project plan, we realised it was not detailed enough.
g Putting all those illustrations in won't get you any extra marks for your essay.
h If you don't know the meaning, why don't you the word look up in the dictionary?
i Antonio figured out the answer without much difficulty.
j We were advised to brush our computer skills up as our coursework would all be done on the computer.

2 Replace the underlined words with a single word + prefix in the correct form.

a She left her last job because she was made to work too hard.
b If you don't cook this meat for long enough there is a risk of food poisoning.
c In some countries it is considered bad manners not to take off your outdoor shoes when you go into someone's home.
d The debate was very interesting as the speakers had different views on every topic.
e We shouldn't form our opinion about the new prime minister before she has had a chance to put her ideas into practice.
f I am going to study for a few hours every night before the exams to make sure I do not have to do any of them again next year.
g I really hate going in lifts. It's not based on any clear thought or reason but it makes me feel panicky!
h If you continue to be rude and naughty, you will not be allowed to meet your friends tonight.

Grammar

3 Complete the letter using the reporting verbs in the box. Use each reporting verb once only.

refuse   ask   explain   promise   inform   apologise   remind   tell

Dear Sir/Madam,

I am writing to you to complain about a conversation I had with a member of your customer service staff (Mark Smith) yesterday, who was unprofessional in the manner in which he dealt with my complaint about a book I had ordered from your website.

When I called customer services, I _____(1) Mark that I had ordered a book from your website a month ago as I thought it would help me with my Biology International GCSE revision. It says on the website that delivery will take 2–3 days, but I had to wait two weeks for my book to arrive. Mark _____(2) for the late delivery and _____(3) that there had been a problem with the delivery system recently.

I _____(4) Mark that when I received my book I was expecting it to be 'nearly new' as this was the website description. However, when I opened the parcel, I was shocked with the condition of the book. There were pages missing and the cover was torn. In response to this, Mark _____(5) me to send the book back and said I would be sent a replacement. I _____(6) Mark that I needed the book for revision and my exams were in a month. He _____(7) to send a replacement book out within 3 days of receiving the one I returned; a week later and I am still waiting.

Mark _____(8) to arrange for a new book to be sent out to me until I had returned the one I already had. I have already done this, so please could you confirm this and send me out a replacement book as my exam is now in three weeks' time.

Yours faithfully,

Sally North
Sally North

Paper 1: Reading and Writing

 Part 6: Writing a summary

You have to produce a summary of specific information in the text – two or three bullet points indicate this information, so make sure you read the bullet points carefully before you begin to write your summary. You are allowed to write between 100 and 150 words only, so you must filter out all unnecessary detail and focus on just these bullet points. The bullet points follow the order the information is presented in the text.

In the Edexcel IGCSE ELS Paper 1 in November 2008, the bullet points were:

- **two** reasons why recycling is important
- **two** things students can do at school
- **two** things students can do at home.

The first step is to read through the whole text so that you understand the gist and identify which section of text refers to which bullet point.

The extract reproduced below is the section of text you need to consider in order to address the first bullet point.

Having read through the extract, you need to underline or highlight all the information relevant to that bullet point:

REDUCE, REUSE, RECYCLE

Recycling and Rubbish
Last year we collected 33,000 tonnes of household rubbish in our town – that's the same weight as 64 jumbo jets! Of this, 77% was buried in a landfill site and with this hole set to fill up in less than four years' time, it's vital that we all play our part in reducing waste and recycling more. We have set ourselves a target of 40% by 2009. We can only achieve this with everyone's participation.

Recycling
Our borough council has 23 recycling points located at supermarkets, shopping parades and in some residential areas. This means that people don't have to store materials in their houses for long periods and they needn't drive to a site, which makes the whole process more environmentally friendly.

Why should we recycle?
There are many advantages. Recycling

- saves on natural resources. Recycling glass uses 20% less energy than making it from raw materials. Recycling aluminium saves 95% of the energy needed to make it from its raw material bauxite. And recycling paper uses around 20% less energy than paper produced from virgin materials. It also uses less water.

- maintains the countryside. By recycling we reduce the need to use more raw materials that are needed to produce the products from scratch.
- reduces the amount of waste we throw away.
- reduces the cost of collection and disposal.

Now go back to the question to check who this summary is for – this will decide the kind of language you use. For this task, you are told to *write a short summary for your school magazine*. Therefore, the language will be semi-formal.

When you write your summary, you should use your own words and phrases as far as possible. This means that you should not copy sentences or chunks from the text – however, there may be a couple of key words in the text that you will have to re-use.

It is always a good idea to jot down some notes first of all.

Two reasons why recycling is important

- *uses less energy and less water than producing from raw materials*
- *reduces quantity of raw materials needed and thus protects countryside*
- *reduces amount of rubbish*
- *saves money – less rubbish to get rid of*

You have to mention two reasons only, so decide which ones you will focus on before you turn your notes into sentences. You should also write a brief introduction – one sentence is likely to be enough:

Recycling is very important for a number of reasons.

The landfill site where our rubbish is buried will soon be full. The more we recycle, the less rubbish we produce. Producing less rubbish saves money since less money is spent on collecting and getting rid of it.

Check your word count to make sure you have kept to the word limit. The paragraph above contains 47 words: an introductory sentence (9 words) and a summary of information relevant to the first bullet point (38). You will then need to repeat this process to cover the two remaining bullet points. Make sure that your final summary contains no more than 150 words.

Getting started...

1 What different kinds of mysterious, weird or puzzling things can you see in the pictures?

2 Complete the phrases in these questions using the words in the box. Use each word only once. Use a dictionary if necessary.

> haunted   suspense   cryptic   illusions
> treasure   unanswered   solving   working

a Do you like films or books about ghosts and _____ *houses*?

b Do you like _____ *out* the answers to 'Whodunnit' type films or books?

c Can you think of any films or books which are *full of* _____?

d What do you think of shows in which magicians perform tricks and *optical* _____?

e There are many _____ *questions* about UFOs. Can you think of any other things which are mysterious?

f Do you know anyone who is good at doing _____ *crosswords*?

g Have you ever taken part in a _____ *hunt*?

h Are you the sort of person who is good at _____ *problems*?

3 Work with a partner and discuss the questions from Exercise 2.

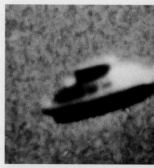

Exam hint

Exercise 1 is a practice task for Part 1 of the Speaking Paper.

👄 Speaking

1 Work with a partner and decide who is going to answer the Student A questions and who is going to answer the Student B questions. Student A needs to answer all four questions, taking no more than 3 minutes. Repeat the process for the Student B questions.

Student A
Let's talk about films
What kinds of films do you enjoy watching? (Tell me about that.)
Why do you prefer those types of films? (Tell me about that.)
Where do you usually watch films? (Why is that?)
Who do you usually watch them with? (Why is that?)

Student B
Let's talk about books
How do you choose which books to read? (Tell me about that.)
What kinds of books do you enjoy reading? (Why is that?)
Why do you prefer those types of books? (Tell me about that.)
Do you ever borrow books? (e.g. *from a library or friends*) (Why is that?)

Reading

1 Work with a partner and discuss these questions:

● Have you ever done a Sudoku puzzle?

● If yes, do you enjoy doing them? What do you enjoy about them?

● If no, why not? Do you enjoy doing any other puzzles?

2 Read the article *The History of Sudoku* and answer the questions.

Exam hint

Exercise 2 is a practice task for Part 2 of the Reading and Writing Paper.

The History of *Sudoku*

Sudoku has a fascinating history. "Su" means number in Japanese, and "Doku" refers to the single place on the puzzle board that each number can fit into. Although its name is Japanese, the puzzle's origins are actually European and American, and the game represents the best in cross-cultural fertilisation. Unlike many games which spring from one culture and are then absorbed by others, *Sudoku's* development reveals it to be a true hybrid creation.

The 18th century Swiss mathematician Leonhard Euler apparently developed the concept of "Latin Squares" where numbers in a grid appear only once, across and up and down. In the late 1970s, Dell Magazines in the United States began publishing what we now call *Sudoku* puzzles using Euler's concept with a 9 by 9 square grid. They called it Number Place, and it was developed by an independent puzzle maker, Howard Garnes.

In the mid-1980s, the president of the Japanese puzzle giant Nikoli Inc., Mr. Maki Kaji, urged the company to publish a version of the puzzle that became a huge hit in that country. Nikoli gave the game its current name and helped refine it by restricting the number of revealed or given numbers to 30 and having them appear symmetrically. Afterwards the game became increasingly popular in Japan and started becoming a fixture in daily newspapers and magazines.

Almost two decades passed before the game was taken up by *The Times* newspaper in London as a daily puzzle. This development was due to the efforts of Wayne Gould, a retired Hong Kong judge originally from New Zealand. He first came across a *Sudoku* puzzle in a Japanese bookshop in 1997. Over the next six years he developed a computer programme to produce puzzles quickly. Knowing that British newspapers have a long history of publishing crosswords and other puzzles, he promoted *Sudoku* to *The Times* in Britain. In the autumn of 2004, he was able to convince *The Times* to start publishing daily *Sudoku* puzzles developed using his software. The first game was published on November 12, 2004. Within a few months, other British newspapers began publishing their own *Sudoku* puzzles. Once again, *Sudoku's* popularity crossed the oceans. By the summer of 2005, major newspapers in the United States were also offering *Sudoku* puzzles like they would daily crossword puzzles. It is interesting to note that while software is critical to being able to supply the growing demand for *Sudoku* puzzles, as it can take hours of processing time to generate one unique puzzle, it was old media in the form of newspapers that have done so much to encourage the spread of *Sudoku* around the world.

Sudoku's future development is unknown. While the 9 by 9 grid is the most common form of *Sudoku*, there are many variants of the game. Four by four *Sudoku* with

2 by 2 sub-sections are simpler, fun for younger audiences and easy to deliver to mobile devices like phones. There are 5 by 5 games, 6 by 6 and 7 by 7 games. For the truly addicted, there are even 16 by 16 grids, not to mention a 25 by 25 grid apparently offered by Japanese game developer Nikoli. *Sudoku* puzzles using letters and symbols, some even spelling words in their final solutions, are also becoming available.

Sudoku software is very popular on PCs, websites and mobile phones. Software has also been released on video game consoles, such as the Game Boy Advance, Xbox Live Arcade, the Nooke-book reader, several iPod models and the iPhone.

One of the most popular video games featuring *Sudoku* is *Brain Age: Train Your Brain in Minutes a Day!* Critically and commercially well received, it generated particular praise for its *Sudoku* implementation and sold more than 8 million copies worldwide. Due to its popularity, Nintendo made a second *Brain Age* game entitled *Brain Age 2*, which has over 100 new *Sudoku* puzzles and other activities.

Where this rapidly developing fad leads to, no one can tell. What is clear though is that *Sudoku* is a fun and challenging way for people of any age and culture to hone their logical and deductive abilities. Who knows, played often enough, *Sudoku* may help make the human race a tiny bit smarter.

Questions

1–5

Choose **true**, **false** or **not given** for each statement.

	True	False	Not given
1 'Doku' relates to the number of puzzle squares.	☐	☐	☐
2 The *Sudoku* puzzle was first developed in Japan.	☐	☐	☐
3 *Sudoku* is based on the idea of Latin Squares.	☐	☐	☐
4 The puzzle first went out to the public in America.	☐	☐	☐
5 In Japan, the puzzle was renamed and adapted.	☐	☐	☐

6–10

Complete these sentences using no more than **three words** and/or **numbers**.

6 Wayne Gould _____ for the first time in 1997.

7 Wayne Gould spent a number of years working out how to _____.

8 On _____ *Sudoku* appeared in *The Times* newspaper.

9 The use of _____ is necessary when creating *Sudoku* puzzles.

10 The _____ is due to the existence of newspapers.

11–15

Answer these questions using no more than **three words** and/or **numbers**.

11 Which *Sudoku* grid size is the easiest ?

....

12 Which *Sudoku* grid size is the most challenging?

....

13 In *Sudoku* puzzles, what is now being used as an alternative to numbers?

....

14 How many sales did *Brain Age* generate?

....

15 What skills does *Sudoku* help you to practise?

....

Grammar: possibility and certainty

1 Work in a small group and discuss these questions:

● Have you ever seen the series *Lost*?

● If so, tell other students about it. Did you like it? Why/why not?

● If no, find out as much as you can about the series.

2 R.38 ▶ Listen to two people discussing the TV drama series *Lost*. Which two mysteries in the programme are they talking about? What different theories do they have about them?

3 Look at these sentences and decide if one or both of the modal verbs in *italics* are grammatically possible.

a I'm absolutely certain that the monster *must/might* be something really weird – not just an ordinary wild bear.

b I'm sure that the monster *can't/couldn't* be a normal wild bear. It's just not possible.

Grammar hint

may, might, could, can

Which one of these sentences is grammatically incorrect? Why?

1 *I think it might rain today.*

2 *It's possible she may be late today.*

3 *It could be the best thing that's ever happened to me.*

4 *I'm not sure, but I suppose he can still be at work.*

Grammar reference: see page 245

c I'm certain that the island is real. The survivors *can't/mustn't* be imagining the whole thing.

d I'm not sure, but I think the whole thing *might have/may have* been set up as a huge scientific experiment.

e I'm not certain, but possibly they *could/can* be in the middle of some sort of a scientific experiment.

f It's possible that the scientists *could/might* be doing some research into how people behave in a crisis.

g I feel certain that the survivors *can't have/couldn't have* known anything about the island before landing on it.

h I'm certain the crash was an accident. The scientists *couldn't have/mustn't have* made it happen on purpose.

4 Complete the second sentence so that it has a similar meaning to the first sentence, using the word given. Do not change the word given. You must use between two and five words, including the word given.

a Jenny will possibly lend me the first series of *Lost* on DVD.

   might

   Jenny _____ me the first series of *Lost* on DVD.

b I can't work out how people managed to build the Great Pyramid.

   have

   I can't work out how the Great Pyramid _____ .

c It's possible that there's a piece missing from this jigsaw puzzle.

   be

   There _____ a piece missing from this jigsaw puzzle.

d It's impossible that they have finished the treasure hunt already.

   have

   They _____ the treasure hunt already.

e She's really good at crosswords – I'm certain she does them a lot.

   do

   She's really good at crosswords – she _____ them a lot.

f I don't know what's going on in this episode of *Lost* – I'm pretty sure I missed the last one.

   must

   I don't know what's going on in this episode of *Lost* – I _____ the last one.

g It's not possible for a watch to disappear like that – it's just an illusion.

   could

   A watch _____ like that – it's just an illusion.

h It was obvious who the murderer was from the start – you certainly weren't concentrating properly.

   been

   It was obvious who the murderer was from the start – you _____ properly.

5 Read this story. After each sentence answer the question by speculating about a reason for what happened at each stage.

> On Monday last week, a smartly-dressed man was walking along the beach. *[1 Why? He might have been going to a party.]* He was completely soaked to the skin. *[2 Why?]* When a member of the public spoke to him, he didn't answer. *[3 Why?]* Later that day, he was taken to hospital by the police. *[4 Why?]* Despite the staff talking to him, he stayed silent for weeks. *[5 Why?]* One day, someone gave him a piece of paper and pencil. *[6 Why?]* He drew a detailed sketch of a grand piano. *[7 Why?]* The hospital staff took him to a room with a piano. *[8 Why?]* He played the piano for hours at a time, day after day. *[9 Why?]* Police have put his picture in the newspaper. *[10 Why?]*

6 Find out more about the mysterious pianist on page 228.

Vocabulary: speculating

1 Work with a partner. Look at phrases and sentences i–x.
Discuss questions a, b and c with your partner.

  i   I knew right from the start …

  ii   I've got a feeling …

  iii   I think it's probably some sort of …

  iv   At first I thought … but now I'm not so sure.

  v   I just can't work out how …

  vi   I think it's more likely …

  vii   I don't see how it could be …

  viii   I suppose you're right.

  ix   It doesn't make sense.

  x   I hadn't thought of that.

  a   In which four of the phrases is the speaker fairly sure of his/her ideas?

  b   In which three of the phrases is the speaker not sure of his/her ideas or has no ideas?

  c   In which three of the phrases is the speaker responding directly to someone else's ideas?

2 Cover the phrases in Exercise 1 and then complete the phrases in *italics* in the dialogue.

A: Who do you think they are?

B: *I've got a* _____ (1) *that* they're university students. They definitely look as though they're in a classroom studying and none of them are wearing uniforms.

A: *I think it's more* _____ (2) *that* they're college students. They don't look old enough to be university students and you don't wear a uniform at college either, do you?

B: No, you don't. *I* _____ (3) *you're right*. It does look more like a college setting, I suppose.

A: *At first I thought they were just in a lesson but now I'm not so*_____ (4). I think they could actually be in an exam. They're not speaking to each other and they look as though they're concentrating on what is in front of them.

B: *I hadn't* _____ (5) *of that.* Actually, if you have a look at what's on the tables in front of them, it looks as though they have exercise books and text books, so I don't see _____ (6) *it could be an exam.*

A: Yes, you're right. *It doesn't make* _____ (7). I think I can see a bag and a pencil case and they don't usually let you take your bags and normal pencil cases into an exam, do they? Also, the student at the back of the picture is staring at the student next to her, which you wouldn't really do in an exam.

B: Also, *I just can't* _____ (8) *out how* they would be sitting so close to one another if they were in an exam. *I do think it's just probably some* _____ (9) *of* lesson taking place in a college classroom.

A: Yes, I agree with you. *I knew right from the* _____ (10) that they were college students anyway.

Speaking

1 Work with a partner and each choose one of the topics below. Prepare to time your partner – give them 1 minute to prepare and then ask them to start speaking. Tell them to stop speaking after 2 minutes. Did your partner answer the question on the card?

Exam hint

Exercise 1 is a practice task for Part 2 of the Speaking Paper.

Student A
You are going to talk about **books and films**. You can use some or all of the ideas listed below in your talk but you must answer this question:

Describe a film which is a favourite of yours. Why do you like it?
You must talk for 1 to 2 minutes. You have 1 minute to think and make notes before your talk begins.

Here are some ideas to help you:
· Film type
· Story
· Characters
· Special effects

Student B
You are going to talk about **books and films**. You can use some or all of the ideas listed below in your talk but you must answer this question:

Describe a book which is a favourite of yours. Why do you like it?
You must talk for 1 to 2 minutes. You have 1 minute to think and make notes before your talk begins.

Here are some ideas to help you:
· Book type
· Story
· Characters
· Author

2 Work with a partner and take it in turns to ask and answer the following questions. Remember to give as much information as possible and try to keep talking for at least 5 minutes.

Part 3

We have been talking about **books and films** and I would like to ask you some more questions on this topic.

- Do you prefer to watch a film or read a book? (Why is that?)
- When are you most likely to watch a film? (Why is that?)
- Do you prefer watching films at home or at the cinema? (Tell me about that.)

- For what different reasons do people read? (Tell me about that.)
- Do you think it is important for people to read for pleasure? (Why is that?)
- Do you think it matters what people read (e.g. *comics*, *novels*, *magazines*), as long as they read something? (Tell me about that.)

- What are the benefits of being able to read books in electronic format? (Tell me about that.)
- Do you think that at some point in the future 'paper' books will disappear altogether? (Tell me about that.)
- If they did disappear, what advantages and disadvantages would there be to this happening? (Tell me about that.)

◁))) Listening

1 Work with a partner and check that you understand what the following are:

- a number puzzle

- a crossword puzzle

- a TV game show

- a detective story

- a science fiction film

- a children's treasure hunt

- a dream/nightmare

- an Internet game.

2 Work with a partner and say which three of the above things you are most interested in and why.

3 R39 ▶ Now listen to five people each talking about one of the strange or puzzling things from Exercise 1 and answer the questions.

Questions

1–15

Complete these notes using no more than **three words** and/or **numbers**.

Speaker 1
- Would like to appear in _____ (1) called *Lost*
- Three teams with two people in each team
- Given a rucksack containing _____ (2)
- Left in unknown desert after being blindfolded
- The teams have to race each other to the _____ (3).

Speaker 2
- Talking about Perplex City
- First person to find the Receda Cube qualified for _____ (4)
- 40,000 worldwide played the game.
- To try and work it out, you had to find clues and _____(5).
- Found it so addictive that it started _____ (6) her life

Speaker 3
- On holiday with _____ (7)
- Trying to find their way out of a big house
- The _____ (8) which was very confusing
- Did get out but then fell and _____ (9)
- Fell out of bed and woke up

Speaker 4
- Nina Pell is 18 years old and a student.
- She is the current _____ (10).
- She solved the hardest UK version of the puzzle.
- It took her _____ (11) to solve the puzzle.
- Trained every day by doing puzzles
- The speaker would prefer to _____ (12).

Speaker 5
- Mark, who is 11 years old, knows the location of _____ (13).
- Knowing this secret involves him with the FBI and the mafia.
- The FBI want Mark to _____ (14) the secret location.
- The mafia are against this.
- The speaker recommends _____ (15) due to their unpredictable endings.

4 R39 ▶ Listen again and check your answers.

5 Work with a partner and decide which of the things in Exercise 1 each speaker was talking about.

Grammar: -*ing* forms/infinitives

Grammar reference: see page 246

1 Look at the verb forms in *italics* in the sentences. Match them with the correct rules i–viii.

a It must *get* so boring doing puzzles all the time.

b I went to my friend's house to *play* on his computer.

c *Reading* detective stories is one of my favourite hobbies.

d I'd rather *read* a book than do crosswords.

e I find those TV game shows really exciting *to watch*.

f I'm too impatient *to bother* with those *Sudoku* things.

g My brother makes me *play* computer games with him.

h She trained for the competition by *doing* five puzzles a day.

Use the infinitive without *to* (e.g. *do*)

i after modal verbs

ii after *make* and *let*

iii after *I'd better* and *I'd rather*

Use the infinitive with *to* (e.g. *to do*)

iv after certain adjectives

v after the construction '*too ... to ...*'

vi to express purpose

Use the -*ing* form (e.g. *doing*)

vii after prepositions

viii when an action (not a noun) is the subject or object of a sentence

2 Choose the correct alternatives in the following text.

A man has praised the honest people in Utah, USA for *to return/returning*[1] his wallet forty years after he lost it. Fifty-seven-year-old Doug Schmitt left his wallet on the counter of a petrol station in Logan, Utah in the spring of 1967. 'I've wondered about it occasionally,' he said. 'But I knew that it was too long ago *having/to have*[2] any hope of getting it back. I couldn't *remember/to remember*[3]

where I'd lost it anyway, and I thought I'd better just *to give up/give up*[4] the idea of ever *find/finding*[5] it again.

The owner of the petrol station, however, put the wallet in a drawer *keep/to keep*[6] it safe until Mr Schmitt came back to *collect/collecting*[7] it. Decades later, the owner's son found it in the drawer. '*Having/Have*[8] a student identity card in

the wallet was great,' he said 'because I could track Mr Schmitt down on the Internet and *sending/send*[9] the wallet back.' The wallet also contained $5 in cash, some stamps and a dry-cleaning ticket. 'It makes me *to wonder/wonder*[10] if I've still got some dry-cleaning out there!' said Mr Schmitt.

3 Complete these sentences with the correct form of the verb in brackets.

a I *managed* _____ (work out) who the murderer was in the end.

b She *offered* _____ (help) me with my next task.

c Do you *fancy* _____ (watch) that murder mystery film tonight?

d I *meant* _____ (phone) Marco earlier, but I totally forgot.

e In my dream, the stairs *kept* _____ (disappear).

f I was *expecting* _____ (see) him at the meeting, but he wasn't there.

g I really don't *enjoy* _____ (waste) my time playing computer games.

h When I went camping, I really *missed* _____ (have) a proper bed.

4 Look at the two definitions for each verb pattern and then complete the pairs of sentences with the correct form of the verb in brackets.

a i I love *trying* _____ (work out) all the answers in 'Whodunnit' books.

   ii I *tried* _____ (write) down all the possibilities for each gap in a *Sudoku* puzzle, but I still couldn't do it.

> try to do = attempt to do/make an effort to do
>
> try doing = do something as an experiment or test

b i Did you *remember* _____ (programme) the DVD player to record the match?

   ii I only *remember* _____ (go) inside a dark building, but then I woke up.

> remember to do = remember about something
> and then do it
>
> remember doing = do something and then
> remember about it

c i He only *stopped* _____ (play) that computer game when the computer crashed!

   iii I stopped _____ (have) a coffee on my way to work this morning.

> stop to do = stop doing an action in order to do
> something else
>
> stop doing = stop doing an action while in the
> middle of that action

5 Work with a partner and tell each other about five of these things.

Something you ...

- intend to do
- regret doing
- have given up doing
- usually avoid doing

- don't often remember to do
- miss doing
- sometimes pretend to do
- expect to do soon

Vocabulary: feelings

1 Look at the words/phrases in the box. If there are any you don't know, check the meaning and pronunciation, using a dictionary if necessary.

> elated enthusiastic exhilarated inspired
> relieved thrilled to bits distraught downhearted
> overwhelmed scared stiff staggered traumatised

2 Choose the correct alternatives in these sentences.

a She's a positive person and is always *enthusiastic/relieved* about her studies.

b Don't be *relieved/downhearted* about your driving test. I'm sure you'll pass next time.

c I was *staggered/exhilarated* when he told me he was going bungee jumping. It's so out of character.

d There are several people away at work and I'm feeling *inspired/overwhelmed* by the amount I have to do.

e My cat was like my best friend and I was *downhearted/distraught* when she died.

f After watching the Olympics on TV, I was *elated/inspired* to become a member of a running club.

g She was *traumatised/thrilled to bits* for a while after the car accident.

h I usually feel *exhilarated/scared stiff* in job interviews, but I felt quite relaxed for this one.

3 Complete these sentences. Make three of them true and three of them false.

a Something I always feel enthusiastic about is ...

b Above all, I felt relieved when I ...

c I usually feel scared stiff when ...

d I felt completely elated as soon as I'd finished ...

e I can say that I was absolutely thrilled to bits when ...

f I've never felt as exhilarated as when I ...

4 Work with a partner and try to guess which of your partner's sentences in Exercise 3 are true and which are not. Tell each other more details about the ones that are true.

 Writing

1 You have been asked to write an article for the school magazine titled 'Something I intend to do this year'.

In your article you should:

● give two details about what you intend to do

● give two reasons why you intend to do it

● say how it will make you feel.

Write your article using between 100 and 150 words.

Exam hint

Exercise 1 is a practice task for Part 4 of the Reading and Writing Paper.

Summarising

1 Read the article about the history of *Sudoku* and write a summary for your teacher.

In your summary you should:

- say how *Sudoku* developed

- say what different versions of *Sudoku* are available

- say what *Sudoku* software is available.

Write your summary using between 100 and 150 words.

The History of *Sudoku*

The 18th century Swiss mathematician Leonhard Euler apparently developed the concept of "Latin Squares" where numbers in a grid appear only once, across and up and down. In the late 1970s, Dell Magazines in the United States began publishing what we now call *Sudoku* puzzles using Euler's concept with a 9 by 9 square grid. They called it Number Place.

In the mid-1980s, the president of the Japanese puzzle giant Nikoli Inc., Mr. Maki Kaji, urged the company to publish a version of the puzzle that became a huge hit in that country. Nikoli gave the game its current name and helped refine it by restricting the number of revealed or given numbers to 30 and having them appear symmetrically. Afterwards the game became increasingly popular in Japan and started becoming a fixture in daily newspapers and magazines.

Almost two decades passed before the game was taken up by *The Times* newspaper in London as a daily puzzle.

This development was due to the efforts of Wayne Gould, a retired Hong Kong judge originally from New Zealand. He first came across a *Sudoku* puzzle in a Japanese bookshop in 1997. Over the next six years he developed a computer programme to produce puzzles quickly. He then promoted *Sudoku* to *The Times* in Britain and, in the autumn of 2004, he was able to convince *The Times* to start publishing daily *Sudoku* puzzles developed using his software. The first game was published on November 12, 2004. Within a few months, other British newspapers began publishing their own *Sudoku* puzzles. By the summer of 2005, major newspapers in the United States were also offering *Sudoku* puzzles like they would daily crossword puzzles.

Sudoku's future development is unknown. While the 9 by 9 grid is the most common form of *Sudoku*, there are many variants of the game. Four by four *Sudoku* with 2 by 2 sub-sections are simpler, fun for younger audiences and easy to deliver to mobile devices like phones. There are 5 by 5 games, 6 by 6 and 7 by 7 games. For the truly addicted, there are even 16 by 16 grids, not to mention a 25 by 25 grid apparently offered by Japanese game developer Nikoli. *Sudoku* puzzles using letters and symbols, some even spelling words in their final solutions, are also becoming available.

Sudoku software is very popular on PCs, websites and mobile phones. Software has also been released on video game consoles, such as the Game Boy Advance, Xbox Live Arcade, the Nooke-book reader, several iPod models and the iPhone.

One of the most popular video games featuring *Sudoku* is *Brain Age: Train Your Brain in Minutes a Day!* Critically and commercially well received, it generated particular praise for its *Sudoku* implementation and sold more than 8 million copies worldwide. Due to its popularity, Nintendo made a second *Brain Age* game entitled *Brain Age 2*, which has over 100 new *Sudoku* puzzles and other activities.

Language recap

Grammar

1 There are mistakes in the verb forms in *italics* in these sentences. Find the mistakes and correct them.

A: I can't find my keys anywhere. I must *left*[1] them at Sally's house.

B: They *mustn't be*[2] at her house because you drove home using them.

A: Oh, yes, so I did. Oh dear, they *can't have be stolen*[3], can they?

B: I don't think so. Where did you go after Sally's?

A: Well, I went to the supermarket – so I suppose I *can have dropped*[4] them somewhere there ...

B: No, you *can't do*[5] because you drove home from there as well, didn't you?

A: Of course I did! Well, they *must to be*[6] somewhere in the house, then.

B: Have another look in your bag – you *could have miss*[7] them.

A: They're really not in there. Perhaps I *must have left*[8] them in the front door ...

B: No, they're not there. They're probably somewhere really obvious – like in your pocket. Have a look, they *might have be*[9] in your pocket.

A: Oh, yes! Here they are – after all that! They're right here!

2 Match the sentence halves a–j with i–x to make complete sentences.

a   I'd rather ...
b   I usually avoid ...
c   I think you're too young ...
d   I've always dreamt of ...
e   You can ...
f   I want ...
g   I really regretted ...
h   My parents don't let me ...
i   I borrowed his puzzle book ...
j   He said he regrets ...

i   ... going to a desert island.
ii ... play computer games much.
iii ... to watch such scary horror films.
iv ... watch a detective film than a horror film.
v   ... borrowing things if I can.
vi ... borrow my puzzle book if you like.
vii ... to borrow Steve's puzzle book for the journey.
viii ... to have something to do on the journey.
ix ... to say that he won't be lending you any more money.
x   ... borrowing all that money from my parents last time.

Vocabulary

3 Six of these sentences have a word missing. Write the missing words in the correct place.

a   I suppose you right.
b   It doesn't make sense me.
c   I hadn't thought of that.
d   I've got feeling that someone's watching me.
e   I think it's some sort charity fund-raising event.
f   I don't how it could be brand new – it looks dirty.
g   At first I thought she was a bit unfriendly, but now I'm not so sure.
h   I knew right the start that he wasn't going to fit in with the team.

4 Choose the correct alternatives.

Hi Tim,

I just wanted to tell you about this fantastic holiday I'm on. It's a sort of adventure type holiday and we've been doing really exciting but sometimes scary things! At the end of every day, I'm exhausted but completely *distraught/exhilarated*[1] by my achievements. The staff are lovely – very friendly and *enthusiastic/elated*[2] about all the sports.

On the first day, we went abseiling. At first, I really didn't want to do it – I stood at the top of the enormous cliff and was *staggered/scared stiff*[3]. Then I watched James – he was the first person to go over the edge and down the side of the rock. In the morning, he had been really *distraught/relieved*[4] at the whole idea of it. You have ropes and everything, but it's still scary! He did it though and I was really *inspired/downhearted*[5] when I saw him – and suddenly I really wanted to do it myself.

When it was my turn, I was *staggered/overwhelmed*[6] that I didn't feel more scared actually ... I went over the edge at the top quite easily. It was a bit scary on the way down and I was very *exhilarated/relieved*[7] when I reached the bottom in one piece – but I would definitely recommend it.

I'll write more tomorrow. By the way, well done about your exam results. You must be *enthusiastic/thrilled to bits*[8]!

Michael

Exam tips

Paper 2: Listening

🔊 Part 3: Listening (10 marks)

Text type

In this part you will listen to a longer recording which may be a monologue in the form of a talk, or a dialogue in the form of an interview or a guided dialogue. The monologues or dialogues are on themes which you are likely to encounter in a range of everyday situations – in social, educational or employment contexts.

Skills

This section tests your ability to listen to a more complex argument or discussion. You are expected to understand the overall message of what is being said as well as the essential and finer points of detail. In addition, you have to identify attitudes and opinions (both stated openly or just implied).

Task types

There are 10 marks available in this part and there will be 10 questions, each worth one mark.

Task types in this section include:

● **Notes and sentence completion:** you have to write your answers out in words for this task type. The prompts indicate clearly what parts of speech you should use in your answer, so you need to bear that in mind as you listen – the answers are all words you hear in the recording. Don't change the form of the words you hear – just lift them directly from the recording. The answer required will be either a number or one, two or three words (check the instruction for the exact number).

● **Chart or table completion:** this task type is similar to notes and sentence completion. You write your answers out in words, the answers are all words you hear in the recording, and you should not change the form of the words you hear. The instruction tells you the maximum number of words (or numbers) you need for the answers.

● **Multiple-choice questions:** you have to decide which option is the correct answer to the question, or which option best fills a gap in a sentence. There are generally three options for each question.

● **Short-answer questions:** again, you have to write your answers out in words for this task type. The answers are all words you will hear in the recording, and, remember, don't change the form of the words you hear. You will need to write a number or one, two or three words for your answer – this will be made clear in the instruction.

Let's look at the Edexcel IGCSE ESL Listening Paper in November 2008:

This is an extract from what you hear:

> The Solar Decathlon is a competition in which 20 teams of university students compete to design, build and operate the most attractive and energy-efficient house. But the ... houses they build must only use the power of the sun to provide all the energy needs of a typical household.
>
> During the competition, students will test their houses in 10 contests – these range from architecture and comfort to how well the homes perform tasks such as heating water and powering appliances.
>
> .... They transport their solar houses to the competition site and rebuild them in a solar village. ...

This is an extract from the task:

> Listen and complete the sentences. Write no more than **three words and/or numbers** for each answer.
>
> **SOLAR DECATHLON**
>
> The houses the students build must be both energy efficient and **[21.]** .... – and use solar power.

The prompt indicates that you need to pick out an adjective: *energy efficient* is already given and acts as a clue. You will be listening out then for another adjective – the correct answer is *attractive*.

> The competition includes tests on **[22.]** ...., architecture and the performance of household tasks.

This time the prompt indicates you need a noun, and you are given further clues with *architecture* and *performance of household tasks* – a paraphrase for *heating water and powering appliances*. The only other noun in that section of the text is *comfort* so this is the correct answer.

> The houses are moved to the competition site where students **[23.]**...................................... them.

You are listening out for a verb this time – what do the students do with the houses when they get them to the competition site? You know *move* is a synonym for *transport* so that part is taken care of, thus you are left with *rebuild*.

Getting started...

1 Look at the pictures, which show people earning money in different ways. Say what you think each job is and what skills or personality characteristics you would need to do these jobs well.

2 Work with a partner. Explain the difference in meaning between the phrases in *italics* in these pairs of sentences.

a i I *got the sack* on Friday.

   ii I was *made redundant* on Friday.

b i I'm on *maternity leave*.

   ii I'm on *sick leave*.

c i He's in a *dead-end* job.

   ii He's got a *promising career* ahead.

d i She has a *demanding* job.

   ii She has a *high-powered* job.

e i I was *promoted* to this job.

   ii I was *headhunted* for this job.

1

2

3

4

Exam hint

Exercise 1 is a practice task for Part 1 of the Speaking Paper.

🗣 Speaking

1 Work with a partner and decide who is going to answer the Student A questions and who is going to answer the Student B questions. Student A needs to answer all four questions, taking no more than 3 minutes. Repeat the process for the Student B questions.

Student A
Let's talk about future jobs
What kind of job would you like to do in the future? (Why is that?)
What skills or qualifications do you need for that job? (Tell me about that.)
Would you enjoy working in a different country? (Why is that?)
Which country/ies would you like to work in? (Why is that?)

Student B
Let's talk about part-time jobs
Have you ever had a part-time job? If yes, what was/is it? If not, why not?
What part-time job do you think you would most enjoy? (Why is that?)
What are the benefits of having a part-time job? (Tell me about that.)
What would you do with the money that you earned? (Tell me about that.)

Listening

1 Work with a partner and discuss these questions:

- How would you feel about being fired out of a cannon?

- Would you enjoy working as a 'human cannonball'? (e.g. *in a circus*)

- What talents/skills are needed to be a 'human cannonball'?

2 R.40 ▶ Listen to part of a radio programme about unusual jobs and answer the questions.

Exam hint

Exercise 2 is a practice task for Part 1 of the Listening Paper. In the Listening Paper, Part 1 will have 10 questions and not 15 as with this practice test.

Questions

1–5

Complete these sentences using no more than **three words** and/or **numbers**.

1 Diego always knew he was going to have a job in _____.

2 His parents worked as _____ with an Eastern European circus.

3 Diego was _____ when he started his circus training.

4 Before he became a human cannonball, he worked on the _____ and the trapeze.

5 Diego starts his circus act, by standing _____.

6–10

Complete these notes using no more than **three words** or a **number.**

- Diego climbs inside his cannon and stands on a platform.
- The space under his feet is filled with _____ (6).
- Final checks then take place.
- The gun that Diego is fired from is _____ (7) long.
- He travels at speeds reaching 100 kilometres per hour.
- His flight ends with him landing in the _____ (8).
- Diego says the feeling is similar to bungee jumping.
- After he has finished, children often ask for his _____ (9).
- Diego enjoys the working hours but the work is not easy.
- He is always nervous, and to make sure everything goes smoothly he must _____ (10).

11–15

Choose **a**, **b** or **c**.

11 For his act, Diego has to
 a keep his body locked in one position.
 b finish the act by landing on his feet.
 c turn several times during his flight.

12 When the circus relocates,
 a the cannon has to be redesigned.
 b a dummy is used in the cannon.
 c the acrobat wires are adjusted.

13 Working as a human cannonball for a circus, you
 a have to rent accommodation nearby.
 b are well paid for the risks you take.
 c have to take part in the whole show.

14 Diego has also used his skills by
 a making a movie about his job.
 b taking part in circus advertising.
 c playing a short part in a film.

15 To prepare physically for his job, Diego
 a has put himself on a special diet.
 b takes regular physical exercise.
 c frequently attends training courses.

3 R.40 ▶ Listen again and check your answers.

Grammar: passives

1 Look at these sentences. What do the parts in *italics* have in common?

a Diego, 'the human cannonball', is *fired* from a four-metre gun and travels through the air at speeds of up to 60 mph.

b He says that he *has* always *been* well *looked after* by the circus.

c Last year he *was offered* a part in a Hollywood movie.

2 Work with a partner. Discuss which of these you think are common reasons why we use the passive.

a We are not interested in who or what did the action.

b We are writing a formal letter.

c We want to keep a piece of new information until the end of a sentence.

d We are describing a process.

3 Complete the text with the verbs in brackets in the correct tense. Use the active or passive as appropriate.

HIGH FLYER!

She (make) ____**makes**____ (1) swinging on a trapeze look far too easy, but acrobat Corinne Pierre is well aware of the dangers. 'I (have) _____ (2) no serious injuries during my career so far, but I know it could happen at any time.' This is very obvious when you see her dangling from a ten metre rope swing, waiting to (catch) _____ (3) by another acrobat. As she says, 'Safety standards need to (establish) _____ (4), but without taking away the excitement.'

Corinne (join) _____ (5) the circus in 1985 at the tender age of ten. While other children (read) _____ (6) Harry Potter stories, she (teach) _____ (7) how to do the Chinese balancing chair act. A couple of years later she (see) _____ (8) by a scout for the world famous 'Cirque du Soleil' and invited to join them for a two-year tour. Since then she (never look back) _____ (9).

Luckily for us she (recently settle) _____ (10) in London and set up her own performing company. She now directs as well as performs what she calls 'physical theatre'. Money is an important issue for the company. As she points out, 'We (fund) _____ (11) by government grants and these seem to be harder and harder to get.' Nevertheless, her company's ambitious productions (amazingly well receive) _____ (12) by audiences and I, for one, have no doubts that we (see) _____ (13) a lot more of this remarkable new talent in the future.

👄 Speaking

1 Work with a partner and each choose one of the topics below. Prepare to time your partner – give them 1 minute to prepare and then ask them to start speaking. Tell them to stop speaking after 2 minutes. Did your partner answer the question on the card?

Grammar hint

the passive with make, let, allow

Which of these sentences are grammatically possible?

a i His boss made him finish the report before he went home.
 ii He was made finish the report before he went home.
 iii He was made to finish the report before he went home.

b i She let him have the day off work.
 ii He was let to have the day off work.
 iii He was allowed to have the day off work.

Grammar reference: see page 247

Exam hint

Exercise 1 is a practice task for Part 2 of the Speaking Paper.

Student A

You are going to talk about **jobs and working**. You can use some or all of the ideas listed below in your talk but <u>you must answer this question</u>:

What would be your ideal job and why?
You must talk for 1 to 2 minutes. You have 1 minute to think and make notes before your talk begins.

Here are some ideas to help you:
- Salary
- Enjoyment
- Working hours
- Challenge

Student B

You are going to talk about **jobs and working**. You can use some or all of the ideas listed below in your talk but <u>you must answer this question</u>:

Which job would you least like to do and why?
You must talk for 1 to 2 minutes. You have 1 minute to think and make notes before your talk begins.

Here are some ideas to help you:
- Salary
- Enjoyment
- Working hours
- Challenge

2 Work with a partner and take it in turns to ask and answer the following questions. Remember to give as much information as possible and try to keep talking for at least 5 minutes.

Exam hint

Exercise 2 is a practice task for Part 3 of the Speaking Paper.

Part 3

We have been talking about **jobs and working** and I would like to ask you some more questions on this topic.

- What are the benefits of working from home? (Tell me about that.)
- What are the disadvantages of working from home? (Tell me about that.)
- What kind of person would be suited to working from home? (Why is that?)

- Do you think it is more important to do a job that you enjoy or one that pays well? (Why is that?)
- Do you think that everybody should have the opportunity to learn new skills in their job? (Why is that?)
- Do you think that it is important to stay with the same employer throughout your working life? (Why is that?)

- In the last twenty years, what changes have there been in the way that people work? (Tell me about that.)
- Do you think that improvements in technology have made work easier for people? (Why is that?)
- What changes do you think will take place in the way that people work over the next twenty years? (Tell me about that.)

Grammar reference: see page 248

Grammar: ability

1 Look at these examples and answer the questions that follow.

- *I hope **I'll be able to** do more work in films in the future.*

- *You must **be able to** fly straight and keep your body rigid if you want to be a human cannonball!*

- *I **can** use this new design programme quite easily. I did a training course on it last month.*

- *I **could** speak Portuguese quite well when I was working in Brazil.*

- *I **managed to** communicate quite well on my school trip to Italy although I have never studied Italian properly.*

- *I **haven't been able to** attend many meetings recently.*

    a   What is the past of *can* (when it refers to ability)?

    b   When do we use *able to* rather than *can* or *could*?

2 Which of the alternatives in sentences a and b are correct? Why?

    a   He *managed to/could* get to the meeting on time in spite of the traffic.

    b   When Beatrice was younger, she *managed to/could* sing like an angel.

3 There are mistakes in six of these sentences. Find the mistakes and correct them.

    a   How did he manage to finish writing the report so quickly?

    b   I can't to speak any louder. I've got a sore throat.

    c   I've been able to touch type since I was at college.

    d   Apparently, a secretary got stuck in a lift this morning, but they were able to get her out quite quickly.

    e   He could juggle quite well when he worked as a clown.

    f   We've looked everywhere for the caretaker, but we don't be able to find him.

    g   I was used to be able to work through the night if necessary.

    h   We didn't managed to persuade Mikey to take the day off work.

    i   The window in the conference room was stuck but we're able to open it in the end.

    j   They must can lend us some money. They're very rich.

4 Complete the text with one word in each space.

> James was always something of an unusual child. To start with, he _____ (1) walk by the time he was nine months old and then he was _____ (2) to speak in proper sentences before he was a year and a half. There are other examples, but I particularly remember when he took us all by surprise shortly before his tenth birthday when he _____ (3) to memorise every capital city for fun one weekend. He does have an incredible memory. For example, if you ask him what he was doing on a particular day a year ago, he _____ (4) tell you exactly where he was, who he was with and what they were doing. James left university last year and unfortunately he hasn't _____ (5) able to find a job that really suits him yet. We really hope he'll _____ (6) able to put his talents to good use. He's a very special person.

5 Work with a partner and tell each other about something you:

- could do when you were younger that you can't do now.

- have managed to do recently which you are really pleased about.

- can do quite well but not as well as you would like.

- hope you will be able to do in the future.

 Writing

1 Work with a partner. Discuss these questions about writing a job application letter in English.

a What style should the letter be written in?

b How long should it be?

c About how many paragraphs should there be?

d What should go in each paragraph?

e What should you do once you have written your letter?

2 Read this text and check your ideas from Exercise 1.

Get it Write

Never underestimate the __C__ (0) of the covering letter that you send for a job application. It is your _____ (1) to sell yourself to the employer and to get the opportunity of an interview for the _____ (2). There is no strict formula for an application letter as different jobs may require different approaches. Employers can _____ (3) standardised letters, so you must tailor every letter to be uniquely relevant to each job you apply for. You will need to make sure that the letter is essentially formal in style but also friendly and that you pay _____ (4) to your spelling, punctuation and grammar. Many application letters are far too long. Try to keep to one side of A4 paper and no more than three to four paragraphs, otherwise you will lose the interest _____ (5) the person reading it!

The first paragraph of the application letter is the most important. It _____ (6) the tone and focus. It is a good idea to begin by addressing the letter to a _____ (7) person if you can get hold of this information. This paragraph should be brief and to the point, indicating which job you are applying for as well as the _____ (8) of your information and an explanation as to why you have applied for this job.

In the _____ (9) parts of the letter, present your work experience, education, training – whatever makes the connection between you and the job you are seeking. Highlight why you are right _____ (10) the job and list any relevant achievements. Be positive and confident and focus more on the future than the past.

In the final paragraph you should indicate how the prospective employer can get in _____ (11) with you and when are the best times for an interview. It is important to end the letter strongly and on a positive note. Once you have written your letter, check it several times for any mistakes you may have made and check all the information you have provided them with is _____ (12).

3 Read the text again and decide which answer, a, b, c, or d, best fits each gap.

0 a status	*b influence*	*c importance*	*d grandeur*
1 a luck	b chance	c fortune	d gamble
2 a position	b place	c spot	d site
3 a watch	b notice	c observe	d spot
4 a regard	b thought	c attention	d concentration
5 a by	b from	c with	d of
6 a sets	b starts	c presents	d shows
7 a unique	b special	c particular	d peculiar
8 a cause	b source	c root	d base
9 a majority	b chief	c main	d prime
10 a for	b with	c to	d on
11 a meet	b connect	c touch	d hold
12 a accurate	b legitimate	c authentic	d faithful

4 Work with a partner and discuss these questions:

● Have you ever written any job application letters?

● If yes, what job(s) were you applying for and what happened?

● If not, and you were going to apply for a part-time job, what sort of work would you like to do and why?

Writing reference: see page 258

5 Work with a partner. Read the advert and the letter of application and then discuss these questions:

● Do you think it is a good letter?

● Does it have any problems?

● If so, what are they?

English-speaking Tour Guide Wanted

Our client is an English family with two young children who would like to spend two weeks travelling around the country, visiting all the most important tourist sites.

The successful applicant for this position will spend two weeks accompanying the family, ensuring they have a comfortable and informative trip.

You will have a good level of English and a good knowledge of the major tourist sites.

There is very generous remuneration for this position and all (first-class) travel and living expenses will be paid.

Please apply in writing to: Marsha Thorpe, LuxHolidays, 15 Cavendish Square, London W1 3PN.

Dear Ms thrope i am writing to apply for the position you advertised in 'english Language Weekly' on 14th June

I am twenty-one years old and in the third year of a degree in tourism Im also studying English as a subsidiary subject. I have a good knowledge of all the major Tourist sites and can communicate well in English Last summer I worked as a tour guide for Thomas Holidays in addition I have two younger brothers and have always enjoyed being with and looking after children I am available during the months of july and august and would very much value the opportunity to work with this English family

I can be contacted at the above address or by phone on 07941127123 if you have any further questions please don't hesitate to call me. I look forward to hearing from you.

yours sincerely,

Silvia Nero
(Silvia Nero)

6 Work with a partner. Read the section on punctuation in the Writing reference on page 253. Correct all the errors you can find in the letter.

7 Read the advert and then write a letter applying for one of the volunteer positions.

Exam hint

Exercise 7 is a practice task for Part 5 of the Reading and Writing Paper.

Get Away From It All!

We have a few limited places for volunteers to join our round-the-world sailing expedition, which will carry out scientific research in various remote islands and other parts of the world. You can be part of this unforgettable experience for three months. No experience of working on boats is necessary, but it is important that you are flexible, hard-working and can be an enthusiastic member of a team. Food and accommodation provided.

Apply to Voyage International, PO Box 294, Croydon, Surrey.

In your letter you should:
● give two details about yourself
● give two reasons why you are interested
● give two reasons why you are suitable.

Write your letter using between 100 and 150 words.

Vocabulary: phrasal verbs (work)

1 **R41** ▶ Listen to a conversation between two work colleagues. What are they both worried about?

2 Look at the audioscript on page 227. Match the <u>underlined</u> phrasal verbs to these meanings.
   a depend on
   b reduce (x 2)
   c arrive
   d postpone
   e fire (for economic reasons)
   f take control
   g employ
   h expand
   i arrange

3 Complete these sentences with the correct forms of the phrasal verbs in Exercise 2.
   a The government needs to _____ _____ the level of inflation urgently.
   b We have three candidates for the new job _____ _____ to see you this afternoon.
   c We've decided to _____ _____ our usual Tuesday staff meeting until Friday because so many people are off sick.
   d Steve finally _____ _____ nearly twenty minutes after the presentation had started.
   e We really must _____ _____ on travel expenses. From now on, all junior managers must fly economy class.
   f Our local big supermarket has _____ _____ into selling designer jeans and t-shirts.
   g Why does she want to leave? We only _____ her _____ in March.
   h Who do you think will _____ _____ as manager when Sue goes on maternity leave?
   i You know you can always _____ _____ Jamie in a crisis.
   j Apparently, due to falling demand EngCom have _____ _____ another 300 workers.

4 Work with a partner and discuss these questions:
   ● Have you ever been surprised by somebody *turning up* to see you when you weren't expecting them?

   ● Is there anything that you *put off* doing because you don't enjoy it?

   ● If you had a problem, is there anybody you could *count* on to help you?

Reading

1 Work with a partner and discuss these questions:

● Is there a difference between a shop sales assistant and shop floor assistant?

● What is the difference between a cashier and a shop floor/sales assistant?

● What do you think an in-store demonstrator does?

2 Read this list of jobs and match each of the statements that follow to one of the jobs. You must choose answers based on the information given. Each job should only be used once.

Exam hint

Exercise 2 is a practice task for Part 1 of the Reading and Writing Paper.

Jobs

A   Shop Sales Assistant

Previous retail experience would be an advantage. Applicants must have the ability to work alone and be a confident people person. Duties include selling, stock counts, re-stocking of the shop, taking payments and other associated tasks as required. This is a temporary position for three weeks only.

B   Shop Floor Assistant

Working on the shop floor, you have an important part to play in helping meet sales targets, whether it's by recommending a product to a customer or making sure the shelves are stocked with the things they want to buy. A smart uniform will be provided.

C   Multi Drop Van Driver

Multi drop van drivers required. Previous multi drop experience of 75 deliveries a day an advantage and must be able to provide relevant references. Duties include multi drop deliveries in Leeds and surrounding areas. A minimum of 8 hours pay per day and overtime is paid at time and a half after 10 hours.

D   Nursery Nurse

Typical work activities include: helping children with their learning, play and educational and social development, and assisting children in gaining independence within the class and when using playground environment. Also, you will be responsible for general care and maintenance of materials and equipment, and keeping records. Applicants must have proven work experience.

E Support Assistant

Seeking an enthusiastic and organised person to work in our graduate school office. You will provide high quality support to all core student administrative functions, from enquiry and application to final examination and graduation. This is an exciting opportunity for a highly motivated individual who enjoys working as part of a team.

F Cashier

Applicants must be aged 18 as they will be serving petrol. Previous experience is preferred; however, full training will be provided. Duties include selling at the till, merchandising and general cleaning. Hours are available on a rota basis. Applicants must be flexible with working days and hours.

G Bowling Coordinator

This is a varied position working in a busy bowling and family entertainment centre. You will have responsibility for managing the bowling operation, coordinating customer care activities, customer bookings, taking payments and liaising with customers face to face and over the telephone. Experience is preferred but not essential as full training will be provided.

H In-Store Demonstrator

Previous experience within a similar role is preferred but not essential as full training will be given. Must have a confident manner and be able to approach people. You will be working within a retail outlet, demonstrating company products from a stand and making appointments for double glazing fitters to visit clients.

I Travel Consultant

Enthusiastic and confident candidate required to join busy retail travel team. Working hours are three full days – Thursday, Friday and Saturday. Responsibilities include selling all aspects of travel face-to-face, on the telephone and by e-mail, and booking tailor made travel itineraries to suit client needs.

J Customer Care Executive

This is a fixed term contract for 12 months. Experience of providing telephone based customer care as part of a team a distinct advantage. You will have the ability to balance the handling of inbound and outbound calls with the need to ensure customer requests are actioned correctly in a timely manner.

	Statements	A	B	C	D	E	F	G	H	I	J
1	To apply for this job you must have worked in a similar role.										
2	You are paid at a higher rate for working longer hours in this job.										
3	This job relies on you being able to start conversations with strangers.										
4	You will be helping people plan routes and accommodation in this job.										
5	Work clothes will be given to you by the company for this role.										
6	This job lasts for only one year.										
7	You will be helping those in higher education in this role.										
8	You will be in charge of running a service in this role.										
9	You should be happy to work unsupervised in this job.										
10	You have to be of a certain age to apply for this job.										

Summarising

1 You are doing a project for your teacher on work and jobs. Read the article and write your summary.

In your summary you should:

● give **two** ways in which job opportunities have changed

● give **two** ways in which working conditions can vary

● give **two** ways in which employers can support the needs of their employees

Write your summary using between 100 and 150 words.

Exam hint

Exercise 1 is a practice task for Part 6 of the Reading and Writing Paper.

What type of work would suit you?

Jobs are now more flexible than ever; not all workers are simply employed by a company. There are lots more people working on short and fixed term contracts, instead of full-time, permanent ones. Some people choose to get temporary jobs through an employment agency. This means that they work for different companies for a set amount of time. Other people work on a freelance basis, meaning that they work for themselves, but take on short-term contracts for companies. Freelancers often have a great deal of experience in a specialised area. The workforce is now more skilled and qualified than ever. With employers having a larger group of candidates to choose from, it can be hard to get into work if you cannot show that you have certain qualifications or skills.

Starting at 9.00 a.m. and finishing at 5.00 p.m., with an hour for lunch somewhere in the middle, may still be considered a working day, but for more and more people it is not a reality. Some jobs, like nursing or manufacturing, depend on using shift patterns, which means working during the night and early morning. Some jobs will be outside, some will be in an office, some will be in a workshop or industrial environment and some will be more physically demanding than others. When you are applying for a job or planning a career, it may be worth thinking about what sort of environment you work best in and whether you have other commitments or responsibilities that could prevent you from having different working hours. This will make sure that your working schedule fits in with the rest of your life.

Working patterns are now more flexible so that workers can balance career and personal commitments. Many companies or organisations see the benefit in allowing their staff a certain amount of flexibility in their working hours. Some people have a right to ask for flexible working, but a lot of employers now let employees organise their work around their home life. Types of flexibility include working from home, flexi-hours and jobsharing. If you are working, it does not mean that you stop learning. There will be lots of opportunities for you to learn new things, so make the most of any chances you get. Remember that even skills that do not seem relevant at the moment may come in useful later on. Some employers may pay for the costs of training courses that you may want to take if they feel it would benefit you in your current role. If you are in a job that does not offer any training opportunities, you may be entitled to time off if you want to study for certain qualifications.

Planning a career can be tough in an ever-changing job market. It is not just the job itself you have got to consider, but also the working hours, work environment and pay and training opportunities as well.

Language recap

Grammar

1 Rewrite this text with correct punctuation.

> the leaning tower of pisa in italy was begun in 1174 as a bell tower for the nearby cathedral the foundations were laid in sand and only three of the eight storeys were finished before it began to lean the plans were altered to compensate for the problem and the building was eventually completed in 1350 the 54.5 m tower continued to lean a little more each century until 1990 when engineers did work to help correct the problem the work cost $25m but the tower should now survive for another 200 years at least

2 There are mistakes in six of these sentences. Find the mistakes and correct them.
a I think my bike has been stole.
b Your new computer will been sent as soon as possible.
c Have you any idea when this picture was taken?
d The gym can be used by any of our members.
e I'm afraid this flat has already being sold.
f Eddie, our dog, needs be taken for a good walk at least once a day.
g All personnel are requested to make their way towards the nearest fire exit.
h The hole in the road was being repair when I left home this morning.

i My boss has said that I'm going to be given a company car from the start of next year.
j When I finally got to the meeting, everyone had already told about the disastrous sales figures.

3 Complete these sentences with one word connected with ability.
a I'd like to _____ able to swim.
b Did you manage _____ change Derek's mind?
c They haven't _____ able to decide where they want to get married.
d Surely you _____ ask your boss for a few hours off on Friday?
e You must be _____ to work evening shifts in this job.
f My brother and I _____ both play tennis quite well in our teens.
g I hope you _____ be able to come to the party on Saturday.
h I'm afraid they didn't _____ to finish painting the kitchen.

Vocabulary

4 Match the sentence halves a–j with i–x to make complete sentences.
a When you didn't turn up on Friday,
b You can't put off
c His daughter will probably take over
d We want to avoid laying off
e Better farming methods have brought down
f We're thinking of branching out
g It might be a good idea to take on
h The government is going to cut back
i We've lined up some
j You can always count on

i any of our permanent members of staff.
ii into new markets in Asia.
iii making your decision again.
iv the price of food.
v fantastic bands for Saturday night.
vi its funding for adult education colleges.
vii we tried to call you.
viii the business when he retires.
ix Marta to have an interesting idea.
x another marketing assistant.

5 Match the definitions a–h to the words/phrases in the box.

> headhunt   demanding (job)   maternity leave
> promising (career)   promote   be made redundant
> high-powered   get the sack

a time that a mother is allowed to spend away from work when she has a baby
b when someone is dismissed from their job
c find someone with special skills and experience needed for a particular job and persuade them to leave their present job
d give someone a more responsible, higher paid job in a company
e important or influential
f showing signs of being successful or good in the future
g needing a lot of ability, effort or skill
h when someone has to leave their job because there is not enough work.

Paper 3: Speaking

As you know, the speaking examination is in three parts and lasts about 12 minutes altogether. An interlocutor – most probably a teacher within your centre – will interview you. She/He will record your speaking exam and then send it to an Edexcel examiner to be marked.

 ## Part 3: Extended discussion (maximum 5 minutes)

The interlocutor will bring Part 2 of the test to a close after 2 minutes and will then introduce Part 3 – this is an extended discussion of the same topic used in Part 2.

The interlocutor will have a set of questions provided by Edexcel which she/he will ask you in order to extend the topic you covered in your talk in Part 2. All of the questions encourage you to talk at length. They range from the concrete and familiar to the more complex and abstract. The interlocutor will start with the more familiar and everyday questions, and then move on to questions that ask for opinion and hypothesis and which are designed to stretch and challenge you to find the extent of your ability in English. Don't worry: Edexcel examiners do not make any judgements on the views and opinions you express.

Remember: if you don't understand the occasional word in a question, you may ask the interlocutor to explain it, but she/he is not allowed to give you a detailed explanation nor paraphrase the question for you.

Your oral is assessed over all three parts for:

● **Communicative ability and content:** your ability to express opinions and information, to initiate and to respond to questions appropriately.

● **Pronunciation and fluency:** your ability to produce clear and understandable language.

● **Lexical accuracy and range:** how accurately and appropriately you use vocabulary to communicate, and how well you cope with any vocabulary problems, e.g. if you forget a word during the test.

● **Grammatical accuracy and range:** range and accuracy of the grammatical structures you use.

Let's have a look at a Part 3 interlocutor's card from the Edexcel International GCSE ESL Speaking Paper in November 2009.

Remember in Part 2, you had to answer the question *What things should people know if they want to visit your country?* and you were given these ideas to help you:

* *Clothes*
* *Behaviour*
* *Customs and traditions*
* *Weather*
* *Other*

In Part 3, the interlocutor will ask you some questions on the topic, which you, the candidate, do not see.

PART 3

We have been talking about **visiting your country** *and I would like to ask you some more questions on this topic.*

* *Why do people travel to your country?*
* *What do you think a visitor to your country would find particularly interesting?*
* *Has tourism had an impact on your country? (Tell me about it.)*

* *How do you show politeness in your community/country?*
* *What do you particularly like about your community/country? (Why is that?)*
* *How do you think your community/country will change in the future?*

* *What things are important to consider when visiting other countries?*
* *What have you found out when you have met people from other places?*
* *What are the main benefits of international travel?*

The questions are set out in groups of three. If you look closely at them, you will see that you can give factual answers to the questions in the first group. As you progress through the second to the third group, you can see that you need to offer opinions in answer to these questions. It is important to remember that there are not really right or wrong answers to these questions – you are being invited to give your point of view and explain them, i.e. give reasons for your opinions. As long as what you say is relevant to the question, then all is fine. It is useful to note that the questions in the first two groups target your country specifically, whereas the questions in the final group widen the theme and ask about visiting other countries in more general terms.

These questions give you plenty of opportunity to use a wide range of structures, e.g. past, present and future tenses, conditional, passive, modal verbs, superlatives, relative and other subordinate clauses. Try your best to take advantage of this opportunity to demonstrate your capabilities. Since the questions ask about different aspects of visiting your country and then other countries, you are also given the chance to use an extensive range of vocabulary in your answers.

Getting started...

1 Look at the pictures. What does each one make you think about?

2 Check that you understand the words in the box. Which syllable has the main stress in each word? (Refer to a dictionary if necessary.)

> memory subconscious health
> depression feeling mind
> psychologist interpretation
> mood experiment analysis

3 Complete these sentences using words from the box in Exercise 2.

a Blood samples were sent to the laboratory for _____.
b He managed to recite the entire poem from _____.
c I thought the director's _____ of *Hamlet* was very interesting.
d Billy seems to have a lot on his _____ at the moment.
e Why are you in such a bad _____? Has something happened?
f I've decided to re-train and become a child _____.

Exam hint

Exercise 1 is a practice task for Part 1 of the Speaking Paper.

Speaking

1 Work with a partner and decide who is going to answer the Student A questions and who is going to answer the Student B questions. Student A needs to answer all four questions, taking no more than 3 minutes. Repeat the process for the Student B questions.

> **Student A**
> **Let's talk about moods**
> Would you say that you are usually a happy person? (Why is that?)
> What puts you in a good mood? (Tell me about that.)
> What puts you in a bad mood? (Tell me about that.)
> Is there somebody you know who always puts you in a good mood? (Tell me about that.)

> **Student B**
> **Let's talk about memory**
> Do you think you have a good memory? (Why is that?)
> Do you find it easy to remember names and faces? (Tell me about that.)
> What techniques do you use when revising for exams? (Tell me about that.)
> Is there anything that you always forget to do? (Tell me about that.)

Reading

1 Work with a partner and discuss these questions:

● What kinds of things make people happy?

● Do you think that people are happier now than in the past? Why/Why not?

2 Read the article *How to be happy* and answer the questions.

Exam hint

Exercise 2 is a practice task for Part 3 of the Reading and Writing Paper.

How to be happy

Happiness is hard to define. For some people it's about being in love or the birth of a child, for others, winning the lottery or being in touch with nature. In scientific terms, happiness has different dimensions. Positive psychology expert, Sheila Panchal, explains: 'Psychologists have identified three elements to happiness – having pleasures in life, being engaged and using your strengths on a regular basis, and experiencing a sense of meaning by feeling part of something greater than yourself.'

Happy people have stronger immune systems – when exposed to the flu virus, they are more able to resist it – and they recover from surgery faster. Happy people also tend to live longer. That's the conclusion from an analysis of the attitudes of new nuns entering an American convent in 1932. Psychologists rated each of them for the level of positive feeling expressed and found a correlation with how long each nun lived.

The relationship between money and happiness is complex. 'If you're below the breadline, then extra money makes a difference to your happiness,' says Panchal. But after a certain level of income, extra money does not make you that much happier. One key factor seems to be that we start to compare ourselves with others and this creates discontent. In one study, Harvard students were asked what they would prefer – a world where they got $50,000 a year and everyone else got $25,000, or one where their income was doubled to $100,000, but others got

more – $250,000. The majority preferred the first world, where they got less in absolute terms, but at least it was more than everyone else.

Studies on twins show a strong genetic component in happiness and depression. This is not just because twins share the same environment – research on identical twins brought up apart shows the same. However, the genes involved in happiness are unknown and, as with all psychological attributes, it is likely that many different genes are responsible. One group of genes that may be involved in positive mood are those dealing with the brain chemical serotonin. Low levels of serotonin are linked to depression. Drugs like Prozac boost serotonin levels and so lift depression and improve mood. But even if you are born miserable, you can still learn to be happier by changing your outlook and attitude.

Relationships are one of the most important sources of our happiness. Socioeconomic surveys in Germany suggest that both men and women become happier when they marry. Happiness increases as the marriage approaches, peaks in the first year and then decreases a little as people get used to their new status. However, it still remains at a higher level than in the single state. Children, as you might expect, are a source of joy when they are born, but within two years, their parents' happiness tends to revert to its former level.

Happiness around the world is tracked by projects such as the World Database of Happiness. It seems that populations

in Western countries, such as Britain, have not got any happier since 1950. This appears to be true despite massive increases in the standard of living and quality of life. Dr Stevens identifies two major barriers to achieving happiness in the 21st century – the car and the media. Cars isolate you from the local community so that your neighbourhood and town centre more often feel like threatening places rather than a positive resource. Television (and to a lesser extent print media) exposes people to violence, bad news and consumer pressures which create fear and discontent. TV watching is also passive and takes away time that could be used for much more satisfying activities.

According to the US General Social Survey, the main sources of happiness are, in order of importance: family relationships, finances, work, social networks and health. Added to that are personal values and freedom. Based on his long-standing research, Dr Stevens claims happiness comes from the body, relationships and learning to direct your thoughts in a positive way. That doesn't just mean vaguely wishing that things in your life were different. It means taking definite steps to improve your life. 'Take exercise and watch your diet, work at caring, loving relationships and give them the time they need,' he says. 'Smile at strangers, make small gestures and, above all, to make a list of the good things you have to be grateful for. If you think like this, wellbeing and good feelings will follow.'

Questions

1–5

Choose **true**, **false** or **not given** for each statement.

	True	False	Not given
1 Happiness is calculated using a scientific formula.	☐	☐	☐
2 There are three aspects to happiness.	☐	☐	☐
3 Happy people are likely to be physically stronger.	☐	☐	☐
4 Having more money always makes people happier.	☐	☐	☐
5 Comparing yourself to others is not beneficial.	☐	☐	☐

6–10

Complete these sentences using no more than **three words** or **a number**.

6   A person's genes greatly influence how they feel; this has been proven by conducting research using _____.

7   It is _____ which genes, and how many, are involved in what makes us happy.

8   The lack of _____ has been associated with depression.

9   Research has shown that _____ makes people happier than remaining single.

10   Global data indicates that since 1950 people have not become _____.

11–15

Answer these questions using no more than **three words** or **a number**.

11   According to Dr Stevens, which two things stop us from being happy?

....

12   Due to having more transport options, what have we lost touch with?

....

13   Which pastime takes the place of more beneficial pursuits?

....

14   According to Dr Stevens, what type of thinking contributes to happiness?

....

15   How should you go about remembering the positive things in your life?

....

3 Read the 'Happy Hints'. Work with a partner and discuss these questions:

● Which do you think are the three best pieces of advice? Why?

● Is there one which you would consider trying to follow?

● Could you add one more 'happy hint'?

HAPPY HINTS – TIPS TO IMPROVE YOUR MOOD

1 Go nuts > Instead of eating sweets and crisps, snack on nuts, seeds, bananas and avocados – they all help to boost levels of serotonin, the brain's 'feel good' chemical.

2 Be optimistic > Learn to be an optimist. Look for temporary and specific explanations when things go wrong – 'I wasn't on top form', rather than 'I'm useless'. Take time to identify what you are really good at.

3 Get a pet > Consider getting a pet to look after. Choose an animal that suits your personality or lifestyle.

4 Socialise > Do something to connect you to the community – join an evening class, volunteer for a campaign or invite a neighbour in for coffee.

5 Keep dancing > See what happens if you cut your TV watching and newspaper reading in half. Replace with something more active, e.g. try a dance class, learn a new language, etc.

6 Smile > Be really daring – smile and say 'hello' to someone you don't know; even consider stopping for a chat.

7 Keep a diary > Keep a journal of the good things that happen – aim to list three to five items, however small, every day.

8 Go running > Twenty to thirty minutes exercise, outside if possible, three times a week will boost your mood.

9 Say thank you > Develop the habit of gratitude and learn the art of forgiveness – let go of the bad things that happened in the past. Live as much in the present as you can.

10 Happy talking > Take time to talk. Schedule an hour-long conversation with your partner or closest friend every week and guard the time jealously.

Vocabulary: mispronounced words

1 Look at the dictionary entry and then discuss the questions with a partner.

a What is the correct pronunciation of *scientific*?

b Which letter is not pronounced?

c How many syllables does it have?

d Which syllable has the main stress?

2 Look at the word families a–e. What is:

i the correct part of speech of each word in the family?

ii the position of main stress in each word?

iii the correct pronunciation of each word?

a science, scientist, scientific

b psychology, psychologist, psychological

c analyse, analysis, analytical, analytically

d photograph, photographer, photographic, photography

e economics, economist, economy, economical, economise

> **scientific** /saɪən'tɪfɪk‹ / *adj*
>
> **1** relating to science: *scientific discoveries / a **scientific experiment** / advances in **scientific research***
>
> **2** using an organised system: *we keep records, but we're not very scientfic about it*
>
> —**scientifically** /-kli/ *adv*

3 Look at the words in the box. Make a note of the ones you feel confident about pronouncing and the ones you don't feel confident about.

> secretary   recipe   comfortable   cupboard   cough   receipt   muscle
> interesting   apostrophe   scissors   law   chocolate   comb   dessert

4 Work with a partner and go through the list. Compare how you think you pronounce each word.

5 R42 ▶ Listen and check the correct pronunciation of each word in Exercise 3.

6 Work with a partner and take turns to read these sentences out loud. Pay special attention to the pronunciation of the words in *italics*.

a   Is it against the *law* to take a *comb* on a plane?

b   He wanted to know the *recipe* for the *chocolate* cake which they had for *dessert*.

c   It's *interesting* the way an *apostrophe* can change the meaning of a sentence.

d   Do you have a *receipt* for the *scissors* that you want to return?

e   The *secretary's* chair isn't very *comfortable*.

f   You can see his *muscles* in that *photograph*.

g   William can't decide whether to study *law*, *economics* or *psychology*.

h   My grandmother keeps the *cough* medicine in the top *cupboard*.

Grammar: hypothetical meaning

1 Look at these statements. Work with a partner and discuss these questions:

● Who do you think is speaking?

● Why do you think they each say this?

● What is the context of the statement?

a   I wish I *lived* by the sea.

b   I wish I *could spend* more time with my family.

c   I wish I *had travelled* more when I was younger.

d   I wish you *wouldn't worry* so much.

2 R43 ▶ Listen and check your ideas.

3 Work with a partner and discuss the questions.

a   Look at the tenses of the verbs in *italics* in Exercise 1 sentences a–d. What is surprising about them?

b   How is a person usually feeling when they say *I wish you wouldn't ...!*

Grammar hint

wish + would(n't)

Which of the following sentences is not possible? Why?

1   I wish they wouldn't play their music so loudly.

2   I wish I would lose weight.

3   I wish it would stop raining.

Grammar reference: see page 248

4 Read this extract from an e-mail and complete each space with the correct form of the verb in brackets.

In your last message you asked me how everything was going. Well, to be honest, I really wish I (have) _____ (1) a bit more money coming in every month. I'd really like to pay off some of my credit card debts and start renting a flat on my own. I also wish I (live) _____ (2) a bit closer to my parents. It takes me nearly three hours to go and see them, which is quite hard especially if it's just for a day.

In terms of work, as you know, I've had a few problems getting a decent job recently. I suppose now I really wish I (do) _____ (3) a more practical degree at university. I mean I did enjoy psychology, but it's not very relevant to the jobs I've been applying for. The other thing I regret a little in terms of getting a good job is not making more effort with Spanish. You know my mum's Spanish and she tried to speak to me in Spanish at home when I was younger, but I never wanted to. In fact I really wish I (can speak) _____ (4) Spanish fluently now because it would be a big help in my job interviews!

Oh, yes, and while I'm doing all this wishing ... the only other thing I wish is about my best friend! I really wish he (not whistle) _____ (5). It's never in tune and it's very annoying!

5 Complete these sentences so that they are true for you. Work with a partner and tell each other about your wishes and explain why they are your wishes. Also, say if there is anything you can do to make your wishes come true.

● *I wish I ...* (+ past simple)

● *I wish I ...* (+ past perfect)

● *I wish I could ...*

● I wish (name of someone you know) *would/wouldn't ...*

6 The expressions in *italics* are also followed by past tense forms to show hypothetical meaning. Complete the second sentence so that it has a similar meaning to the first sentence. Decide if you need to add to or change the form of the words in the first sentence.

a *If only* she hadn't left the meeting early.
   I wish ...

b *It's time* I joined a gym. I need to get fit.
   I should ...

c *I'd rather* you painted the bathroom first.
   I would prefer it ...

d *Suppose* you were offered the job. Would you accept it?
   Imagine ...

Grammar reference: see page 248

7 There are mistakes in six of these sentences. Find the mistakes and correct them.

a I wish I can afford to buy a new car.

b If only I'd listen to my dad!

c She'd rather we helped her in the garden.

d It's time you to found somewhere to live.

e Suppose he asked you to marry him, what would you say?

f She wishes she had never borrowed his car.

g If only she knows how sorry we were.

h I wish she wouldn't spend so much time with Terry.

i It time we had a chat about your exam results.

j Suppose someone asked you where you did get the money from.

8 Work with a partner and discuss these questions:

- If you were to give yourself one piece of advice for this week beginning: *It's time I ...*, what would the advice be?

- Suppose you had the chance to meet one famous living person. Who would you choose and why?

 # Writing

1 Work with a partner. Make a list of the characteristics of a good article. How many different points can you think of?

An interesting title

2 Check your ideas on Writing reference page 252.

3 Read this task. Make a note of the important words and phrases.

> **Writing task**
>
> You see the following notice in an airline magazine.
>
> > *Are young people in your country happier today than 50 years ago?*
> >
> > Write us an article giving your opinions. The best article will be published and the writer will receive £200.
>
> Write your **article** for the magazine.

4 Read this answer to the task in Exercise 3. Work with a partner. What are the main strengths and weaknesses of the article?

Happy young people

This is a very interesting question. It is something I have thought about a lot. I have also talked to many of my friends about this. They have many different opinions. I am going to present my points in order.

Young people have many more opportunities than in the past. They have more money, more chances to get a good education and more freedom to do what they want. There is also a lot of new technology for young people to enjoy. There are mobile phones and the Internet. These make lots of possibilities for communicating with friends, getting to know new people and learning about the world.

On the other hand, there are many pressures on young people now to get a good degree, to have a career, to earn lots of money, to look good and to be in a happy relationship. When things don't go well, you can think you are a failure.

5 Complete these expressions for comparing and contrasting with the words in the box.

comparison contrast opposed unlike compared

a Young people today have much more freedom _____ with young people in the past.

b There's quite a bit more pressure on young people now in _____ with a few years ago.

c Children seem to spend much more time indoors using or playing with technology _____ when I was growing up. We were always outside, running around or playing with a ball.

d In _____ to most of her friends, my daughter hates mobile phones.

e Our teachers encourage us to have our own ideas as _____ to just learning other people's opinions off by heart.

6 Write your answer to the task in Exercise 3. Try to improve on the areas of weakness you identified in the sample answer. Use appropriate expressions for comparing and contrasting from Exercise 5. Remember you are writing your article for an airline magazine.

In your article you should:

● give **two** reasons why young people are happier

● give **two** reasons why young people are not happier

● give your opinion about how happy young people are.

Write your article using between 100 and 150 words.

Exam hint

Exercise 6 is a practice task for Part 4 of the Reading and Writing Paper.

Vocabulary: Love and relationships

1 Work with a partner and look at these sentences. What do the phrases in italics mean?

a I am *going out* with Marie from my photography club on Friday.

b She is very popular at work and *gets along with* everybody.

c The man *got engaged* to his wife several years before they got married.

d Many university students have little money so they often *go dutch* when they go out.

e The couple *split up* after dating for more than three years.

f Before actually deciding to *pop the question*, he thought about things carefully.

g She decided to get married and *settle down* after years of travelling.

h The couple had a big fight but they *made up* and things quickly got back to normal.

i After thinking about marriage for a long time the couple decided to *set a date*.

j I *hit it off* with a woman in my painting class and we have been friends ever since.

2 Match the phrases in Exercise 1 to these meanings.

   i   to end a relationship

   ii   to establish a regular routine after getting married

   iii   to decide to marry someone

   iv   to ask someone to marry you

   v   to forgive each other after an argument

   vi   to get along well with someone (from the first time that you meet that person)

   vii to go on a date or be dating someone

   viii to decide on a date for a wedding

   ix   to have a friendly relationship with someone

   x   to go on a date where each person pays half of the expenses

3 Choose the correct alternative in each sentence.

   a After knowing each other for five years, they decided to *hit it off/get engaged*.

   b He *settled down/popped the question* while they were on holiday in the Bahamas.

   c They *hit it off/made up* when they first met in primary school and have been friends ever since.

   d After years of thinking about it and saving for the big day, they decided to *split up/set a date*.

   e They are complete opposites so it is surprising how well they *go dutch/get along with each other*.

   f Nobody thought she would ever *settle down/split up* as she only had time for her career.

   g As it was an expensive restaurant, they decided to go *dutch/split up* on the bill.

   h They soon realised they didn't have much in common, and they *split up/set a date*.

   i They had a big argument last week and they still haven't *made up/settled down*.

   j They *went out/made up* last night after becoming friends at the tennis tournament.

4 Work with a partner and discuss these questions:

   ● Do you usually *go dutch* when you go out with your friends?

   ● Who in your family do you *get along* with best?

   ● Are you *going out* with anyone at the weekend?

   ● When you fall out with someone does it take you a long time to *make up*?

Grammar: subject-verb agreement

Grammar reference: see page 249

1 Choose the correct alternative in these sentences. Both alternatives are possible in two sentences.

a All of my choices *is/are* connected to the subject of 'memory'.

b Hardly anyone *is/are* prepared to help her.

c My family *is/are* very good at making plans.

d None of these films *has/have* been a major success.

e The police *has/have* asked for help from the public in finding a missing teenager.

f Two years *is/are* a long time to be unemployed.

g The news *is/are* much the same as it was last night.

h Politics *was/were* my main subject at university.

i These jeans *is/are* similar to my old ones.

j Our local football team *need/needs* to practise more.

k Scissors *is/are* not allowed on the plane.

l The United States *is/are* the home of baseball.

2 Read this extract from an e-mail message. Complete each gap with one word.

I'm afraid my news _____ (1) not very exciting at the moment – everything _____ (2) much the same as usual. I'm working hard on all my courses – especially economics. _____ (3) is a really difficult subject but the staff _____ (4) been very helpful. One professor has been giving extra tutorials for anyone who _____ (5) questions. Even so, almost nobody I know _____ (6) they're going to pass the end-of-term exams!

Did I tell you that our house was broken into? The police _____ (7) great and came round straight away but _____ (8) is not a lot they can do. Can you believe it my Gucci sunglasses _____ (9) taken? I was so upset. They cost me nearly £100! And £100 _____ (10) a lot of money to me at the moment!

3 Write five sentences which are meaningful for you, with words/phrases from the box.

> the news   politics   hardly anyone   jeans   my family
> the majority of   £5   one of my   everybody   the police

One of my sisters has just got married.

4 Work with a partner and tell each other your sentences.

Speaking

1   Work with a partner and each choose one of the topics below. Prepare to time your partner – give them 1 minute to prepare and then ask them to start speaking. Tell them to stop speaking after 2 minutes. Did your partner answer the question on the card?

Student A
You are going to talk about **feelings and memories**. You can use some or all of the ideas listed below in your talk but <u>you must answer this question</u>:

Describe a photograph that brings back happy memories. Why is it special to you?
You must talk for 1 to 2 minutes. You have 1 minute to think and make notes before your talk begins.

Here are some ideas to help you:
- Subject
- Place
- Situation
- Photographer

Student B
You are going to talk about **feelings and memories**. You can use some or all of the ideas listed below in your talk but <u>you must answer this question</u>:

Describe a happy time in your life. Why was this time special to you?
You must talk for 1 to 2 minutes. You have 1 minute to think and make notes before your talk begins.

Here are some ideas to help you:
- People
- Place
- Situation
- Age

2   Work with a partner and take it in turns to ask and answer the following questions. Remember to give as much information as possible and try to keep talking for at least 5 minutes.

Part 3
We have been talking about **feelings and memories** and I would like to ask you some more questions on this topic.

- How do you usually record your memories? (e.g. *diary, photos, video*) (Tell me about that.)
- Do you prefer taking pictures with a camera or a mobile phone? (Why is that?)
- What are the advantages of having cameras on mobile phones? (Tell me about that.)

- Why do you think people say that school days are the happiest days of your life? (Tell me about that.)
- What skills do you learn from going to school? (Tell me about that.)
- How does school prepare you for the real world? (Tell me about that.)

- Even though we have more now compared to in the past, people do not seem any happier? (Tell me about that.)
- What could people do to lead happier lives? (Tell me about that.)
- Do you think that people will become happier in the future? (Why is that?)

Vocabulary: idioms with *mind*

1 Work with a partner and look at these sentences. What do the phrases in *italics* mean?

a Do you have something *on your mind*? You look worried.

b It never *crossed my mind* that Arthur might be lying.

c When I looked at the first exam question, my *mind* just *went blank*.

d He found it difficult to *keep his mind* on what she was saying.

e I meant to get my dad a present, but it completely *slipped my mind*.

f She couldn't *make up her mind* whether to accept the job or not.

g If it'll *put your mind at rest*, why don't you go and see a doctor?

h I'd definitely be interested in buying your car, if you want to sell. Will you *keep it in mind*?

i I was worried my dad would *change his mind* and say he wouldn't give me a lift to the airport.

j 'Patient' is not the word that *springs to mind* when you think of Bill.

2 Match the phrases in Exercise 1 to these meanings.

i to forget about something

ii to continue paying attention to something

iii to be unable to think of anything

iv to decide

v to help someone to stop worrying

vi to remember information when deciding to do something

vii to think about something for a short time

viii to change your decision, plan or opinion about something

ix to think of something immediately

x to be worrying you

3 Choose the correct alternative in each sentence.

a I'm afraid we don't have any jobs at the moment but we will certainly *keep you in mind/put your mind at rest* if anything comes up.

b Have you *crossed your mind/made up your mind* where you're going to go on holiday?

c I'm afraid the meeting completely *crossed my mind/slipped my mind*. Was anything important decided?

d The interviewer asked me quite an easy question, but *my mind just went blank/it slipped my mind*.

e I'll phone you as soon as we land in Costa Rica if that will *cross your mind/put your mind at rest*.

f After the phone call with his girlfriend, he couldn't *keep his mind/change his mind* on his revision.

g What's on your *mind/put your mind at rest*? You're very quiet!

h I have no ideas for a present for Amy. Nothing *keeps it mind/springs to mind*.

4 Complete these sentences so that they are true for you.

a Something I do to keep my mind on my work when I am studying is to ...

b I sometimes find it difficult to make up my mind when I ...

c The last time my mind just went blank was when ...

d Something which can occasionally slip my mind is ...

5 Work with a partner and compare your sentences.

Summarising

Exam hint

Exercise 1 is a practice task for Part 6 of the Reading and Writing Paper.

1 Read the article *How to be happy* and write a summary for the school magazine. In your summary you should:

- state **two** things that make people happy according to UK experts

- state **two** things that the American survey adds to the UK findings

- state **two** things that the World Database of Happiness shows.

Write your summary using between 100 and 150 words.

How to be happy

Happiness is hard to define. For some people it's about being in love or the birth of a child, for others, winning the lottery or being in touch with nature. In scientific terms, happiness has different dimensions. UK psychologists have identified three elements to happiness – having pleasures in life, being engaged and using your strengths on a regular basis, and experiencing a sense of meaning by feeling a part of something greater than yourself.

UK experts also state that if you're living below the breadline, then extra money makes a difference to your happiness, but after a certain level of income, extra money does not make you that much happier. Relationships have also been proven to be one of the most important sources of our happiness. Research suggests that both men and women become happier when they marry and remain at a higher level of happiness than in the single state. Children, as you might expect, are a source of joy when they are born, but within two years, their parents' happiness tends to revert to its former level.

An American survey has gone one step further and put the main sources of happiness in order of importance: family relationships, finances, work, social networks and health. Added to that are personal values and freedom. Based on his long-standing research, it has been claimed that happiness comes from the body, relationships and learning to direct your thoughts in a positive way. That doesn't just mean vaguely wishing that things in your life were different. It means taking definite steps to improve your life. Taking exercise and watching your diet, working at caring, loving relationships and giving them the time they need is important. Also, smiling at strangers, making small gestures and, above all, listing the good things you have to be grateful for. If you think like this, wellbeing and good feelings will follow.

Happiness around the world is tracked by projects such as the World Database of Happiness. It seems that populations in Western countries, such as Britain, have not got any happier since 1950. This appears to be true despite massive increases in the standard of living and quality of life. Two major barriers to achieving happiness in the 21st Century have been identified as the car and the media. Cars isolate people from the local community so that neighbourhoods and town centres more often feel like threatening places rather than a positive resource. Television (and to a lesser extent print media) exposes people to violence, bad news and consumer pressures which create fear and discontent. TV watching is also passive and takes away time that could be used for much more satisfying activities.

If you do work out *how to be happy* there are recognised health benefits. Happy people have stronger immune systems; when exposed to the flu virus, they are more able to resist it, and they recover from surgery faster. Happy people also tend to live longer. Another two very good reasons to remain positive.

Grammar

1 There are mistakes in five of these sentences. Find the mistakes and correct them.

  a The majority of our class was at the end-of-term party.
  b Two weeks wasn't a long enough holiday.
  c A number of local people has asked for better lighting in this street.
  d A rugby team are made up of fifteen players.
  e My company has given €100,000 to charity this year.
  f The police is sure that the thief must have been in the house before.
  g These jeans aren't very comfortable.
  h The statistics shows that people who live in the south live longer than those who live in the north.

2 Complete these sentences with the words in the box.

> had   rather   suppose   time   only
> could   would   wish

  a I wish I _____ shut all the windows before it started to rain.
  b I'd _____ you tidied up your room before you went out.
  c I wish I _____ develop my own photographs.
  d It's _____ you got a proper job.
  e They _____ they had never bought their house in the country.
  f _____ someone asked where you got the money, what would you say?
  g If _____ I hadn't invited so many people to my birthday party!
  h I wish Simon _____ be a bit more friendly to my sister.

3 Complete these sentences using the prompts.

  a This car / making / strange noises. / Time / we buy / new one.
  b I wish / go / university / instead / get / a job / straight after I left school.
  c Suppose you / have / chance / be part / a scientific expedition / the Amazonian rainforest, / you go?
  d Julian / rather / we get / something to eat / before / go / the cinema.
  e I wish / he / not do / his trumpet practice / so early / Sunday morning.
  f It's time / you get / new jacket. / This one / have holes / the elbows!

Vocabulary

4 Unscramble the letters in *italics* to make words.

  a Everyone was in a confident *odom* and they were sure that they would win.
  b I think that being in good *lhhaet* is much more important than being rich.
  c I've been *gneilef* quite anxious about my job recently.
  d Our conclusion is that further *sasaiyln* of the data is needed.
  e They carried out an *teeemnpxri* on a group of university students to test their theory.
  f He's been suffering from a kind of *nersdeoips* ever since he lost his job.
  g I don't know where it comes from but my therapist says I have a *ccssoobiuuns* fear of failure.
  h Do you know what qualifications you need in order to become a *ohcysigoltps*?

5 Put the words in the box into the correct columns according to the underlined sounds.

> ec<u>o</u>nomy   ph<u>o</u>tograph   s<u>e</u>cretary   c<u>o</u>mfortable
> c<u>ou</u>gh   m<u>u</u>scle   ap<u>o</u>strophe   c<u>u</u>pboard   l<u>aw</u>
> ch<u>o</u>colate   c<u>o</u>mb,   r<u>e</u>cipe

s<u>u</u>n	d<u>oo</u>r	<u>e</u>gg	h<u>o</u>t	n<u>o</u>

6 Rewrite the sentences using an idiom with the word *mind* to replace the words in *italics*.

  a I meant to go to the bank today but *I forgot about it.*
  b I wish Michael would *decide* – does he want to go out tonight or not?
  c I promise I'll be home by 11.00 p.m. if that *makes you feel less worried.*
  d Please try to *concentrate on* your homework. Your exams are coming soon.
  e If you need anyone to do overtime, I'd be grateful if you could *remember that I'm interested.*
  f What's *worrying you*? You can always talk to me about your problems.
  g It was awful. I recognised him but then *I couldn't remember anything* about him.
  h What's *the first thing you think* of when I say 'childhood'?

General tips

You are not allowed to use a dictionary in any of the Edexcel International GCSE ESL papers so make sure you learn words regularly throughout your course – this way you will have more chance of understanding the reading and listening texts and you will be able to use lots of different words in your writing and speaking.

 Tips for Reading

1 Make sure you read the instructions at the beginning of each task – they tell you exactly what you have to do, e.g.

*Read **Top Tips for Saving Money at College** and answer questions 1 to 10.*

Identify which paragraphs (A–H) contain the information listed in questions 1 to 10 by marking (X) for the correct answer. Paragraphs may be used more than once or not at all. If you change your mind, put a line through the box (X) and then indicate your new answer with an (X). (Edexcel International GCSE ESL November 2008)

2 Look carefully to note the number of words needed to answer the questions. When you write your answer, you must not exceed the given word limit – if you do, you will not be able to gain the mark even if you include the correct words in your answer:

*Complete the following sentences. Write **no more than TWO** words and/or numbers taken from the text.*

3 In your answers, use only words and phrases taken directly from the passage. Do not try to paraphrase:

*Complete the following sentences. Write no more than TWO **words and/or numbers taken from the text**.*

4 Spelling is very important, so when you copy the words from the text into your answer, make sure you spell them correctly.

5 Have a go at answering every question – in this way, at least you have a chance of gaining the mark.

 Tips for Writing

1 The most important thing to remember when you are producing your pieces of writing is the word count. You will read the following instruction in every part of the writing section: *You should write between **100 and 150 words**.* This means that any material over the 150-word limit will not be assessed. If you write fewer than 100 words, you will probably not have covered the content

properly and the range of language you demonstrate will be limited. This means you could score a low mark.

2 Every task will have a number of bullet points or questions which you must address. Make sure you cover them all.

3 Bear in mind who you are writing to and why you are writing – this will determine the tone and register. Take care to use the right words and expressions for the context.

4 Your writing needs to be well organised with clear paragraphs, and your sentences should be linked logically. You may find it helpful to use headings for your paragraphs – but you don't have to if you prefer not to.

5 Plan your time carefully. It is a good idea to go back through your writing and check your writing for errors.

 Tips for Listening

1 Reading tips 1, 2, 3 and 5 also apply to the Listening Paper. However, in the Listening Paper you are allowed to make some minor spelling mistakes as long as the word is still recognisable. This piece of advice is offered to candidates on the front cover of the exam paper:

Provided that your answers can be understood, marks will not be deducted if you spell words incorrectly.

2 You will hear the recording for each part twice. Try making notes in pencil when you listen to the recording the first time and then confirm your answer in pen after the second listening.

 Tips for Speaking

1 Remember to speak up during the speaking test: it is important that the interlocutor can hear you!

2 In order to score well, you need to offer opinions as well as information. It is also important to expand your responses – you could offer reasons for your opinions.

3 Try to keep going! Answer all the questions you are asked as fully as possible and don't be afraid to take the initiative and volunteer extra information.

4 Use as wide a range of language as possible – both vocabulary and structures.

Progress Check 3 Chapters 11–15

1 Complete the sentences with the correct form of the verbs in brackets.

a If you _____ (mix) yellow and blue, you _____ (get) green.
b If I _____ (bring) more cash with me, I _____ (have) enough to lend you some now.
c As long as you _____ (not mind) sleeping on the floor, you _____ (be) welcome to stay.
d If only you _____ (tell) her how much you loved her. It's too late now.
e Unless you _____ (start) being more punctual, we _____ (have) to reconsider your position.
f I'd rather you _____ (not interrupt) me while I'm on the phone.
g Suppose you _____ (be) the manager. What would you do?
h I _____ (tell) you what she said provided you _____ (promise) not to tell anyone.

2 There is a mistake in *italics* in each of these sentences. Correct the mistakes.

a Go and talk to her and put your mind at *peace*.
b I tried to remember his name but my mind went completely *blind*.
c It's important to keep your *recipe* if you want to bring something back to the shop.
d I'm working long hours and getting paid a lot of *overwork* as well as my regular salary.
e They want someone who's good with figures and Diana *screams* to mind.
f I don't like borrowing money and I've never been *with* debt in my life.
g It is against the *legal* to use a mobile phone while driving.
h The company didn't need him anyone more and he was made *refund* after twenty-five years.
i You must take *over* insurance before you travel in case something happens.
j I'd like to be a psychologist and work with people with *mind* health problems.

3 Complete the gaps using the correct form of the verbs in brackets.

Have you read these Agatha Christie novels?

Dead Man's Folly
Sir George and Lady Stubbs fancy _____[1] (do) something different for the village fête and eventually decide _____[2] (stage) a 'mock murder mystery'. The well-known crime writer, Ariadne Oliver, agrees _____[3] (organise) the murder hunt with the help of Hercule Poirot. But it seems that something weird is about to happen ...

Dumb Witness
Emily's fall on the stairs seems _____[4] (be) an accident. She remembers _____[5] (trip) on a ball belonging to her dog. But the more she thinks about it, the more she feels that one of her relatives is trying _____[6] (kill) her. She writes to Hercule Poirot about her suspicions but, mysteriously, by the time he receives the letter, Emily is already dead ...

Black Coffee
A famous physicist, Sir Claud Amory, tells Poirot that he fears someone in his household is attempting _____[7] (steal) his latest discovery, a formula critical to England's defence. Poirot rushes to Amory's house and tries _____[8] (stop) the thief. He fails _____[9] (achieve) his mission, however, as Amory has died, his formula is missing and anyone could have been responsible ...

4 Complete the second sentence so that it has a similar meaning to the first sentence, using the word given. Do not change the word given. You must use between two and five words, including the word given.

'Why don't we buy her a CD?' Jules said.
suggested
Jules *suggested buying her* a CD.

a It's a pity I didn't know you were going to be here.
   wish
   I _____ you were going to be here.
b Alex got the sack because he was always late.
   not
   If Alex _____ , he wouldn't have got the sack.
c She said she would never tell anyone else our secret.
   promised
   She _____ anyone else our secret.
d 'Do you like horror films?' she asked me.
   if
   She _____ horror films.

e I didn't ask David because I wasn't able to contact him.
   managed
   If _____ David, I would have asked him.

f He deceived us with all the lies he told us.
   taken
   We _____ by all the lies he told us.

g 'You stole my bicycle,' he said to me.
   accused
   He _____ his bicycle.

h She works such long hours and I really don't like it.
   not
   I wish _____ such long hours.

5 Read the text and decide which answer, a, b, c or d, best fits each gap.

> A survey carried out last year by a recruitment agency investigated the influence of the small screen on our big decisions. These days, it seems, more and more students say that their choice of job was _____ (1) by a TV show. 62% of eighteen to twenty-four-year-olds said that CSI and other crime programmes made forensics look so _____ (2) that they would consider it as a _____ (3).
>
> An obsession with the CSI series led Emma Wade, twenty-two, to study forensic science at university. She explains, 'It was something that had never _____ (4) my mind before seeing that show. But I found I could identify with the characters – I wanted to be one of them. I wanted to _____ (5) in investigations and help _____ (6) the right people for crimes they have _____ (7). At first, I wanted to go for a _____ (8)- powered job in the FBI, but my teachers _____ (9) me to think about forensic science.'
>
> Engineering organisations, worried about low numbers of young people _____ (10) to train as engineers, are _____ (11) about using the TV to address this shortfall. They are going so far as to _____ (12) scriptwriters a £35,000 prize if they create a positive engineering character for TV.

1 a excited	b inspired	c elated	d interested
2 a enthusiastic	b thrilled	c puzzling	d exciting
3 a career	b promotion	c living	d work
4 a changed	b crossed	c slipped	d made
5 a turn out	b work out	c make sense	d take part
6 a punish	b permit	c forbid	d let
7 a done	b made	c punished	d committed
8 a high	b fast	c quick	d strong
9 a insisted	b encouraged	c promised	d warned
10 a studying	b advising	c applying	d graduating
11 a enthusiastic	b staggered	c exhilarated	d overwhelmed
12 a encourage	b offer	c blame	d congratulate

6 Complete the text with one word in each gap.

> Oxfam is a charity whose main aims are to achieve change and save lives. _____ (1) provides help in emergencies as well as setting up longer-term development projects. Cecil Jackson-Cole, _____ (2) was a London businessman in the 1940s, was one of the first pioneers of Oxfam and led the charity for many years. After World War II, Oxfam _____ (3) involved in helping people to rebuild their lives, and food parcels and clothing _____ (4) sent to many parts of Europe.
>
> In 1951, Howard Leslie Kirkley _____ (5) appointed. By insisting _____ (6) a rapid response to emergencies and by his own presence in disaster situations, he _____ (7) to bring Oxfam to the attention of a wider audience than before. The 1960s brought even bigger changes and Oxfam's income trebled _____ (8) the decade. The charity's success depends _____ (9) public donations and it now raises millions of pounds every year.

7 Use the word given at the end of some of the lines in this text to form a word that fits in the gap *in the same line*.

How to make small talk	
It's time to stop pretending to be *invisible* (0) at parties and start mastering	visible
the art of small talk. Small talk can be a big challenge, but a little _____ (1) is all	prepare
you need. You may know how to nod and smile, but you need to talk, too – it's	
_____ (2) to stay completely silent. So,	polite
make the _____ (3) not to be shy any	decide
more and just follow the tips below.	
Tips:	
1 Practice. Talk to all kinds of people; those similar to you, but also people	
_____ (4) yourself, from older	like
people to teenagers to tourists.	
2 Keep a diary. Write down _____ (5)	usual
or funny stories you hear, beautiful things you see, quotes you like and interesting	
_____ (6) you have with people.	converse
3 Give yourself some _____ (7).	encourage
Talk to yourself in the mirror and retell stories you've heard. Make a random list of topics and see what you have to say on the subjects. Baseball, Russia, butter, hip-hop,	
shoes … the more _____ (8) the	vary
better.	
4 Read everything, however	
_____ (9) it might seem at the time:	relevant
cookbooks, newspapers, magazines, reviews, signs and catalogues. Everything is a source	
of _____ (10) that can be discussed.	inform
Remember, the more you know, the more you know you can talk about!	

8 Complete the sentences with the correct particle.

a   When I go shopping, I always take a list with me and I cross _____ the items as I buy them.

b   I am going to look _____ the telephone number because I can't remember it.

c   The director is ill so the meeting has been put _____ until next week.

d   She turned _____ five minutes after the film had started.

e   The restaurant is taking _____ extra staff for the busy summer period.

f   His writing is so bad I couldn't make _____ what his note said.

g   The company is cutting _____ on how much they spend on marketing.

h   Our local supermarket is being taken _____ by a huge multinational company.

Chapter 1

R.02

a <u>block</u>buster
the dress <u>circle</u>
a <u>gig</u>
<u>ceramics</u>
<u>a</u>rchitecture
<u>water</u>colours
a <u>dance</u> floor
a <u>DJ</u>
<u>house</u> music

Chapter 7

R.19

As you know, at the moment,
I'm working in the marketing department
of a small advertising firm.
I have some exams in June
and then I'll probably take a few months off
and go travelling.
I'm not sure what I'll do after that.
If I enjoy it, I might do a course
to learn to be an English teacher.
The one thing I'm sure about
is that I won't still be working in an office
this time next year!

Chapter 8

R.23

1 The habit of chewing gum was first popular with <u>the Ancient Greeks</u>. They chewed mastic gum, a resin obtained from the mastic tree. Modern chewing gum, however, originated around the 1860s in <u>America</u>. A substance called chicle was found in the sapodilla trees of Mexico and made a smoother, more elastic gum than previously. William Wrigley, <u>a flour factory owner</u>, found a way to flavour it with mint and started making the first mass-produced gum. Nowadays 90% of chewing gum is manufactured by Wrigley, and the basic process has changed little since manufacture began in 1892.

2 Sales of chewing gum are at record levels; last year in <u>the UK</u>, £317 million was spent on gum. This figure has risen nearly 40% in the last five years, with the sugar-free brands now making up three-quarters of the total market. Consumer analysts say it's no longer considered just a sweet. It's become more relevant to today's consumer with people regarding it as a kind of two-in-one: a sweet fix and a breath-freshener at the same time. <u>Stress relief</u> is another factor, although not so many gum users admit to that one.

3 I've just heard <u>the most incredible</u> story about Britney Spears' chewing gum! Apparently, she's always spitting her chewing gum out onto <u>the pavement</u> and one day, someone saw her spit some out, picked up <u>the piece of gum</u> and decided to sell it online ... you know, on eBay. Basically they sold her piece of chewed chewing gum by online auction! Nobody could guarantee it was real, of course, but lots of people bid for it – and in the end, it was sold for about $100. I can't believe anyone would want chewing gum that's been in someone else's mouth – whoever that person is!

4 An incredible three and half billion pieces of gum are disposed of in the UK every year. In <u>London</u>, there are 300,000 pieces of discarded chewing gum on the pavement in <u>Oxford Street</u> alone. Better enforcement of fines has helped to reduce the problem slightly, but it is almost impossible to catch people spitting out their gum. Some areas have installed special boards which people are invited to stick their used gum to. Meanwhile, biodegradable gum is being developed which in the end may well be the ultimate answer to the seemingly never-ending problem of chewing gum litter.

5 <u>A man</u> from north London has come up with a new idea for dealing with chewing gum on our pavements – not by removing it or cleaning it, but by painting on it. forty-one-year-old Ben Wilson says he intends to paint <u>gum</u> all the way across London, from north to south. Using acrylic paint and varnish, and a little burner to dry it, he paints different things including <u>animals</u>, flowers and tiny landscapes. Many people stop and look at his work and most have praised him for trying to make beautiful what is, ultimately, just rubbish on our pavements.

Chapter 10

R.29

1 A: I'm really nervous about my presentation later ...
   B: Oh, don't worry – you'll be fine. Just remember, it's a big room so you'll need to <u>speak loudly</u> so that everyone can hear.

2 A: How's your new job going?
   B: Well, to be honest – I'm not really enjoying it. My boss spends his whole time talking <u>to me like I'm a bit stupid</u> ... or like he's better than me.

3 A: What's the matter? You're looking really stressed out ... what's been going on?
   B: Ohh! I've spent the whole morning on the phone trying to <u>contact someone</u> about fixing my TV. They just give you a machine ... but never a real person to speak to ... it's so frustrating!

4 A: Have you heard? Sylvia and Mark have just got engaged. They're getting married in June, I think.
   B: Oh really? <u>Say congratulations to them from me</u> when you see them, won't you?

5 A: He's such a good speaker, isn't he?

B: Yes, what I like about him is that <u>he communicates his point clearly</u> but he's not boring ... Actually, often he's quite funny ...

6 A: How did the council meeting go today?

B: Well, it was good to see so many people <u>standing up and complaining</u> about the new parking restrictions round here ... I'm just not sure how much difference it will really make ...

7 A: Have you ever had Spanish lessons?

B: No, I just <u>learnt it</u> while I was living in Spain – obviously everyone around me was speaking Spanish, so I had to learn pretty quickly.

8 A: You know all that unpaid rent you told me about? Have you talked to your flatmate about it yet?

B: No, I really must ... I find it so hard to <u>start talking about</u> a subject like money ...

Chapter 14

R.41

A: Did you hear that Steve <u>turned up</u> half an hour late for his meeting with Michael Tate, the Marketing Director!

B: Really?

A: And he'd already <u>put</u> the meeting <u>off</u> once from last week.

B: Was Michael annoyed?

A: What do you think? And it's really not very clever of Steve. You know that Michael will probably be <u>taking over</u> as Regional Director in October.

B: I heard that, too.

A: And if he does, they say that he intends to <u>lay off</u> quite a big part of the workforce.

B: That's ridiculous!

A: Apparently he's determined to <u>bring down</u> labour costs.

B: But we should be <u>branching out</u> into new areas, opening new stores. We should be <u>taking on</u> new people, not <u>cutting back</u>! I think they should fire Michael!

A: I couldn't agree more.

B: So, are *you* worried about being laid off?

A: Well, put it this way, I've made a few calls and I've got one or two interviews <u>lined up</u>.

B: Really? Listen, if you get anything ... will you mention my name?

A: Of course I will. You know you can <u>count on</u> me.

Chapter 8 page 108, Exercise 2

Group B

Read your text quickly and check your ideas from Exercise 1.

Encounter, Los Angeles, USA

It's the most recognisable landmark at Los Angeles International Airport and one of the most famous buildings in Los Angeles as a whole. I am, of course, talking about the amazing landmark Theme Building situated at the USA's third busiest airport; this twenty-one-metre-high monster looks like a giant futuristic insect. With its unique arches and multiple lighting changes, the building has been a fixture since 1961 and is now home to Encounter – restaurant with a difference.

For many years, the structure housed a coffee shop providing snacks for travellers waiting to board the next flight. Just a few years ago, Walt Disney Imagineering completely redesigned the interior.* It was converted into a kind of *Star Trek* restaurant, complete with multi-coloured patterns on the carpeting, blue and red lights and moon-cratered walls. You might hear sci-fi or James Bond music in the space-age elevator that takes you up to the top of the building.

There seems to be a separate life at the crater-shaped, metallic bar, too. There are guns that emit laser lights and sound effects when bartenders pour a drink. The barstools seem to hang in mid-air. The overall scene looks like some kind of a vision of an alternate universe in the distant future. Visually, there's nothing like this place anywhere.

But then there's the food. Encounter's management has a daunting challenge on its hands. The building itself is a major attraction with its unusual location and famous architecture. It's easy in such a scenario for the food to become an afterthought. However, you will be in for a surprise if you stop in for dinner at the Encounter, as the cuisine is fabulous.

The Encounter's Executive Chef, Michel Audeon, continues the tradition at the restaurant of a menu featuring 'art-food'; a Los Angeles speciality that focuses not only on taste but also on creating incredible sculptural arrangements on the plate. Whatever your taste, you're sure to find something you will enjoy looking at as well as eating: my favourites are roast chicken, grilled salmon and best of all, the delicious California Summer Spinach Vegetable Wrap. And if you're coming with kids, don't worry; there's a menu for them and Encounter's party atmosphere ensures they'll enjoy themselves without **disrupting** the ambience a bit.

The sceptics may think Encounter is just a 'theme park' with second-rate food. Don't make that mistake. The chef has a good thing going here. At Encounter, Audeon incorporates his flair for genuinely good food, eclectic menus and innovative presentation. You wouldn't want to miss his mouth-watering menu, regardless of the location and décor. In fact, I'd take a bet you wouldn't want to miss the location and décor either.

*Walt Disney Imagineering were contracted by CA One Services, Inc. now trading as Delaware North Companies Travel Hospitality Services, Inc.

Chapter 9 page 125, Exercise 4

The original moral of the story was '*When force fails, gentleness often succeeds*'.

Chapter 13 page 184, Exercise 6

The mysterious pianist

Andreas Grassl (born October 25, 1984) is a German man who was found in England in April 2005. He remained unidentified for a long time due to his refusal to speak; he communicated instead through drawing and playing the piano. When he was first brought to a piano, he reportedly played music from various genres (ranging from classical music by Tchaikovsky to pop by The Beatles) non-stop for four hours.

During the more than four months that passed until he revealed his identity, the mysterious story created interest and speculation across the world, and he became known as the 'Piano Man'.

Many of the questions in the story remain unsolved, however. It is still unclear why he was so smartly-dressed or why he was soaking wet. In fact, nobody knows quite how and why he came to be on a beach in Kent, but it is assumed he either suffered some kind of mental breakdown or that he was pretending all along and it was a complete hoax.

Index

Chapter 1

Question forms

Direct questions

There are three main types of direct questions:

A **Yes/No questions** (which expect the answer '*yes*' or '*no*')

1 Most verbs need to use the auxiliary *do*/*does*/*did* to make questions.

Do you like nature documentaries?

2 Verbs with be, *can* and *have (got)* don't need the auxiliary *do*/*does*/*did*.

Is he playing computer games?

Can you play the guitar?

Have you got the tickets?

3 Negative *Yes*/*No* questions expect a particular answer.

Didn't she go to Barcelona last weekend? (expected answer '*yes*')

Aren't you going to the party? (expected answer '*yes*')

Hasn't he paid you back yet? (expected answer '*no*')

B **Wh- questions**

1 Question words (*who, what, where, when, whose, why, which* and *how*) come at the beginning of the question.

Where did you go last night?

What do you think about horror films?

2 If *who, what* or *which* is the subject of the sentence, we don't use the auxiliary *do*/*does*/*did*, and we use normal sentence word order (not the inversion of subject and verb as for other questions).

Who gave you that CD?

What happened yesterday?

Compare:

Who gave you that CD? (asking about the subject)

Who did you give that CD to? (asking about the object)

3 If there is a preposition, it comes at the end of the question (unless it is very formal speaking or writing).
Who did you buy that for?

(Very formal: *For whom did you buy that?*)

What were you talking about?

(Very formal: *About what were you talking?*)

C **Alternative questions** (which expect the answer to be one of two options)

There are two types of alternative questions; (a) a *Yes/No* type and (b) a *Wh-* type.

Do you want to go to the cinema or watch a DVD?

Which would you rather do, book tickets now or buy them on the night?

Other types of questions

Indirect questions

Indirect questions use statement word order (you don't invert the subject and verb). They are often used to be more polite or tentative when you're asking a question (e.g. if you don't know someone very well/at all, if you're asking for something quite big or difficult). We use *if/whether* for *Yes/No* type indirect questions.

Common ways of starting indirect questions are in **bold**:

I'd like to know *if you're coming to the cinema with us.*

Could you tell me *where the theatre is, please?*

Would you mind telling me *how long the performance lasts?*

Do you know *if the single has been released yet?*

Question tags

Question tags are short questions at the end of a statement. The speaker often expects a particular answer and is using a question tag to confirm what he/she already knows.

The most common question tags are formed as follows:

1 positive statement + negative question tag
She loves singing, doesn't she?
You've seen that film before, haven't you?

2 negative statement + positive question tag
You didn't get me a ticket, did you?
*He isn't learning the piano, is he?*h

Prepositions of place, time and movement

A **In 'time' phrases:** *at/in/on*

1 *at*
Used for clock times, points of time in the day, weekends and holidays, points in time, e.g. *at 9.30 a.m., at midnight, at lunchtime, at the weekend, at New Year, at the moment, at the beginning, at the end*

2 *in*
Used for the main parts of the day, months, years, seasons, centuries, a point of time during a period or at the end of a period, e.g. *in the morning, in August, in 2006, in the summer, in the 21st century, in the night, in an hour, in a couple of minutes*

3 *on*
Used for specific dates and days, e.g. *on 20th May, on Friday, on New Year's Day, on Sunday morning*

B **In 'place' phrases:** *at/in/on*

These prepositions can be used to show where something is or where something is happening. These prepositions can also be used in expressions.

1 *at*
Shows a point in space where something is happening, e.g. *at the bus stop, at the bottom, at the top, at the corner (of a street), at home, (sitting) at the table, at the party, at the end*

2 *in*
Shows that something taking place is inside (not outside), e.g. *in a chair, in bed, in a book, in the centre, in the corner (of a room), in the country, in the world, in the park, in Italy, in an area*

3 *on*
Shows that something taking place is on something (not inside); e.g. *on the sofa, (put something) on the table, on page 1, on the beach, on a trip, on the coast, on an island, on the pavement, on TV, on the radio*

C **In 'movement' phrases:** *at/to/into/towards*

1 *at*
We use *at* with 'arrive', e.g. *We <u>arrived at</u> the party.*

We use *at* to show the person or thing the action is aimed at, e.g. *She <u>shouted at</u> me.*

Compare:

He threw the ball <u>at</u> her. (implies it's aimed at her and he wants to hit her)

He threw the ball <u>to</u> her. (implies he wants her to catch it)

2 *to*

We generally use *to* with verbs of movement e.g. *come, go, travel, run, send, take, return, get, walk*; e.g. *I walked to work yesterday.*

We usually use *to* with nouns that suggest movement e.g. *journey, trip, welcome*; e.g. *I'm going on a trip to Italy.*

Compare:

I've been to Spain three times. (implies travelling/movement)

I've been in Spain for three weeks. (implies staying/place)

3 *into*

We use *into* with verbs that mean 'to move from outside to an inside area'; e.g. *Everybody looked at her when she walked into the room. I got into bed to read my book.*

4 *towards*

Towards means moving or pointing in a particular direction; e.g. *I saw someone coming towards me.*

We also use *towards* with nouns to suggest aiming to achieve; e.g. *I'm working towards my gold medal in swimming.*

at the end/in the end

At the end is a prepositional phrase which is usually followed by a noun. It refers to the final point or part, e.g. *At the end of the film, they all live happily ever after.*

At the end is also an adverb which refers to the point at which something occurs, e.g. *We'll read it through at the end.*

In the end is a linking phrase which means 'finally, after a long time', e.g. *In the end, we found a bank and got some money out.*

Chapter 2

Present simple

USE

We use the present simple:

1 With routine or regular repeated actions (often with adverbs of frequency like *always, often, sometimes, never, every Saturday morning, once a week*).
My father goes to the gym twice a week.
We visit my grandmother in Scotland every summer.
I always have a coffee before I leave for work.

2 When we are talking about permanent situations.
I come from Innsbruck.
He lives with his family.

3 When we are talking about the future as expressed in timetables, regulations and programmes.
The tour of the castle starts at 11.00 a.m.

4 With scientific facts.
Water boils at 100 degrees Celsius.
The sun rises in the east.

5 With 'state' verbs which are not normally used in continuous forms: *be, have, depend, know, think, understand, disagree, like, want, hear, love, see, smell, taste.*
I don't have any brothers or sisters.
Do you know why your father is upset?
This soup tastes delicious.

6 In time clauses with a future meaning after *when, as soon as, if, until.*
Please tell Mike to call me if you see him.
I'll start making dinner when/as soon as I get home.
I can't afford to buy a new car until I get a pay rise.

Present continuous

USE

We use the present continuous when we are talking about:

1 Actions happening now.
She's revising for tomorrow's exam.

2 Changing/developing situations.
The hole in the ozone layer is getting bigger.

3 Temporary situations.
I am staying with my sister for the next few weeks.

4 Plans and arrangements in the future.
I am visiting my brother for New Year.

5 Annoying or surprising habits with *always.*
She's always borrowing money from me.

Modifiers

1 *Fairly* usually modifies gradable adjectives (e.g. *large, hot,* etc.) and adverbs.
It's a fairly large flat but I don't think there's enough space for all our furniture.
Pete works fairly hard, but he could do more.

2 *Quite* suggests a higher degree than *fairly* and can be used with gradable adjectives, nouns, verbs and adverbs.

- *Quite* can be used before *a/an* + (*gradable adjective*) noun, i.e. to modify adjectives and nouns.

It's quite a large flat so there should be space for all our furniture.

It's quite a flat; four large bedrooms and a good living space.

● *Quite* can also be used to modify verbs and adverbs.

Sarah quite likes science but she wants to study languages at university.

Pete works quite hard; he is doing well at work.

3 *Pretty* is stronger than *quite*. It can suggest 'more than was expected' and similar ideas. It is more informal than *fairly* and *quite* and is more often used in speaking than in writing.

● *Pretty* can be used to modify gradable adjectives and adverbs.

It's a pretty large flat…

Sarah is pretty good at science…

Pete works pretty hard…

4 *A bit* is often used with the same meaning as *a little*.

He's a bit more interested in sports than his brother.

When *a bit* or *a little* are used with non-comparative adjectives, the meaning is usually negative or critical.

She's a bit young to go to school on her own.

5 *Really* is used to show emphasis. It can be used with adjectives (gradable and non-gradable), adverbs and verbs.

It's a really large flat…

That was a really awful film.

Sarah is really good at science…

Pete works really hard…

6 *Extremely*, *incredibly* and *terribly* are used to show emphasis and the meaning is stronger than *very*. They are used with gradable adjectives, verbs and adverbs.

It's an extremely large flat…

Sarah is extremely good at science…

Pete works extremely hard…

Chapter 3

Comparison

Types of comparison

There are three types of comparison of adjectives and adverbs:

A to a higher degree (comparative form + *than* and *the most*)

The town centre is **busier than** five years ago.

In our family, my mother drives **the most carefully**.

B to the same degree (*as … as*)

The town centre is not **as busy as** five years ago.

My mother drives **as carefully as** my father.

C to a lower degree (with *less* + *than* and *the least*)

The town centre is **less busy than** five years ago.

In our family, my mother drives **the least carefully**.

1 The comparative and superlative forms of **one-syllable adjectives and adverbs** are generally made by adding -*er*/-*est*.

Petrol prices are **higher** than they were this time last year.

Of our friends, Mary walks **the fastest**.

Exceptions:

● Adjectives which end in a vowel plus a consonant. These comparatives and superlatives are made by doubling the consonant and adding -*er*/-*est*.

They've just moved to a **bigger** house.

● Adjectives which end in -*e*. These comparatives and superlatives are made by adding -*r*/-*st*.

That's **the nicest** thing you've ever said to me.

2 The comparative and superlative forms of **two- and three-syllable adjectives and adverbs** are generally made by using *more* and *most*.

This holiday is **more expensive than** the one we took last year.

The last week of the holiday passed **the most quickly**.

Exceptions:

● Two-syllable adjectives ending in -*y*. These comparatives and superlatives are made by changing the *y* to *i* and adding -*er*/-*est*.

She is usually here **earlier than** this.

Mary was **the earliest** to arrive this morning.

3 (*not*) *as … as*

A We use *not as … as* to compare things which are different.

Jacob is **not as good** at the guitar **as** Racquel is.

B We use *as … as* to compare things which are the same.

The film is **as boring as** the book.

Some adjectives and adverbs have irregular forms.

The most common irregular forms are:

1 Adjectives

good better best

bad worse worst

little less least

much more most

far further/farther furthest/farthest

old elder eldest (used for people only; the regular forms, *old older oldest*, are used for buildings, towns, animals, trees, etc.)

*Carol is a **better** player than I am, but Tess is **the best**.*

*That was **the worst** book I've ever read.*

*I live **further** from school **than** I used to.*

*David is **the eldest** of seven children.*

2 Adverbs

well better best

badly worse worst

late later last/latest

much more most

little less least

*I can speak English **better than** I could six months ago.*

*I don't see Mike **much** but I see him **more than** I used to.*

Reflexives

There are three main ways we use reflexive pronouns:

1 When the object is the same person/thing as the subject. In this case, the reflexive pronoun is essential to the grammar of the sentence.

*I **forced myself** not to watch television for two whole weeks.*

*The computer **turns itself off** after fifteen minutes of no use.*

● Common verbs which take reflexive pronouns include: *enjoy yourself, behave yourself, help yourself, make yourself at home.*

● Common verbs which don't take reflexive pronouns include: *relax, concentrate, hurry, feel.*

2 When you want to emphasise the subject or object (to say 'that person/thing and nobody/nothing else'). In this case, the reflexive pronoun is not essential to the grammar of the sentence, but is added for emphasis.

*I'd like to speak to the director **himself**.*

*The film **itself** is very good, but some of the acting is a bit weak.*

3 With *by* to mean *alone*.

*More and more people in their twenties live **by themselves** these days.*

own

There are three main ways we use *own*:

1 *on my own/on his own*, etc. to mean '*without the help of others*'

*I organised the whole thing **on my own**, which was tiring but satisfying in the end.*

2 *on my own/on his own*, etc. to mean '*alone*'

*She doesn't seem to mind going to the cinema **on her own**.*

3 *my own/her own*, etc. to mean '*belonging to no other person*'

*I've just bought **my own** flat.*

Chapter 4

Past simple

FORM

verb + *-ed* (remember there are many irregular verb forms)

USE

We use the past simple:

1 To talk about events in the past that are now finished.

We had a great skiing holiday in Austria in January.

2 To talk about habits in the past.

My family went to the south of Spain for a two-week holiday every summer.

3 In reported speech.

She said she didn't want to go out for the evening.

Past continuous

FORM

was/were + *-ing*

USE

We use the past continuous:

1 To talk about actions in progress in the past.

She was lying on the grass, looking at the stars.

2 To talk about temporary situations in the past.

Last June I was doing part-time work in my father's insurance company.

3 To talk about an event that was in progress when another event happened.

He was reading a holiday brochure when Pete called him on his mobile.

4 To talk about actions in progress at the same time in the past.

While Tara was preparing dinner, Cassie was making a list of everyone they wanted to invite to the party.

Past perfect simple

FORM

had + past participle

USE

We use the past perfect simple:

1 To refer to a time earlier than another past time.

   The next time I spoke to Josie, she had had the baby.

2 In reported speech.

   She said she had already sent us an invitation.

Past perfect continuous

FORM

had been + *-ing*

USE

We use the past perfect continuous:

1 To talk about actions or situations which had continued up to the past moment that we are thinking about.

   I decided to take my bike to a garage as the engine had been making some strange noises.

Time conjunctions

1 *As*, *when* and *while* can introduce a background action/ situation which is going on while something else happens.

   I heard the phone ring while I was having a shower.

   ● *As-*, *when-* and *while-* clauses can go at the beginning or middle of sentences, but *as-* clauses usually introduce less important information and often go at the beginning of sentences.

     As I was sitting in my car, I saw two masked men run out of the bank.

   ● We usually use *while* to describe two longer actions or situations going on at the same time.

     While I was making dinner, Tina was finishing her essay.

   ● *As* is used (with simple tenses) to talk about two situations which develop or change together.

     As I get older, I don't worry about things so much.

   ● We often use *when* to refer to periods of life.

     When I lived in London, I had a lot more money than I do now.

2 *Eventually* and *finally* mean 'in the end'. We use them to say that something happens after a long time or a lot of effort.

   It was a very close match which lasted for hours but eventually Tim won.

3 *At first* and *to begin with* refer to the beginning of a situation, to make a contrast with something different that happens later.

   At first she enjoyed her new job, but after a while she wanted more of a challenge.

4 *As soon as* and *then* can be used to talk about two actions or events that happen very quickly one after the other.

   As soon as I saw him, I gave him the letter.

5 *Afterwards/After that* can be used to talk about one action following another.

   We're going to see an early film and afterwards we're all going out for a drink.

6 *By the time* is used before a clause (subject + verb) and means 'not later than'.

   I will have finished painting the bedroom by the time you get home.

Chapter 5

Asking for and giving permission

1 *can*

We use *can* to ask for and give permission.

You can go to your friend's house on Saturday.

You can come with me to watch the football match if you help me in the garden on Sunday.

2 *could*

We use *could* to ask for permission when you are not sure what the answer will be.

Note: *could* is not used for giving permission

A: **Could** *I see you for a minute?*

B: *Not now, but after lunch will be possible.*

3 *may*

We use *may* to ask for or give permission in formal situations.

May *I take these files home with me tonight?*

You **may** *have the rest of the day off.*

Obligation: *should* and *ought to*

1 We use *should* and *ought to* to talk about obligations and duties in the future, present and past.

Oughtn't *we* **to/Shouldn't** *we do some revision tonight for tomorrow's exam?*

You **ought to/should** *do more exercise.*

Shouldn't *we have/***Oughtn't** *we* **to** *have bought Sara a birthday present?*

2 *Should* + *have* + past participle is often used to criticise your own or other people's behaviour.

We **should have won** *yesterday's match.*

She **shouldn't have taken** *my car without asking.*

Strong obligation and necessity

1 *must*

We use *must* to:

- Talk about present and future strong obligations and necessities that come from the speaker.

  You **must** *drink lots of water after having a sauna.*

  I **must** *remember to ask the tennis coach for another lesson this week.*

- Ask about what the listener wants you to do.

  Must *I wear any special clothing?*

- Tell people not to do things.

  You **mustn't** *use your mobile phone in here.*

2 *have to/have got to*

We use *have to/have got to* to:

- Talk about present and future strong obligations that do not come from the speaker.

  We **have to** *pay our rent on the first of every month.*

  When do we **have to** *register for the exam?*

  I **have got to** *go to team practice tomorrow.*

- Talk about past and reported obligations of all kinds.

  She told me I **had to** *change my diet.*

  We **had to** *do a cross-country run every term when I was at school.*

Lack of obligation

1 *needn't, don't need to* and *don't have to*

We use *needn't, don't need to, don't have to* to talk about a lack of obligation in the present or future.

You **don't need to/needn't** *come and watch me on Saturday. It's not an important match.*

We **don't have to** *get up early tomorrow. It's a holiday.*

2 *needn't* + *have* + past participle

We use *needn't* + *have* + past participle to say that somebody did something, but that it was unnecessary.

You **needn't have done** *all the washing-up. I was going to do it.*

3 *didn't need to* + infinitive

We use *didn't need to* + infinitive to say that something wasn't necessary without saying whether the person did it or not.

We **didn't need to** *bring our sweaters.*

Used to

FORM

Positive statements

used to + infinitive

Negative statements

did/didn't + *use to* + infinitive

Questions

did you/she/they, etc. *use to* + infinitive

USE

We use *used to* to talk about past habits and states that do not occur now or no longer exist.

I **used to** *play a lot of sport, but now I hardly ever do.*

How did they **use to** *keep in touch without e-mail?*

He **used to** *be great at volleyball, but he's put on a lot of weight recently.*

Notes:

1 *Used to* is not used to say how often things happened or how long they took.

2 *Used to* can be used for things you still do now but the place or time has finished.

I **used to** *ride a motorbike when I lived in Egypt. I still do, but now I live in Portugal.*

3 Be careful not to confuse *used to* with *be/get used to* + noun/gerund which means 'be/become accustomed to something' because you have been doing it for a while.

I'm **used to** *getting up early.*

I can't **get used** *to living in the middle of the city.*

Do you think we'll ever **get used to** *the heat?*

Would

Would is also used to talk about past habits and repeated actions but not about past states.

When I was a child, I **would** *go to the park after school and kick a ball around with my friend Peter for hours.*

Chapter 6

Present perfect simple

FORM
have/has + past participle

USE
We use the present perfect simple:

1 To talk about an experience or an action in the past when the time is not important or not known. (Often used with *ever* and *never*.)
*I've **never** been to Greece.*
*Have you **ever** been on a skiing holiday?*

2 ● To talk about an action that started in the past and continues to the present. (It is often used with *for* and *since*.)
  ● When you're focusing on the finished action.
    I've revised everything I can for the test tomorrow.
  ● When you're focusing on the number of times the action has been completed up to the time of speaking.
    I've seen that film three times since it came out.
  ● With 'state' verbs, e.g. *be, have, like, believe, know.*
    He's known about the letter since last week.

3 To talk about an action that happened or should have happened in the past but has the result in the present. (It is often used with *just, yet* and *already*.)
*She's **just** had her hair cut.*
*Have you booked that holiday **yet**?*
*I've read that magazine **already**.*

4 To talk about our first/second experience of something with the phrase *This is the first/second time ...*
This is the first time I've driven a car on my own.

5 When used with the superlative. (Often used with *ever*.)
My first job interview was the most difficult thing I've ever done.

Present perfect continuous

FORM
have/has + *been* + *-ing*

USE
We use the present perfect continuous:

1 To suggest that an action is not complete.
I've been reading this book all morning and I'm halfway through.

2 To emphasise how long the action has been going on for.
He's been having driving lessons for over a year.

3 To describe a recent activity when you can still see the results of that activity.
  A: *What's all that mess?*
  B: *I've been painting the bathroom.*

ever
Ever indicates that the speaker is talking about 'at any time in your life'. It generally comes before the past participle in questions.
Have you ever tried Thai food?

for/since
For is used to talk about a period of time.
I've lived here for three years.
Since is used to talk about the starting point.
We've been friends since 1999.

just/yet/already
● *Just* means a short time ago. It usually comes between *has/have* and the past participle.
I've just seen David.

● *Yet* shows that the speaker expected something to happen before now. It is used at the end of negative sentences and questions.
I haven't bought the tickets yet.
Have you heard from Paula yet?

● *Already* shows that something happened sooner than expected. It usually comes between *has/have* and the past participle or at the end of the sentence.
He's already passed his driving test.
She's invited me to the dinner party already.

so/such

MEANING
So and *such* are used to emphasise the great extent or high degree of what you're talking about.
*I wish he wouldn't drive **so fast**.*
*I'm lucky to work with **such interesting people**.*
*We had **such a lovely time** at your party.*

FORM
1 *so* + adjectives and adverbs
  *He's **so kind**.*
  *She speaks **so quickly**.*

2 *so* + quantifiers (*much, many, few, little*)
  *I've got **so many** books.*
  *There's **so little** time left.*

3 *such/such a* + nouns and noun phrases

such good weather

such lovely trousers

such a beautiful day

4 Use *so* (not *very*) in *that* clauses.

*We were **so late that** we took a taxi there.*

*He wanted to make her feel **so ashamed** of her bedroom **that** she would tidy it up.*

too/enough

MEANING

Too is different from *very*:

too = more than is necessary or wanted

enough = as much as is necessary or wanted

Compare:

*It's **very hot** today.*

*It's **too hot** to sit in the sun today.*

*It's **hot enough** to sit in the sun today.*

FORM

1 *too* + adjectives and adverbs

*These trousers are **too small for me.***

*Don't eat **too quickly** – you'll be sick.*

2 *too much/too many* + noun phrases

*There's **too much salt** in this soup.*

***Too many people** wanted tickets.*

3 adjectives and adverbs + *enough*

*I'm not **old enough** to vote.*

*You're not speaking **slowly enough**.*

4 *enough* + noun

*Have you got **enough milk**?*

Also:

adjective + *enough* + noun OR *enough* + adjective + noun

Compare:

*These aren't **fresh enough vegetables**.*

*I haven't got **enough fresh vegetables**.*

5 *too/enough* + infinitive

*It's **too cold** for me **to go out** today.*

*She's **old enough to make** her own decision.*

*This food is **too spicy** for her **to eat**.*

(NOT: *This food is too spicy for her to eat ~~it~~.*)

Chapter 7

like and *as*

FORM

1 *like* as a verb

- *like* + object
  I like my new flat, but I would prefer to be closer to the centre of town.

- *like* + *-ing* (= enjoy doing)
  Do you like working for a small family firm?

- *like* + *to* + infinitive (= choose to do)
  I like to go to the gym for an hour before work.

  Note: short answers to *Yes/No* questions with *like* are always formed with *do, does* or *did*.

  A: *Do you like going to the gym?*

  B: *Yes, I do.*

- *Would like* + (object) + infinitive with *to* is used as a polite way of saying 'want'.
  I'd like you to help me paint the spare room this evening.

2 *like* as a preposition. This means 'similar to' or 'in the same way as'. We use *like*, not *as*, before a noun or pronoun to talk about similarity.

This perfume smells like the one my grandmother used to wear.

My brother looks very like me.

3 *like* which means 'such as/for example'

I want to do something active this afternoon, like going swimming or playing tennis.

4 *feel like* + object/-ing, This is used to talk about something that we want or want to do

I feel like going for a long walk by the sea.

5 *As* is a conjunction. We use it before a clause and before an expression beginning with a preposition.

I think the stock market will crash soon, as it did in 1989.

6 We can use *as* to talk about function – the jobs that people or things do.

He worked as a waiter over the summer.

7 *As* can be used to talk about actions or situations that take place at the same time.

As I was having my breakfast, I heard a loud crash upstairs.

8 *As if* and *as though* are both used to say what a situation seems like. They can refer to something that we think may be true.

It looks as if the rain will stop soon.

9 Some expressions beginning with *as* are used to introduce facts which are known to both speaker and listener, e.g. *as you know, as we agreed, as you suggested.*

So, we'll all meet back here in an hour, as we agreed.

Overview of future forms

FORMS

will (*shall*) + infinitive

going to + infinitive

Present continuous

Present simple

Future continuous (*will* + *be* + *-ing* form)

Future perfect (*will* + *have* + past participle)

USES

1 will (*shall*) + infinitive

● We use *will* +infinitive for predicting something based on what you know or believe.

I think it will rain later this afternoon.

I'm sure you'll pass your exam because you've worked really hard.

Note: *going to* + infinitive is also possible in this case.

● We use *will* + infinitive for promises, threats, offers and requests.

I promise I won't tell anyone.

If you shout at me one more time, I'll leave.

I'll give you a lift to work if you like.

Will you make the dinner tonight?

Note: We cannot use *going to* in this case.

● We use *will* + infinitive to talk about future actions decided at the time of speaking.

I think I'll lie down for a moment.

I'll make a cup of tea.

Note: We cannot use the present continuous in this case.

2 *going to* + infinitive

● We use *going to* + infinitive for predicting something based on what you can see or hear.

Look at those clouds; It's going to rain.

He's going to fall if he tips his chair back like that.

Note: We cannot use *will* + infinitive or the present continuous in this case.

● We use *going to* + infinitive and the present continuous to talk about things that have already been decided. We usually use present continuous if the plans are more certain and more details have been decided.

I'm going to see that new film at the weekend.

Jim and Sarah are getting married on Saturday.

Note: We cannot use *will* + infinitive in this case.

3 Future continuous (*will* + *be* + *-ing*)

● We use the future continuous (*will* + *be* + *-ing*) to say that an action will be in progress at a definite time in the future.

I'll be lying on a beach this time tomorrow.

4 Future perfect (*will* + *have* + past participle)

● We use the future perfect (*will* + *have* + past participle) to describe something that will be completed before a definite time in the future.

I'll have finished this book by the end of the day.

Chapter 8

Countable and uncountable nouns

Nouns which can be countable or uncountable

The following nouns can be both countable and uncountable:

1 Nouns we think of as single things or substances.

Egg: *I'll have a fried egg and two sausages.*
   You've spilt egg on your shirt.

Chicken: *I bought a chicken to have for Sunday lunch.*
   Would you like some more chicken?

Iron: *I'm going to buy a new iron – this one's broken.*
   They found some old tools made of iron.

Glass: *Could I have a clean glass, please?*
   Did you know that glass is made from sand?

Hair: *I found a hair in my soup.*
   He's got short red hair.

2 Words for drinks, e.g. *coffee, tea, beer, wine.* The countable noun means a glass of, a cup of, a bottle of, etc.

Coffee is very expensive at the moment.

Do you fancy going for a (cup of) coffee?

He usually drinks beer not wine.

There's a (bottle of) beer in the fridge if you want one.

3 *time, space, room*

I won't have time to finish my essay today.

We had a really good time on holiday.

We haven't got space for any more people I'm afraid.

Fill in the spaces with a suitable word.

There's room for a small table in the corner.

I'd like a double room for three nights.

Determiners used with countable and uncountable nouns

Before countable nouns, we can use:

a/an, few(er), a few, not many, several, many, a great many,

Before uncountable nouns, we can use:

(very) little, a little, not much, much, a great deal of, a small/large amount of

Before both countable and uncountable nouns, we can use:

a lack of, some, any, (quite) a lot of, lots of, plenty of

1 *few/a few and little/a little*

Use *few/a few* with plural countable nouns and *little/a little* with uncountable nouns.

A *a few* (for countables) and *a little* (for uncountables) are used to talk about positive ideas. *A few* means 'some but not many' and *a little* means 'some but not much'.

I went out for dinner with a few friends.

There's a little cake left.

B *few* (for countables) and *little* (for uncountables) are used to talk about negative ideas. *Few /little* are generally used to mean 'not enough'/'almost none'.

Few people are interested in coming to the meeting.

Little money was collected for the new roof appeal.

2 *many/much*

Use *many* with plural countable nouns and *much* with uncountable nouns.

How many dogs have you got?

There are many places we could go on holiday.

I haven't got much money left.

How much pasta is in that packet?

3 Some determiners can be used with both plural countable nouns and uncountable nouns.

*I've got **some** paper in my bag if you want to borrow some.*

*The library has got **some** new computers.*

*A **lot of** equipment was stolen from the school.*

*They've got **a lot of** relatives who live in South Africa.*

4 *a slice, a lump, a piece*, etc.

Use specific words to make uncountable nouns countable. The most common ones are:

a slice of bread, toast, cheese, ham, meat

a loaf of bread

a carton of milk, juice

a joint of meat

a bar of chocolate

a lump of sugar, cheese

a tube of toothpaste

an item of news

Articles

The definite article: *the*

Use the definite article *the* to talk about:

- **areas:** *She comes from **the** north of England.*

- **cinemas:** *That new Brad Pitt film is on at **the** Odeon.*

- **deserts:** ***The** Sahara Desert is growing every year.*

- **hotels:** *We spent a week staying at **the** Hilton in New York.*

- **inventions:** *When was **the** jet engine invented?*

- **island groups:** *I'd love to go to **the** Seychelles.*

- **mountain ranges:** *Which are higher: **the** Andes or **the** Dolomites?*

- **national groups:** ***The** British are known for being rather reserved.*

- **newspapers:** *I usually read **the** 'Guardian' during the week and **the** Observer on Sundays.*

- **oceans and seas:** *We went on holiday to an island in **the** Aegean Sea.*

- **rivers:** *We took a boat along **the** River Thames to the London Eye.*

- **species of animal:** ***The** tiger is now an endangered species.*

- **theatres:** *I saw Shakespeare's 'Macbeth' at **the** Globe Theatre in London.*

Also:

- With superlatives.
  *She's **the kindest** friend I've ever had.*

- When there is only one thing.
  *Don't forget to take some sun cream as **the** sun is really hot today.*

- To talk about particular nouns when it is clear what we are referring to.
  *Do you mind looking after **the** cat while I'm away?*

- To talk about previously mentioned things.
  *Take one egg, a small onion and a bunch of parsley. Break **the** egg into a bowl.*

The indefinite article: *a/an*

Use the indefinite article *a/an*:

- With (singular) jobs, etc.
  *She's **an** architect.*

- With singular countable nouns (mentioned for the first time or when it doesn't matter which one).
  *Don't forget to bring **a** pen.*

- With these numbers: 100, 1,000, 1,000,000.
  *There were over **a** hundred people at the party.*

- In exclamations about singular countable nouns.
  *What **a** lovely jacket!*

The zero article

Use no article (the zero article) to talk about:

- **continents:** *They're travelling across Africa on foot.*

- **countries:** *Have you been to Brazil?*

- **illnesses:** *I had chickenpox and measles when I was a child.*

- **lakes:** *What country is Lake Tanganyika in?*

- **magazines:** *I usually read 'Hello' magazine when I go to the hairdresser.*

- **mountains:** *They have reached the summit of Mount Everest.*

- **streets, roads, etc.:** *Oxford Street and Tottenham Court Road are very busy shopping streets in London.*

- **villages, towns, cities:** *Zahara is a village just along the coast from here. I was born in Milan.*

Chapter 9

Participle clauses

Participle clauses can be used to express condition, reason and result. They are often quite formal.

***Maintained regularly**, this dishwasher should last for many years. (If it is maintained regularly …)*

***Hearing a noise in the garden**, I went out to investigate. (After hearing …)*

***Having been left some money by an old uncle**, I decided to go travelling. (As a result of having been left …)*

Expressing purpose

1 We can use the infinitive to talk about purpose with *to, in order to* and *so as to. To* is the least formal.

*John is coming over tonight **to** talk about the holiday.*

In order to and *so as to* are used before negative infinitives. *So as to* is more informal.

*I'm putting on lots of suntan lotion **so as not to** get burnt.*

2 *So that* and *in order that* can be followed by auxiliary verbs, e.g. *can* and *will. So that* is more informal.

*I'd like to do a part-time degree **so that** I'll have a better chance of getting promoted.*

In an informal style, *that* can be dropped after *so*.

*I want to go back to the CD shop **so** I can get a refund for the CD I bought yesterday.*

3 *In case* is used to talk about being prepared for things or taking precautions. To talk about the future, we use a present tense after *in case*.

*You should take your swimming trunks **in case** you decide to go swimming.*

Chapter 10

Adverbs

We use adverbs to modify verbs, adjectives, other adverbs and sometimes whole sentences.

Adverbs and adverbial phrases – different types:

1 Adverbs of manner describe how someone does something, e.g. *angrily, in a friendly way.*

2 Adverbs of place describe where something happens, e.g. *here, in the corner.*

3 Adverbs of time describe when something happens, e.g. *tomorrow, soon.*

4 Adverbs of frequency describe how often something happens, e.g. *usually, once a week.*

5 Adverbs of certainty describe how certain something is, e.g. *perhaps, definitely.*

6 Adverbs of completeness (or degree) describe how much or how strongly something happens, e.g. *nearly, quite.*

7 Emphasising adverbs emphasise the following word, e.g. *very, extremely.*

8 Connecting adverbs join a clause to what came before, e.g. *next, however.*

9 Comment adverbs give the speaker's opinion of an action, e.g. *surprisingly, stupidly.*

How to form adverbs

We form most adverbs by adding *-ly* to the adjective:

slow > slowly; beautiful > beautifully

Exceptions:

1 Adjectives ending in *-le* form adverbs by changing *-le* to *-ly*.
simple > simply

2 Adjectives ending in *-y* form adverbs by changing *-y* to *-ily*.
easy > easily

3 Adjectives ending in *-ic* form adverbs by adding *-ally*.
automatic > automatically

4 Some adverbs which end in *-ly* come from nouns.
day > daily; week > weekly

5 We cannot add *-ly* to adjectives which end in *-ly*. In these cases, we use an adverbial phrase (*in a ... way/manner/ fashion*).
friendly > in a friendly way; silly > in a silly manner; lonely > in a lonely fashion.

6 There are other exceptions which do not fit the rules.
fast > fast; hard > hard; still > still; good > well; full > fully; true > truly; public > publicly

Position of adverbs (and adverbial phrases)

Different types of adverbs go in different positions in a sentence. There are general rules about this (and some exceptions).

1 We do not usually put adverbs between a verb and its object.
She speaks English well.
~~She speaks well English.~~

2 There are three normal positions for adverbs:

A Front position (at the beginning of a clause).
Suddenly*, someone ran through the door.*

B Mid position (before the main verb).
*I've **never** been so upset.*

C End position (at the end of a clause).
*Shall we go to the cinema **tomorrow**?*

3 There are common positions for the different types of adverbs.

A **Adverbs of manner** usually go in end position. (Adverbs ending in *-ly* can also go in mid position if the adverb is not the main focus of the sentence.)

B **Adverbs of place** usually go in end position (but can also go in front position – especially if the adverb is not the main focus of the sentence).

C **Adverbs of time** usually go in end position (but can also go in front position – especially if the adverb is not the main focus of the sentence). *Soon* can go in mid position.

D **Adverbs of frequency** such as *usually, normally, often, frequently, sometimes* and *occasionally* are most common in mid position. (They can also go in front position or end position if they are the main message of the sentence.) *Always, ever, rarely, seldom* and *never* cannot normally go in front or end position.

E **Adverbs of certainty** – *maybe* and *perhaps* usually go in front position. Other adverbs of certainty (e.g. *probably, definitely*) usually go in mid position.

F **Adverbs of completeness (or degree)** usually go in mid position.

G **Emphasising adverbs** go directly before the word they are emphasising.

H **Connecting adverbs** usually go in front position (but can also go in mid position and end position).

I **Comment adverbs** usually go in front position (but can also go in mid position).

4 When there are adverbs of manner, place and time in one sentence, they normally go in that order.
He sat quietly in the corner of the room for hours.

Causative *have* and *get*

1 *Have/get* + object + past participle is used to talk about when somebody else does something for you (often when you arrange and pay them to do so). (*Get* in this case is sometimes considered slightly more informal.)
*We're **having the house painted**.*
*I must **get my watch repaired**.*
*I'm going to **get my hair cut** this afternoon.*

2 *Have/get* + object + past participle is used to talk about an 'experience' or something that happens to you (often something which you have no control over). (*Get* in this case is sometimes considered slightly more informal.)
*We **got our roof blown off** in the storm last week.*
*I've just **had my first article published**.*

3 *Get* + object + past participle is used to talk about completing work on something. (We cannot use *have* in this case.)
*I'll **get the washing up done** and then I'll help you in the garden.*

4 *Get* + object + *to*-infinitive is used to talk about when you make (or persuade) somebody/something do something (often with the idea of difficulty). (We cannot use *have* in this case.)
*You could **get Jim to help** us.*
*I tried to **get someone to listen** to our complaint.*

Chapter 11

Relative clauses and pronouns

Relative pronouns

The most common relative pronouns are:

who, whom: to refer to people

which: to refer to things

that: to refer to people or things

whose: the possessive of *who* and *which*

when: used after nouns referring to time

where: used after nouns referring to place

why: used to refer to reasons

Defining relative clauses

1 The relative clause defines or identifies the person, thing, time, place or reason.

*Kate is the woman **who told me about the new job**.*

*That's the street **where John's just bought a flat**.*

2 *That* can be used instead of *who* and *which*.

*The man **that** (who) is doing the project with me isn't here today.*

*The room **that** (which) is booked for the meeting is locked.*

3 The relative pronoun can be omitted when the clause defines the object of the clause.

The place (where/that) we're going on holiday is supposed to be lovely.

The reason (why/that) I'm late is that the traffic was awful.

4 No commas are used before and after the relative clause.

Non-defining relative clauses

In non-defining relative clauses the relative clause gives extra information which can be left out. Commas are used before and after the relative clause.

David, whose brother already lives in New York, is about to move to the States.

My computer, which I only got two months ago, keeps crashing.

Prepositions in relative clauses

Prepositions can come before the relative pronoun or at the end of the relative clause depending on whether the sentence is formal or informal.

The person to whom you need to speak is not available. (formal)

Stella, who you need to give the money to, will be back later. (informal)

if structures

Linking words in *if* structures

Some common conditional linking words are:

if, when, as/so long as, until, unless , even if, no matter how/who/what/where/when, provided (that)

Punctuation in *if* structures

When the clause with the conditional linking word (*if, unless,* etc.) is at the beginning of the sentence, there is a comma. When the main clause begins the sentence, there is no comma.

If I see her, I'll give her the money back.

I'll give her the money back when I see her.

I won't lend her any money unless she promises to pay me back.

As long as you pay me back by Friday, I'll lend you some money.

Different types of *if* structures

A

FORM

if + present simple + present simple in the main clause

USE

To talk about something which is always true or describe what always happens. (Sometimes called the **zero conditional**.)

If you stroke our cat, she purrs.

Ice melts if you heat it.

B

FORM

if + present simple/present continuous/present perfect + future/present continuous or imperative in the main clause

USE

To talk about something that is a real possibility in the future. (Sometimes called the **first conditional**.)

If she passes her exam, she'll be really pleased with herself.

You'll be improving your qualifications if you decide to go to college.

As long as you've eaten enough breakfast, you won't need to take any food with you.

If you're watching TV, I'm going to do some revision.

C

FORM

if + past simple/continuous + conditional in the main clause

USE

To talk about something:

1 That is impossible and just imagined.

2 Which is very unlikely to happen in the future (Sometimes called the **second conditional**.) Also, this form is often used to give advice.

If she was a bit taller, she'd look really good in that dress.

I wouldn't go parachuting even if you paid me.

If I were you, I'd have an early night.

D

FORM

if + past perfect + *would have* + past participle in the main clause

USE

To talk about something in the past that could have happened, but didn't, or something that shouldn't have happened, but did. (Sometimes called the **third conditional**.)

I wouldn't have put any meat in if I'd known he was vegetarian.

If you'd asked me earlier, I would've given you a lift.

E

FORM

an *if*-clause referring to the past with a main clause referring to the present or the future

USE

To talk about if something had been different in the past, the present (or future) would be different. (Sometimes called a **mixed conditional**.)

If she'd had more practice, she'd feel a lot more confident about passing her test today.

I'd be a wealthy man if I'd got that job I applied for.

F

FORM

an *if*-clause referring to the present or future with a main clause referring to the past

USE

To talk about if something in the present (or in general time) were different, the past would have been different. (Also sometimes called a **mixed conditional**.)

If I knew him better, I would have invited him to the party.

She wouldn't have ordered spaghetti if she didn't like pasta.

Modals in *if* structures

Modal verbs (*may, might, could,* etc.) can be used in all *if* structures, except those expressing general truth (in **A**).

I might go to the cinema if I'm not too tired.

If she studied harder, she could pass the exam.

If they had told me what the course involved, I might never have signed up for it.

Polite expressions using *if, would* and *should*

● *Would* can be used after *if* in polite expressions.

If you wouldn't mind waiting for a moment, the manager will see you shortly.

● *Should* is used in the *if*-clause to make it even less likely. This is common in formal letters.

If you should require any further information, please do not hesitate to contact us.

● *Should* can replace *if* in formal letters.

Should you wish to contact me, I can be reached at the above address.

Chapter 12

Direct speech

This is when we report the exact words that someone says or writes.

'Are you going to call the police?' she asked.

In her e-mail she said, 'I need to see fo urgently.'

Reported speech

This is when we report something that has been said or written. If the report is after the time the thing was said or written, the verb form generally changes as follows:

Direct speech	Reported speech
1 Present simple/ continuous	Past simple/continuous
'I am living with my brother,' she said.	She said she was living with her brother.
2 Past simple/continuous	Past simple/continuous or past perfect simple/continuous
'We arrested Mr Brown this morning,' a police spokesperson said.	A police spokesperson said that they arrested/had arrested Mr Brown that morning.
3 Present perfect simple/ continuous	Past perfect simple/ continuous
'I have played the guitar since I was seven,' he said.	He told me (that) he had played the guitar since he was seven.
4 will	would
'I'll answer the door,' she said.	She said she would answer the door.
5 must (obligation)	had to
'You must tell the police everything you know,' Becky insisted.	Becky insisted that I had to tell the police everything knew.
6 can	could
'I can do a handstand,' said Peter.	Peter said he could do a handstand.

The verb form does not need to change when:

1 The thing being reported is still true.

'The Sun is approximately ninety-three million miles from the Earth,' the teacher told us.

The teacher told us that the Sun is approximately ninety-three million miles from the Earth.

'The bus leaves at 4.00 p.m.,' said the woman at the ticket office.

The woman at the ticket office told us that the bus leaves at 4.00 p.m.

2 The thing reported contains the modals would, could, might, ought to and should as well as must for logical deduction.

'You ought to revise for your exam this weekend,' she said.

She said I ought to revise for my exam this weekend.

'We might not be free on Friday night,' she said.

She said they might not be free on Friday night.

'I think she must be working late', Tim said.

Tim said he thought she must be working late.

3 The thing being reported contains the past perfect.

'He had been helping the police with their enquiries,' she said.

She said he had been helping the police with their enquiries.

Direct speech	Reported speech
tomorrow	the next day, the day after, the following day
yesterday	the day before, the previous day
last week	the week before
here	there
this/that	the
this morning	that morning
today	that day
next Friday	the following Friday
ago	before

Reported statements

FORM

verb (+ that) + clause

'I stole the car,' she admitted

She admitted (that) she had stolen the car.

'He sleeps during most of the day and then studies all night' she said.

She said (that) he slept during most of the day and then studied all night.

Reported questions

Reported Yes/No **questions**

FORM

When there is no question word in the direct speech question, we use if/whether. Word order is the same as in the statement. The verb tense and other changes are the same as for other types of reported speech.

'Are you going to arrest him?' she asked.

She asked if/whether they were going to arrest him.

'Do you like dogs?' he asked.

He asked us if/whether we liked dogs.

Reported *wh-* questions

FORM
When *wh-* question words are used, the *wh-* word is followed by statement word order, that is the subject followed by the verb.

All the tense and other changes are the same as for other types of reported speech.

'Why isn't John here?' she asked.

She asked why John wasn't there.

'Where do you usually have lunch?' he asked her.

He asked her where she usually had lunch.

Reported orders

FORM
verb + (*that*) + clause or verb + object + infinitive with *to*

'Go back to college,' his father said.

His father recommended (that) he go back to college.

'Bring in the washing, will you?' she said.

She told me to bring in the washing.

Reported suggestions

FORM
suggest + *-ing*

suggest + *that* + *should* + infinitive without *to*

suggest + past simple

'Let's make a picnic and take it to the beach,' she said.

She suggested making a picnic and taking it to the beach.

She suggested that we should make a picnic and take it to the beach.

She suggested we made a picnic and took it to the beach.

Reporting verbs

1 Verb + object + infinitive
   They asked us to stay.
   Other verbs with the same pattern are:
   advise, beg, encourage, invite, order, persuade, remind, warn

2 Verb (+ *that*) + clause
   He says (that) he is very angry with you.
   Other verbs with the same pattern are:
   claim, admit, explain, promise

3 Verb + object (+ *that*) + clause
   We told him (that) we had just moved to Manchester.
   Other verbs with the same pattern are:
   remind, warn

4 Verb + gerund
   He admitted taking the shoes without paying for them.
   Other verbs with the same pattern are:
   deny, recommend, suggest

5 Verb + preposition + gerund
   She apologised for lying to me.
   She discouraged me from leaving school early.
   Other verbs with the same pattern are:
   accuse (of), blame (for), congratulate (on), insist (on)

6 Verb + infinitive
   We agreed to write to each other as often as we could.
   Other verbs with the same pattern are:
   decide, offer, promise, refuse, threaten

Chapter 13
Possibility and certainty

A **Factual possibility** – *could, may and might (not)*

   We use *could, may* and *might (not)*:

   1 To say that something is possibly true at the moment of speaking.

      ### FORM
      might/may/could + infinitive

      She might be angry about something you said.

      He may be back earlier than expected.

      He could be late because of the weather.

   2 To talk about the possibility that past events happened.

      ### FORM
      could/may/might + *have* + past participle

      They may have decided to stay the night before.

      He might not have received your e-mail.

      She could have talked to him yesterday.

3 To say there is a chance that something might happen in the future.

FORM

might/may/could + infinitive

We may go to Australia next Christmas.

It could snow tonight.

She might not come and see us after all.

B Theoretical possibility – *can*

We use *can*:

1 To ask, speculate or guess about past events.

Note: This is only in questions.

FORM

(*Wh-* word +) *can* + subject + *have* + past participle

Can he have thought we'd left already?

Where can they have gone?

2 To say that things are possible in the future (without saying what chance there is that they will happen).

FORM

can + infinitive

Anyone can learn to use a word processor.

3 To talk about typical behaviour of people or things.

FORM

can + infinitive

Dogs can be jealous of small babies.

C Certainty – *must*

We use *must*:

1 To talk about something which is certain or highly probable to be true, or for which we have excellent evidence for believing to be true in the present or future.

FORM

must + infinitive

You must be exhausted after all that running.

2 To express conclusions about things that happened in the past when we are certain, or it is highly probable, something was true, or for which we have excellent evidence for believing to have been true.

FORM

must + *have* + past participle

He must have overslept this morning – he's never usually this late.

D Certainty – *can't*

We use *can't*:

1 To talk about something which is certain or highly probable NOT to be true, or for which we have excellent evidence for believing NOT to be true in the present or future.

FORM

can't + infinitive

That can't be Michael at the door – he's on holiday at the moment.

2 To express conclusions about things that happened in the past when we are certain, or it is highly probable, something was NOT true, or for which we have excellent evidence for believing NOT to have been true.

FORM

can't + *have* + past participle

She can't have understood what you meant.

Note: We can also use *couldn't* in this case (to talk about certainty):

That couldn't be Michael at the door – he's on holiday at the moment.

She couldn't have understood what you meant.

We don't use *mustn't* in this case (to talk about certainty): ~~He mustn't have liked the film because he left halfway through it.~~

-ing forms and infinitives

Certain grammatical constructions and certain verbs are followed by:

1 The infinitive without *to* (e.g. *do*).

2 The infinitive with *to* (e.g. *to do*).

3 The *-ing* form (e.g. *doing*).

Grammatical constructions/patterns

1 Use the infinitive without *to* (e.g. *do*):

● after modal verbs

*You **must take** all the medicine.*

● after *make* and *let*

*She **let me borrow** the DVD.*

● after *I'd better* and *I'd rather*

*I'**d better phone** Michael soon.*

2 Use the infinitive with *to* (e.g. *to do*):

● after certain adjectives

  *I'm really **pleased to be** here.*

● in the construction *too ... to ...*

  *It's **too cold to swim** in the river at the moment.*

● to express purpose

  *I go to dance classes **to keep fit.***

3 Use the *-ing* form (e.g. *doing*):

● after prepositions

  *He accused me **of taking** his pen.*

● when an action (not a noun) is the subject or object of a sentence

  ***Smoking** is not permitted inside the building.*

With certain verbs:

1 Some verbs are followed by the *-ing* form (gerund).
  *He **admitted taking** part in the robbery.*

2 Verbs followed by an object + the infinitive without *to*.
  *Would you **help me finish** tidying this room?*

3 Some verbs are followed by an infinitive with *to*.
  *We **arranged to meet** the following week.*

4 Some verbs are followed by object + infinitive with *to*.
  *He **encouraged me to make** an appointment.*

5 Verbs followed by a gerund or an infinitive with a difference in meaning.

  A *remember, forget, stop, try*

  ● *remember:* the gerund is used when the action happens before the remembering; the infinitive refers to an action that happens after.
    *I **remember seeing** someone behaving strangely at the bus stop.*
    *Did **you remember to get** some more bread?*

  ● *forget:* when used with the gerund this means 'forget what you have done'; when used with the infinitive with *to*, this means 'forget what you have to do'.
    *I had completely **forgotten putting** that book on the shelf.*
    *I **forgot to post** the letter you gave me.*

  ● *stop:* when used with the gerund, this means 'stop something you do'; when used with the infinitive with *to*, this means 'stop in order to do something'.
    *I **stopped drinking** coffee because I couldn't sleep.*
    *We **stopped to have** a coffee on our way into town.*

  ● *try:* when used with the gerund this means 'make an experiment' – doing the action may not be successful; when used with the infinitive this means 'make an effort' – the action may be difficult or impossible to do.
    *Try drinking** some warm milk before going to bed.*
    *Try to listen** to English radio for at least half an hour a day.*

  B *can't bear/stand, hate, like, love, prefer*
  When these verbs are used with the infinitive they refer to more specific situations. When they are used with the gerund they refer to more general situations. The difference in meaning is very slight.
  *I **prefer to go** to school by bus.*
  *I **can't bear getting up** so early, but I have to.*

Chapter 14

Passives

FORM
appropriate tense of *be* + past participle

Present simple:	All notebooks **are kept** in the cupboard by the window.
Present continuous:	My computer **is being looked at** just now by someone from the IT department.
Past simple:	We **were** all **given** the day off yesterday.
Past continuous:	The last time I saw Tim, he **was being shown** how to use a new design programme by one of the designers.
Present perfect:	**Have you been told** about the cutbacks in staff they are planning?
Past perfect:	We **had been asked** to meet in the boardroom by 10.00 a.m.
Future *will*:	You**'ll be told** about all your duties when you start work on Monday morning.
Future perfect:	These **will have been** completely **redesigned** by the time we move in.

going to:	The meeting **is going to be chaired** by Philip.
Modals:	The file **must have been put back** in the filing cabinet.
Passive gerund:	Emily hates **being patronised**.

USE

The passive is used to talk about actions, events and processes when the action, event or process is seen as more important than the agent. This is often the case in scientific writing.

The Eiffel Tower was built in 1889.

The subjects in the experiment were given three of the pills every four hours.

by + agent

When we are interested in the agent, we use the preposition *by*.

These documents were found in the cupboard **by** *the secretary.*

Ability

1 *can*

- We use *can* to talk about present ability.

  Can you speak any Arabic?

- We use *can* to talk about future actions which we will be able to do because of present ability, present circumstances, etc.

  I can go to next week's meeting in New York.

2 *could*

- We use *could* to talk about general past ability.

  I could ride a horse quite well by the time I was thirteen.

Chapter 15

Hypothetical meaning

A *wish*

1 We use *wish* + past simple to express a wish that has not come true in the present. We also use *wish* + past simple to talk about wishes that might come true in the future.

I wish I had a dog.

Don't you wish you had your own flat?

2 If the verb is *be*, we can use the past simple (*I/he/she/it was; you/we/they were*) or *were* with all persons (*I/you/he/she/it/we/they were*).

We all wish the weather wasn't/weren't so awful.

I wish she wasn't/weren't quite so noisy.

3 We use *wish* + *would* and *could* to refer to general wishes for the future.

I wish I could see you tonight but I have to work late.

I wish she would be a bit more friendly.

4 *Wish + would* is often used to talk about other people's irritating habits. This form is not often used with *I* or *we*. To talk about our own irritating habits we use *could*.

I wish you would stop humming. It's very irritating.

Don't you wish she wouldn't be so patronising?

I wish I could improve my tennis.

5 We use *wish* + past perfect to refer to things we are sorry about in the past.

I wish I hadn't lost my temper.

She wishes she hadn't resigned from her job.

B *if only*

If only is used with the same verb forms as *wish*, and is used when your feelings are stronger. It is often used with an exclamation mark (!). It is used very commonly with *would/wouldn't* to criticise someone else's behaviour.

If only I could speak Spanish well!

If only I had more time to be with my family.

If only she hadn't read my diary.

If only you wouldn't criticise Tania all the time.

C *it's time*

It's time is used with the past simple to talk about the present or future. We mean that the action should have been done before. We can also say *It's about time* and *It's high time*.

It's time you had a break. You've been working on those spreadsheets for hours.

It's about time we painted the spare room. It's looking very old-fashioned.

It's high time she got a job. She finished her college course months ago.

D *I'd rather (would rather)*

1 We use *I'd rather* + past simple when we want to say what we want someone or something else to do in the present or future.

I'd rather you came and picked me up from the airport.

I'd rather you didn't go out tonight.

2 We use *I'd rather* + past perfect when we want to say what we wanted to happen in the past.

I'd rather you hadn't told them about our engagement.

I'd rather she had asked us before borrowing the car.

3 *I'd rather* + infinitive without *to* is used to talk about our preferences or other people's preferences in the present or future.

I'd rather stay at home than go out tonight.

We'd rather get a takeaway pizza.

E *suppose*

Suppose means 'What if ...?'. It is used with:

1 The present simple to describe something that may possibly happen or may have happened.

Suppose Jane tells someone about what you did.

Suppose someone saw you using Mr Green's computer.

2 The past simple to talk about something that is just imagination or which is unlikely to happen in the future.

Suppose he asked you to marry him. What would you do?

Suppose they offered you a job in the USA. Would you go?

3 The past perfect to talk about something that could have happened but didn't in the past.

Suppose we had known each other when we were teenagers. How well do you think we would have got on?

Suppose you had stayed in Australia. Do you think you would have been happy there?

Verb–subject agreement

● Most words ending in *-ics* (e.g. *politics, mathematics, athletics*) are normally singular uncountable and have no plural use.

Mathematics was my favourite subject at school.

● Some singular uncountable nouns end in *-s*. These have no plurals, e.g. *news, billiards, measles.*

I'm afraid the news about your father isn't very good.

● Singular words which refer to groups of people (e.g. *family, team, government*) can have either singular or plural verbs and pronouns.

Our team is/are going to play this afternoon.

● *Police* is a plural word used to talk collectively. (*Staff* and *crew* are used in the same way.)

The police are hunting a thirty-five-year-old man last seen running from the bank.

● *Trousers, jeans, scissors, glasses* and the names of many similar divided objects are plural and have no singular forms.

Do you know where my glasses are?

● Plural names of countries usually have singular verbs and pronouns.

The United States is represented today by Mr William O'Donnell.

● Sums of money, periods of time, distance, etc. are seen as one thing, so we use a singular verb.

Two hours is a long time to have to travel to and from work each day.

Report

(For work on reports, see pages 71 and 138.)

> **Task**
>
> The school where you study English has decided to spend some money on either buying more computers or improving the library. You have been asked to write a report for the school principal.
>
> In your report you should:
>
> • give **two** benefits of buying more computers
>
> • give **two** benefits of improving the library
>
> • say which option you prefer and why.
>
> Write your report using between 100 and 150 words.

USEFUL LANGUAGE

Introduction

The aim of this report is to ...
This report is intended to ...

Reporting results

Most people seem to feel that ...
Several people said/told me/suggested/thought that ...

Presenting a list

They gave/suggested the following reasons:
They made the following points:

1   ...
2   ...

Making recommendations

I would therefore recommend (that we expand the library/ installing a new coffee machine).
It would seem that (banning mobile phones) is the best idea.

Model answer

DO use headings because this makes it easier for the reader to find the main information.

DO say how you collected the information.

Use of money for school improvements

Introduction

The aim of this report is to compare the advantages of additional computers and of improving the library, and to suggest which of these would be best. I interviewed a number of students to find out their views.

DON'T begin and end your report with Dear Sir/ Madam as you would in a letter.

Buying more computers

DO use a range of specific vocabulary or set phrases, e.g. Some thought this was a good idea ..., other students said they preferred ..., but DON'T use lots of adjectives and dramatic language as you do in a story. A report gives factual information.

Some of the students thought that this was a good idea, saying computers were useful for:

● practising writing;

● using the Internet;

● playing games.

However, other students said that they preferred to use their own computers at home.

DO include at least two points under each heading.

Improving the library

DO use numbering or bullet points to highlight main points.

Most of the students preferred this suggestion, giving the following reasons:

1 The library would be a good place for private study, but at present there are not enough tables and chairs there.

2 They feel that up-to-date dictionaries and reference books are needed.

DON'T include irrelevant details or description.

DO express opinions impersonally. DON'T express recommendations or opinions until the conclusion.

Recommendations

The majority of students felt that improving the library would be more useful. I would therefore recommend this.

DO use formal language.

250

Task

The owner of your school where you study English has decided to make some changes to the school classrooms. He has asked for ideas from students about what should be done to make the classrooms better places to study.

In your report you should:

- give **two** features of a good classroom
- give **two** improvements that need to be made
- give your opinion and make a recommendation.

Write your report using between 100 and 150 words.

Answer

Introduction

This report is to suggest what we need to make the classrooms better in our school. I asked students for their ideas.

Background situation

What it's need to be inside a good school classrooms is that they all have all the equipment students might need starting from the essential things like chair, blackboards, finishing with accessories like televisions.

Suggestions

I certainly believe that two things need to start our plan to improve the school classrooms, they are money and good management. My idea of improving the classrooms is to start with what we have and see what needs to be repared and what has to be thrown away and replaced with a new equipment and some computers that the students might need also having a massive liberrary is one of the more important things that students request. Heating and air conditioning are necessary to make the atmosphere in the classrooms cosy.

Personal opinion

In conclusion, the chance of having a good classrooms looks easy from a distance, in fact it isn't, and that we must try to find the balance between having a very good school and not spending too much.

Comments

The report starts well with an introduction and then gives two features of a good classroom. The paragraph giving suggestions for improvement is confusing and it is not clear what two improvements the student would like to see. The final paragraph does not make any clear recommendations about what classroom improvements are needed. The student does not include all the information asked for in the task.

The student uses a good range of vocabulary ('equipment', 'essentials', 'massive' and 'cosy') and also uses some good phrases ('I certainly believe', 'in conclusion' and 'find the balance'). There are few spelling errors ('repared 'and 'liberrary') and one instance where vocabulary is used inappropriately ('accessories').

There are some grammatical errors in the report. These errors range from subject and verb agreement and errors with use of articles ('a good school classrooms' and 'a new equipment') to errors with tense ('two things need to start our plan'). However, in other cases, the grammar used is correct and the report does show a range of grammar structures.

The student makes use of headings which gives the report a structure and allows for the organisation of ideas and the use of paragraphs. There is a lack of balance between the second and third paragraph, with the third paragraph being much longer. Within the paragraphs, there is a lack of punctuation and also errors with punctuation use. The sentences are too long and the student should have used full stops. Due to lack of punctuation and poor use of cohesive devices, it is sometimes difficult to follow the line of communication.

The report is also longer than 150 words.

Communicative quality 3
Lexical accuracy and range 4
Grammatical accuracy and range 3
Effective organisation 3

Overall mark 13

Writing reference

Article

(For work on articles, see pages 43 and 215.)

Task

The school principal has asked students to write articles for the school magazine. He would like to hear about celebrations around the world and wants articles about celebrations that are important in your country.

In your article you should:

- give **two** reasons why the celebration is important

- give **two** details about what people do

- say what you like most about the celebration and why.

Write your article using between 100 and 150 words.

Model answer

DO think of an interesting title.

Olinda's carnival – something for everyone

Rio isn't the only city in Brazil that knows how to have parties. I live in Olinda, a lovely city in the north-east of Brazil. What can we say about the carnival at Olinda? Just that it's the best in the world!

DO try to involve your readers, e.g. by using a question.

DO use informal language to involve the reader.

Carnival has its origins in ancient Egyptian and Roman festivals. It was introduced to Brazil by the Portuguese, and was influenced by African rhythms and Indian costumes. Now it's a big national celebration.

DON'T forget to express your opinion.

Parades of people wearing costumes typical of our north-eastern folklore dance through the streets. I love the giant street dolls, both the traditional ones such as 'the man of midnight' and the new ones that appear each year.

DO finish your article by summarising your main point and giving your opinion or expressing your feelings.

The best thing about our carnival is that no one has to pay and there are no big stars. Everyone takes part, rich and poor, old and young, residents and tourists. If you come, I promise you'll never forget it!

USEFUL LANGUAGE

Involving the reader

Are you thinking of (getting married in the near future)?
I'm sure you'll agree (it was a great idea).

Developing your points

Let's start with (why it is so important to take plenty of exercise).
Another advantage (of using a computer is that ...)
On top of that, ...

Giving your own opinion

I think that/In my opinion (traditional celebrations are very important).
It seems to me that (people are much more aware of the importance of a good diet nowadays).

Task

The school principal has seen an advertisement in a magazine for young people and wants students from the school to write articles to send in.

The title of the article is **I'd love to have....**

You have to write an article about something you would like to have. The writer of the best article will win a lap-top computer.

In your article you should:

- say what you would like to have

- give **two** reasons why you would like it

- give **two** ways in which it will change your life.

Write your article using between 100 and 150 words.

Answer

I'd love to have a lot of money although I think money is not a perfect solution. Of course not! However, if I had enough money, I could do a plenty of things which I want to do.

Above all, I want to study in other countries, because. It is a good chance to develop my abilities. In this case, I don't need to worry about the fee of education in my life. I can only concentrate on studying as long as I do my best.

Secondly, I would like to prepare a lovely house for my parents. Although they didn't say to me at all, I think the work of electric services is so hard to continue at their ages within ten years. Therefore, I hope that I could make them relax and enjoy their life.

On the other hand, I can help the other people who are suffering from lack of food, illness and so on. When I saw a TV programme which announced those people's stories, I thought if I were them I would get really depressed.

Sometimes, money can be used in a bad way, but if I am a rich person, I will spend them on not only for me, but I also give an opportunity to others.

Comments

The article starts by saying what the student would like to have and continues by giving two reasons as to why the student would like to have a lot of money. However, the student does not clearly indicate two ways in which having a lot of money would change his/her life. The student therefore does not give all the information asked for in the task.

The student uses a mixture of formal and informal language in writing the article, which is appropriate for the task. There are no spelling mistakes in the article and the student does use a good range of vocabulary ('solution', 'suffering', 'announced', 'depressed', 'opportunity'). However, there are several errors with the way in which vocabulary is used ('fee of education', 'I can only concentrate', 'Although they didn't say to me at all', 'make them relax') which makes the line of communication difficult to follow, particularly in the third paragraph.

There are several grammar errors in the article which highlight inappropriate and limited use of tenses ('I don't need to worry about the fee', 'I can only concentrate',' they didn't say to me at all', 'I can help the other people', 'if I am a rich person, I will spend'). These errors are present throughout the article.

The student organises his/her ideas via the use of paragraphs. However, the paragraphs are not balanced in terms of content. The second and third paragraphs could be combined to address the second bullet point in the task. The next paragraph should then give two ways in which having money would change the student's life. There is an error with punctuation in the second paragraph ('I want to study in other countries, because. It is') and there are instances where cohesive devices are not used correctly ('In this case', 'On the other hand'); however, in general, the use of punctuation and cohesive devices is appropriate.

The article is also longer than 150 words.

Communicative quality 3
Lexical accuracy and range 3
Grammatical accuracy and range 2
Effective organisation 3

Overall mark 11

Punctuation

Full stops (.), question marks (?) and exclamation marks (!) are used to finish sentences. After these a new sentence has a capital letter.

Mark got all 'A' grades in his final exams! He's going to Manchester University to study law.

Capital letters are used to start sentences, for names and with *I.*

We like Angela. She's very friendly.
I worked in Kenya for a year.

Commas (,) usually reflect a pause in speech. They are often used to separate items in a list (but not before *and*) and add information.

In the end we went to Peru, Chile, Ecuador and Brazil.
That's my oldest sister, who now lives in Paris.

Colons (:) usually introduce an explanation or a list.

I decided to resign from my job: it no longer gave me any real satisfaction.
I played lots of different sports at school: rugby, cricket, tennis, hockey and squash.

Semi-colons (;) can be used to separate items in lists of phrases.

Before you leave the house, please remember to do what I asked: shut all the windows; leave a light on in the living room; water the plants and put some food out for the cat.

Quotation marks can be single ('...') or double ("..."). They are also called 'inverted commas'. We use them (single or double) when we quote direct speech. We also use single quotation marks when a word is used in a special way.

"Get out of the way," she cried.

Pete said he found my brother 'interesting'. Unfortunately I have no idea what he meant!

Apostrophes (') show where letters have been left out or are used to indicate possession.

I'm sorry I'm late.
This is Simon's coat.

Informal letter/e-mail

(For work on informal letters/e-mails, see pages 26 and 173.)

Task

You have received a letter from your penfriend inviting you for a visit in July. You are now going to write back to your penfriend in response to their letter.

In your letter you should:

- accept the invitation
- suggest **two** things you would like to do
- ask what you should bring with you.

Write your letter using between 100 and 150 words.

USEFUL LANGUAGE

Beginning the letter

Many thanks for your letter (– it was really nice to hear from you again).
I thought I'd better write (and give you some more details about ...)
It's been such a long time since we wrote to each other.
How are you and your family?
How are things with you?
How was (your holiday)?

Introducing the topic

I know you're longing to hear all about (my holiday).
You remember I told you in my last letter (that I was going to ...)

Ending the letter

Once again, (thanks very much for all your help).
Give my love/regards to (your family).
Please write/drop me a line soon.
I look forward to (meeting up again soon).

Model answer

DO mention a letter you have received from the person you are writing to, or refer to a shared experience.

DO mention the next time you will see the person you are writing to.

Dear Carla,

Thanks for your letter – it was great to hear from you. I'm sorry I haven't written for ages, but I've been really busy preparing for my exams.

Thank you so much for your invitation to stay with you for a week in July – I'd love to come. I know that you have a wonderful beach near your house, and I'd really enjoy spending some time there. I expect that the weather will be hot, so I hope we can go swimming.

What sort of clothes should I pack? Casual or formal? Would you like me to bring anything for you? I would like to bring something special for you and your family from my country.

I'd better stop now and get on with my studying. I hope you're enjoying driving your car, and I'm looking forward to seeing you in July! Thanks again for the invitation.

All the best,

Irene

DO invent a name. Don't write Dear Penfriend.

DO say what you've been doing recently.

DO think of some specific details to include in each paragraph – this will make your letter more interesting.

DO use an appropriate informal phrase to end your letter, e.g. Love, All the best, Best wishes. DON'T finish your letter with Yours sincerely/faithfully.

Task

You have received a letter from a penfriend who is planning to visit you in July. You are now going to write back to your penfriend in response to their letter.

In your letter you should:

- describe **two** activities you have planned for his/her visit
- give **two** pieces of advice on what to bring
- ask if he/she has any special requests.

Write your letter using between 100 and 150 words.

Answer

Dear Carria,

Nice to hear from you. I'm so surprised that you are on your way to come here this summer.

First of all, I would like to recommend you some places where you shouldn't miss such as Sentosa island. You can have different activities there. For example, if you would like having sunbathing. I think 'Sun World' is the best choice to relax. Don't forget to bring swimwear.

Secondly, it's the best time come here if you enjoy the shopping. We have big on sale in July. Therefore, I can arrange the shopping table for you. I will be very please to show you how interesting on big sale in here!

I don't think you need to bring any special stuff. That's because you can buy them here. Don't forget to prepare some more empty suitcase for your shopping.

If you have any question just ask me. I'll do my best to solve them.

Best wishes,

Carel

Comments

This letter addresses all the points raised in the task. The student starts the task with 'Dear Mrs Thompson' and finishes correctly with 'Yours sincerely'. The tone and register of the letter is mostly appropriate, although there are two examples where the language may be too formal for this situation ('concerning this point', 'I like to thank you in advance for your assistance').

The language used in the letter is mostly semi-formal and appropriate for the situation. The student uses a good level and range of vocabulary in response to the task ('I am very pleased that', 'I do not mind', 'If it is possible please let me know'). There are no spelling mistakes in the letter.

There are grammatical errors in the letter but they do not affect communication ('*I've received yesterday*', '*I never have been* to the USA', 'at sometime in July', 'I do not mind *both*', 'a free accommodation').

The letter is clearly organised into paragraphs which address each of the bullet points in the task. However, cohesive devices are not used as effectively as they could be and this causes some interruption to the flow of the letter.

Communicative quality 4
Lexical accuracy and range 4
Grammatical accuracy and range 4
Effective organisation 3

Overall mark 15

Writing reference

Formal letter/e-mail

(For work on letters/e-mails, see pages 56 and 158.)

Task

You recently had a short holiday in a large city which you booked through a company called Citibreaks. Read the Citibreaks advertisement for the holiday you booked.

Citibreaks

Enjoy a short holiday in the capital city.

We offer two nights' accommodation in a four-star hotel in a central location.

All rooms have their own bathrooms, and a view of the river.

The price of £150 per person includes all meals as well as a ticket for a show of your choice in one of the city's leading theatres.

This will be a real holiday to remember!

You were very disappointed with the holiday as some things were different from the advertisement. You are going to write a letter/e-mail of complaint to Citibreaks. In your letter/e-mail you should:

• say why you are writing

• state **two** problems you had with the holiday

• say what you want them to do about it.

Write your letter/e-mail using between 100 and 150 words.

Model answer

DO make a clear connection between your letter/e-mail and the task input. DON'T repeat the exact words in the task input.

If you begin your letter/e-mail Dear Sir/Madam, DO end with Yours faithfully. If you begin Dear Ms (or Mr, Mrs, Miss) Jones, etc., DO end with Yours sincerely.

Dear Sir,

I am writing to complain about a short holiday I had recently, which was organised by Citibreaks. I was dissatisfied with several things.

First, your advertisement promised a hotel in a central location, whereas in fact the hotel was a long way from the city centre. This caused problems as we had made holiday plans based around being able to walk to most places, but instead had to pay for transport. I also had to pay extra for dinner, although the advertisement had stated that it was included in the price. To make matters worse, I had no choice of which show to go to.

I had been looking forward to my holiday very much, but it was completely ruined by these problems. I therefore feel that you should refund half the cost of the holiday in compensation for my disappointment.

I look forward to hearing from you soon.

Yours faithfully,

Ursine Schmidt

Ursine Schmidt

DO begin by saying why you are writing. DON'T begin by saying who you are.

DO list your complaints clearly, using linking words to connect your actual complaint with the details.

If you expect a reply to your letter/e-mail, DO finish with this sentence on a separate line.

DO sign and print your full name.

USEFUL LANGUAGE

Complaining

I am writing to you about (several problems related to my city break in June).

I have been waiting for (two weeks for a reply to my letter).

To make matters worse, (we were informed that there was no record of our cheque being cashed).

I would be grateful if you could (refund my deposit as soon as possible).

Requesting information

I am writing in response to (your advertisement in 'The Daily Standard' on July 20th).

I would be grateful if you could (send me further details about the position).

I am writing to enquire whether (you could let me have further details about the holiday).

I would like to know more about (the arrangements for the evening meal).

Giving information/responding to requests for information

In response to your query, I would like to inform you that (I passed the International GCSE in ESL in June).

With reference to your letter of … (I enclose details of my qualifications).

You asked me to tell you about (my travel plans and I enclose further details).

Task

You recently entered a competition for learners of English, and have just received a letter from the organisers of the competition. Read the letter below.

> Congratulations! You have won first prize in our competition – a two-week trip to Vancouver or San Francisco.
>
> Your prize includes:
>
> *FREE return flight to the city of your choice
>
> *FREE two-week course at the Vancouver or San Francisco School of International English
>
> *Two weeks' FREE accommodation with a family
>
> We need to know your choice of city, your preferred dates, and if you would like us to make any special arrangements for you.
>
> We look forward to hearing from you. Once we have the information we will send you your tickets and further details.
>
> Yours sincerely
>
> *Jacky Thompson*
>
> Jacky Thompson
>
> Competition Manager

You are now going to respond to Jacky Thompson's letter. In your letter you should:

- say which city you want to go to and why
- give **two** sets of preferred dates
- give **two** special arrangements you would like.

Write your letter using between 100 and 150 words.

Answer

Dear Mrs Thompson,

Thank you very much for the letter which I've received yesterday. I am very pleased that I've won the prize. I would like to go to San Francisco because I never have been to the USA before.

I would like to go at sometime in July. I do not mind both the first two weeks in July or the last two.

You wrote about a free accommodation with a family. Are the meals included and/or do I have the opportunity to cook by myself? I would like to do this. Also, I would like to ask if it is possible to stay for an extra week. If it is possible please let me know the price I have to pay concerning this point.

I like to thank you in advance for your assistance and I look forward to hearing from you soon.

Yours sincerely,

Lennart Moser

Comments

The letter addresses all the points raised in the task. The tone and register of the letter is mostly appropriate; however, use of the cohesive devices 'First of all' and 'Secondly' are more suited to formal situations.

The language used in the letter is mostly informal and appropriate for one friend writing to another. However, the vocabulary used is frequently inaccurate ('You can have different activities', 'shopping *table*', 'I'll do my best to *solve* them'). Also, the student does not use a wide range of vocabulary.

There are frequent grammatical errors in this letter ('recommend *you* some places *where* you shouldn't miss', 'would like *having sunbathing*', 'enjoy *the* shopping', 'We have big *on* sale in July'). These errors affect communication and do cause confusion at times.

The letter is clearly organised into paragraphs, each addressing different parts of the task. The letter generally reads well although use of the cohesive devices 'First of all' and 'Secondly' is too formal for this situation. In some cases, particularly the second paragraph, misuse of linking and cohesive devices affects the coherence of the paragraph.

Communicative quality 3
Lexical accuracy and range 2
Grammatical accuracy and range 2
Effective organisation 3

Overall mark 10

Letter of application

(For work on writing applications, see page 201.)

> **Task**
>
> You see this advertisement in a local English-language newspaper.
>
> > We are looking for students of English to spend two mornings a week helping in the local tourist office.
> >
> > Good pay and conditions for the right applicants.
> >
> > Write to us, giving information about your level of English, and explaining why you would be suitable for the job.
>
> You are now going to apply for one of the jobs in the tourist office.
>
> In your letter of application you should:
>
> - say what your level of English is
> - say why you would be suitable for the job
> - say when and how you can be contacted.
>
> Write your letter of application using between 100 and 150 words.

Model answer

DO say which job you are applying for and where and when you saw it advertised. You can invent a newspaper and date if you need to.

DO organise your application so that you mention each of the areas in the advertisement.

DO say when and how you can be contacted.

Dear Sir/Madam,

I am writing to apply for one of the positions helping in the local tourist office which were advertised in 'Kent Weekly' on August 23rd.

I am nineteen years old and I have been learning English and French for five years at a comprehensive school. At the moment I'm a student at English International, studying for the International GCSE in ESL.

As I have already spent three months in England, I know the local tourist attractions quite well. I would also say that I have a good knowledge of history and old places. In the near future, I would like to continue studying English, and so the job in your tourist office would be a great opportunity for me to improve my speaking.

I am available for interview at any time. I can be contacted on 0795 51 32 41 after 6 p.m. every evening.

Thank you for considering my application. I look forward to hearing from you.

Yours faithfully,

Gabriella Daniels

DON'T start and finish your letter of application in the same way as a other formal letters.

DON'T make mistakes with time expressions and tenses.

DON'T forget to mention why you think you are suitable.

DO begin and end your letter as you would other formal letters.

USEFUL LANGUAGE

I have always been interested in (using English in my work).
One of the main reasons I am applying for this job is that (I want to work in England).
I have a lot of experience of (dealing with the public).
I am available to start work (at any time/from the end of the month).
Thank you for considering my application.
I would be grateful if you would (send me further details of the job).
I can be contacted (on 0849 58 48 43) at any time.
I can be contacted (at the above address).
I look forward to hearing from you soon.

Task

You recently saw this notice in an international magazine.

> We are looking for ten people from different countries to walk with us to the Base Camp of Mount Everest to raise money for charity. We guarantee it will be the experience of a lifetime! You just need to be fit, be free for two weeks in April and have a reasonable level of English.
>
> Write and tell us why you are one of the people we are looking for and why you would like to be part of this adventure.

You are now going to apply to join the group of walkers to Base Camp.

In your letter of application you should:

- say why you would be suitable for this adventure
- say why you are interested in taking part
- say when and how you can be contacted.

Write your letter of application using between 100 and 150 words.

Answer

Dear Sirs or Madams,

I am writing in reply to advertisement I was seen in international magazine last week. I would like to apply to be part of the group that walks to the Base Camp of Mount Everest.

I play tenis and football a lot and go to my gym two times in every week. So, I am a quite fit person. My level of English is upper-intermediate and I will take my International GCSE in ESL exam in June. My teacher thinks I will succeed! I am on holidays for most April but it depend on the dates of the voyage. I think raise money for charity is a very good way to spend holidays.

I can be contact by phone on 07945 392 693. If I don't answer your call, please leave message and I will phone you after.

I look forward to hearing from you.

Yours faithfully,

Pietro Sampras

Comments

The student starts the letter with 'Dear Sirs or Madams' and although this is correct as we are not given the name of a person to write to, the letter should start 'Dear Sir/Madam'. The letter finishes with 'Yours faithfully', which is correct. The student tries to address all the bullet points in the task, but the information is not clearly laid out and the bullet points are not fully addressed. The tone and register of the letter is mostly appropriate for the task; however there is some irrelevant information included ('My teacher thinks I will succeed').

The language used in the letter is mostly semi-formal and appropriate for the situation. However, the level and range of vocabulary is limited ('two times in every week', 'phone you after'). 'Tennis' is also spelt incorrectly. Some words are also misused ('voyage', 'succeed').

There are frequent grammatical errors in the letter and they do have a negative effect on the line of communication at times ('in reply to advertisement I was seen in international magazine', 'a quite fit person', 'most April', 'I think raise money', 'I can be contact').

The letter has clear opening and closing paragraphs. However, the student could have made better use of paragraphing in the main body of the letter. The second paragraph addresses the first and second bullet points together and this causes some confusion and neither of the bullet points is fully addressed.

Communicative quality 3
Lexical accuracy and range 2
Grammatical accuracy and range 3
Effective organisation 3

Overall mark 11

Review

(For work on reviews, see page 4.)

> **Task**
>
> Your teacher has asked you to write a review of a book you have read recently.
>
> In your review you should:
>
> • say what type of book it is
>
> • say what you liked/disliked about the book
>
> • say whether you would recommend it.
>
> Write your review using between 100 and 150 words.

Model answer

DO give some details of personal interest to catch your reader's attention.

DO use specific vocabulary about the CD/ book/film/play, etc. that you are reviewing

DON'T only describe the CD/book/film/ play, etc., but make sure you give your opinion.

DON'T give away the ending or spoil any surprises in the book/ film/play.

I saw the musical of 'The Phantom of the Opera' and wondered if the book would be as good. The novel was written about 100 years ago by Frenchman Gaston Leroux. He was fascinated by the Opera House in Paris and decided it would be a perfect setting for a detective story.

The book starts with a death and the sighting of a ghost in the Opera House in Paris and continues in the style of a detective novel. It is well-written and the plot was extremely gripping. One of the other strengths of the book is the description of one of the main characters, Erik. He is a complex character because, although he is very talented, he has a terribly deformed face and is therefore rejected by society.

I would highly recommend this book. The various parts of the story are expertly put together and it is very easy to read. Personally, I couldn't put it down!

(171 words)

DO organise your review into clear paragraphs.

DO end your review with a recommen-dation (briefly summa rising the reasons for your opinion).

Giving information (about the CD, book, film or play/musical)

The album was released in 2006 and went straight to number one.

It's a huge production with a cast of about sixty singers and dancers.

This film is produced by the same company that made Toy Story and The Incredibles.

The novel describes the author's childhood in Scotland in the 1960s.

Giving your opinion (about the CD, book, film or play/musical)

One of the strongest things about the book is the plot, which is exciting and unusual.

The acting is very good, especially the main character, who is played by …

My favourite track is …

The song is very lively and has interesting lyrics.

The only negative thing I would say about the … is …

Giving a recommendation

I would definitely recommend buying/seeing/reading it.

It's an easy read and I would say it's perfect for taking on holiday.

If you get a chance, then go and see it as soon as you can.

I would say try to see it at the cinema (not just on DVD) to make the most of the special effects.

Assessment criteria: writing skills assessment grid

This grid should be used for marking Parts 4, 5, and 6 on Paper 1.

Mark	Communicative quality	Lexical accuracy and range	Grammatical accuracy and range	Effective organisation
5	The response communicates most successfully, conveying the information set out in the task using appropriate tone and register for the audience.	Writing shows highly effective use of vocabulary to meet the requirements of the task. Vocabulary is used appropriately and effectively to communicate and is accurate in all respects.	Writing shows very good range and control of grammatical structures which are used appropriately and effectively to address requirements of the task. There are very few errors.	An extremely coherent piece of writing, successfully organised with confident and appropriate use of cohesive devices where necessary. Requires no effort on the part of the reader.
4	The response generally communicates successfully. There may be errors which cause the reader some difficulty but these do not impede communication. Tone and register are generally ppropriate to the task.	Writing shows good use of vocabulary used effectively and appropriately with occasional lapses. Spelling is generally accurate.	Writing shows a sufficiently good range and control of grammar. Structures are generally used appropriately. Despite occasional errors, communication is not hindered.	Very coherent piece of writing with occasional lapses. Generally well organised with appropriate use of cohesive devices. Occasional errors do not affect the reader.
3	The response does not wholly communicate successfully. Errors cause the reader some difficulty in following what the writer is trying to say. Tone and register may not be consistently appropriate to the task.	Writing makes a largely effective use of the vocabulary though at times this does not meet the requirements of the task. Vocabulary is generally spelt correctly with occasional lapses which do not hinder the reader.	A limited range of structures is present, generally used correctly. There are several errors which occasionally hinder the reader who has to think at times about what the student wants to say.	Generally coherent piece of writing though there are several errors in the use of cohesive devices etc, which may affect the reader's ability to follow the line of communication. Writing is generally well organised with slight errors.
2	The response is difficult to follow. Student may not have considered the need to address tone and register.	Insufficient range of vocabulary used to meet the requirements of the task. Vocabulary is sometimes used inaccurately or inconsistently and there are several spelling mistakes that slow the reader down.	The writing is lacking in range and control of structures. There are frequent errors which hinder communication and confuse the reader at times.	A poor piece of writing, generally lacking in organisation, with misuse of cohesive devices. Requires effort from the reader.
1	Response is very difficult to read and does not communicate successfully. Tone and register have not been taken into consideration.	Student shows poor use of vocabulary throughout. Vocabulary is used inaccurately or inconsistently, spelling is generally inaccurate and causes the reader some difficulty.	The writing shows poor range and control of grammatical structures. The writing is generally inaccurate and grammatical errors cause confusion.	Generally incoherent and poorly organised, lacking in use of cohesive devices.
0	The student has made no attempt to address the task. What the student has produced is insufficient and cannot be read or marked.			

Assessment criteria: speaking skills assessment grid

Mark	Communicative ability and content	Pronunciation and fluency	Lexical accuracy and range	Grammatical accuracy and range
5	Confidently expresses opinions and attitudes, and conveys a lot of information. Responds well to all questions and frequently takes the initiative to expand on ideas under discussion.	Pronunciation and intonation are consistently comprehensible and clear. Accent in no way impedes communication. Student is able to sustain the conversation with ease and without undue hesitation.	Uses a wide range of vocabulary appropriately, accurately and precisely. Student has appropriate linguistic resources to be able to overcome problems and maintain interaction.	Uses a wide range of complex structures accurately and appropriately. Full range of tenses, subordinate clauses etc. are used very competently and appropriately to convey information.
4	Expresses opinions without undue difficulty and conveys a significant amount of information. Responds well to a range of questions and expands on some questions.	Pronunciation and intonation are generally comprehensible and clear. Accent is noticeable but does not impede communication. Student generally responds without undue hesitation.	Uses a relatively wide range of vocabulary, generally used appropriately and accurately. Occasional errors impede communication though generally student has resources to maintain interaction.	Generally accurate in straightforward language. Some errors evident, particularly when using more complex language.
3	Expresses simple opinions and offers some personal responses, conveying some relevant information. Generally responds well but rarely expands on ideas under discussion. Student has difficulty with more complex questions. Student needs help to interpret the question.	Pronunciation and intonation are generally accurate though errors may interfere with communication. Accent may impede communication. Student hesitates occasionally.	Student uses an adequate range of structures and vocabulary. Some attempts to use complex language though not always successfully. Student may occasionally lack the resources to maintain interaction.	Generally accurate using simple, basic language. Less accurate in more unfamiliar language situations. Errors are at times significant and impact on communication.
2	Opinions are limited to basic questions and relevant information provided is limited. Answers are short and student shows little or no initiative.	Pronunciation and intonation are generally poor and inconsistent, and may impede communication. Accent regularly impedes communication. There are patches of speech which cannot be understood. Student is hesitant.	Range of vocabulary used is limited and repetitive. Student rarely attempts complex language and often lacks the resources to overcome problems.	Generally inaccurate in basic language. Errors impede communication and student is unable to use any complex structures.
1	Offers little relevant information and is unable to formulate clear opinions. Produces minimal responses and is unable to maintain interaction.	Pronunciation is poor and inconsistent and communication is hesitant and disjointed.	Uses only the most basic vocabulary. Student is unable to overcome problems.	Consistently inaccurate use of structures.
0	Student produces no language worth rewarding.			